I am a fifth-generation entrepreneur, and my three boys were taught the value of money from the age of four. As a result, my children are savvy negotiators, understand investing, and focus on building wealth even as preteens. Finally, I found a book that teaches parents and their children the road map to wealth. I only wish I had this book 10 years ago—bravo to Loral and Kyle for bringing this gift to millions.

> —**Kedma Ough,** MBA, speaker, consultant,
> *Entrepreneur* contributor, and bestselling author of
> *Target Funding*

Loral Langemeier has done it again! She and Kyle have written a much-needed book about creating millionaires, but this time it's about the most significant group of people on earth: our kids. Our children are the future and the seeds we invest in them now determine their path as adults as well as that of the planet. I highly recommend this work that Loral is doing; she has my heart-felt support. Engage with her and let's change and create a massive future for our kids!

> —**Pat Mesiti,** speaker, author, and coach

Loral has always been brilliant on anything investments, education, money, and financial freedom. As a mother—and having known her since her son was a toddler—I know that when she looked at her child at the time, her mind was already working overtime on how she was going to educate him and other children. This is a masterful human being who has a heart of gold and super-intelligence when it comes to financial matters.

> —**Dame Doria (DC) Cordova,** PhD (Hon.), CEO,
> global business developer, and sustainability entrepreneur

This book provides the long-sought-after but never-delivered checklist for busy parents wanting to make sure they teach everything their kids need to know about money! In the information age, it is so important that parents get the right education on HOW to teach their kids about money. This book provides real-world examples from the authors' children that any parent can incorporate and use themselves! It is a must-read!

> —**Bill Walsh,** venture capitalist and top business coach

This book is clear, helpful, and empowering. It provides a concise and comprehensive guide to becoming a millionaire. Loral and Kyle deliver on the much needed HOW to do it and it is a must-read for anyone wanting to transform their financial life and set their kids on a path to financial freedom.

—**Randy Tate,** CEO, Flip Investor Inc.


Lots of books talk about money and your kids. But these books usually leave parents with more questions than answers. Loral and Kyle have written the book that shows parents HOW to teach their children about money! Combining their skills and talents, these two have created the ideal book for any parent looking to lead an honest conversation with their children about financial literacy.

—**Lisa Williams,** wealth educator


Let's be honest: most parents are never given the insight into how to teach their children about money. Most of the time, their parents weren't given it either! This book provides badly needed guidance that parents can take to help their kids get the education about financial freedom they need to hear.

—**Scott Donnell,** founder, Apex Leadership Co. and the
GravyStack banking app for families


As a serial entrepreneur and investor, I know the importance of process and laying out a plan for creating success. What Loral and Kyle have created with *Make Your Kids Millionaires* is the ideal blueprint for teaching kids about money and being realistic about the results. This book is a must-read for anyone who wants to learn about money AND teach their children the right lessons at the same time.

—**Kevin Harrington,** original shark from *Shark Tank* and
pioneer of the As Seen On TV industry

Loral has been my money mentor and inspiration for more than a decade. Money is never really taught well in schools and I used to joke that I had to go to the ATM to find out my account balances. Thanks to her keen insights I more than figured it out, but most importantly, the trainings passed on to my 19-year-old daughter, Makenna, served to help her create a million-dollar company during Covid . . . imagine what other children can become when they truly grasp financial literacy. Loral and Kyle's strategies for children (and parents!) are a profound approach to creating wealth and, ultimately, a legacy lifestyle. This book is a must-read for EVERY parent!

> **—Forbes Riley,** celebrity TV host, motivational speaker, and cofounder of the Ultimate Pitch Academy

This book provides the long sought after but never delivered checklist for busy parents wanting to make sure they teach everything their kids need to know about money! In the information age, it is so important that parents get the right education on *how* to teach their kids about money. This book provides real-world examples from the authors' children that any parent can incorporate and use themselves!

> **—Shawn Shewchuk,** the Number 1 Results Coach and bestselling author of *Change Your Mind Change Your Results*

# MAKE YOUR KIDS
## *Millionaires*

# MAKE YOUR KIDS
## *Millionaires*

### The Step-by-Step Guide to Lead Children to Financial Freedom

## LORAL LANGEMEIER
### and
## KYLE BOECKMAN

New York Chicago San Francisco Athens London Madrid
Mexico City Milan New Delhi Singapore Sydney Toronto

1  2  3  4  5  6  7  8  9    LCR  27  26  25  24  23  22

ISBN      978-1-264-27849-7
MHID       1-264-27849-7

e-ISBN    978-1-264-27850-3
e-MHID     1-264-27850-0

This publication is designed to provide accurate and authoritative information in regard to the subject matter covered. It is sold with the understanding that neither the author nor the publisher is engaged in rendering legal, accounting, securities trading, or other professional services. If legal advice or other expert assistance is required, the services of a competent professional person should be sought.
—*From a Declaration of Principles Jointly Adopted by a Committee of the American Bar Association and a Committee of Publishers and Associations*

**Library of Congress Cataloging-in-Publication Data**

Names: Langemeier, Loral, author. | Boeckman, Kyle, author.
Title: Make your kids millionaires : the step-by-step guide to lead children to financial freedom / Loral Langemeier and Kyle Boeckman.
Description: New York : McGraw Hill, [2022] | Includes bibliographical references and index.
Identifiers: LCCN 2021059311 (print) | LCCN 2021059312 (ebook) | ISBN 9781264278497 (hardback) | ISBN 9781264278503 (ebook)
Subjects: LCSH: Finance, Personal. | Finance—Vocational guidance.
Classification: LCC HG179 .L2636 2022 (print) | LCC HG179 (ebook) | DDC 332.024/01—dc23/ eng/20220204
LC record available at https://lccn.loc.gov/2021059311
LC ebook record available at https://lccn.loc.gov/2021059312

McGraw Hill books are available at special quantity discounts to use as premiums and sales promotions or for use in corporate training programs. To contact a representative, please visit the Contact Us pages at www.mhprofessional.com.

McGraw Hill is committed to making our products accessible to all learners. To learn more about the available support and accommodations we offer, please contact us at accessibility@mheducation .com. We also participate in the Access Text Network (www.accesstext.org), and ATN members may submit requests through ATN.

*This book is dedicated to our kids,*

*Logan Langemeier, Tristin Langemeier,*

*Bryce Boeckman, and Bret Boeckman.*

*They survived our parenting*

*experiments and occasional blunders*

*and still turned out amazing!*

# CONTENTS

## PART 1
# Financial Foundation

## PART 2
# Age-Specific Guide

# MILLIONAIRE KIDS CHECKLIST

**Chapter 4:** *Birth to Age Five*
- [ ] Decide on a Legacy Plan
- [ ] Start a Business and Get Incorporated
- [ ] Employ Your Child
- [ ] Open a Roth IRA for Your Child
- [ ] Set Up a Tax-Advantaged Education Account
- [ ] Create a Will and Advance Directive
- [ ] Create a Trust
- [ ] Purchase Life Insurance
- [ ] Money Buys Things
- [ ] Counting Money
- [ ] Goal Setting Foundations
- [ ] Basic Opportunity Cost
- [ ] Delayed Gratification
- [ ] Never Pay Your Kid an Allowance
- [ ] Pay Yourself First

**Chapter 5:** *Ages Six to Eight*
- [ ] Your Child's Money Goals
- [ ] Family Financial Goal Setting
- [ ] Breaking the Lifestyle Cycle
- [ ] Set Up a Bank Account in Their Name (and Yours)
- [ ] Interest Makes Your Money Work for You
- [ ] Active Income Versus Passive Income
- [ ] Basics of Credit Cards, Debit Cards, Checks, Etc.
- [ ] Financial Discipline
- [ ] Supply and Demand
- [ ] How You Do Anything Is How You Do Everything
- [ ] Teamwork Is Fundamental
- [ ] Leadership Is Vital
- [ ] Play Games with Your Kids That Involve Money

## Chapter 6: *Ages 9 to 11*
- [ ] Spend Only What You Have or Make More
- [ ] Start a Twenty-First-Century Lemonade Stand
- [ ] Taxes
- [ ] Assets Versus Liabilities
- [ ] Good Debt Versus Bad Debt
- [ ] Your Money Isn't Their Money . . . or Is It?
- [ ] Risk Versus Reward for Investments
- [ ] A Stock Is Ownership in a Business
- [ ] Start a Stock Simulator for Your Child
- [ ] The Value of Real Estate Investing
- [ ] Have Your Child Create a Car Account
- [ ] The Importance of Giving Back
- [ ] The Value of Challenging Their Comfort Zone

## Chapter 7: *Ages 12 to 15*
- [ ] Set Up a Checking Account and Debit Card for Your Child
- [ ] Forecasting
- [ ] Advanced Pay Yourself First
- [ ] The Balance Sheet
- [ ] The Income Statement
- [ ] Real World Cost of Living
- [ ] Credit and the Credit Score
- [ ] Get Your Child an Authorized User Credit Card
- [ ] The High Cost of Borrowing
- [ ] Begin Relinquishing Control of Their Stock Investments
- [ ] Due Diligence
- [ ] Buying a Car
- [ ] Insurance

# ACKNOWLEDGMENTS

We would like to first acknowledge our parents, who provided us the solid foundation and fertile soil that allowed us to flourish. We also couldn't have created this book without the loving support of our incredible spouses. Next, we would like to give special appreciation to all our family, friends, and mentors who helped us expand and branch out along the way. Additional thanks go out to all of those who assisted or provided feedback to help this book blossom, including the remarkable people at McGraw Hill. Finally, we would like to acknowledge our kids. They are not only the fruits of our labors but also our inspiration.

# FOREWORD

Some financial self-help books transcend the genre and are capable of helping people from all over the world and from all walks of life. As the coauthor of *Rich Dad Poor Dad* and over 20 bestselling books, I am always honored when someone shares how they took action from something learned from one of my books. To know that my work has had that kind of transcendent impact is both humbling and an honor. When I read *Make Your Kids Millionaires*, I knew right away that Loral and Kyle had written a book with the potential to be transcendent as well.

*Make Your Kids Millionaires* uniquely combines financial and parenting self-help insights and guidance to create a book that is truly greater than the sum of its parts. As a five times *New York Times* bestseller, Loral's hard-hitting style shines through with a proven, no-nonsense, and unapologetic clarity. Kyle's military background and investing experience help make this a systematic, leadership-based, and actionable guide that parents or caregivers can follow along with throughout their child's life.

The fact that both Loral and Kyle came from humble beginnings to eventually achieve financial freedom brings credibility and proof that if people follow their guidance, they truly can bring financial literacy and eventually financial freedom to their children.

Far too few educational systems include the teaching of personal finance, so as caring adults we must make sure our children are prepared for the economic world they will face.

With its age-by-age format, this book provides a guide for parents and caring adults to know which money concepts they should teach their children that are relevant and applicable for each given age. Experiential learning has long been proven to be the best type of education and *Make Your Kids Millionaires* provides experiential lessons to fit your child's age. As a lifelong financial education teacher and advocate, I applaud Loral and Kyle for creating a guide that will undoubtedly have tremendous impact and be a valuable resource to those who read it or have the benefit of learning from the lessons shared in the book.

**Sharon Lechter**

Global Financial Literacy Expert

Author of *Think and Grow Rich for Women*,
coauthor of *Exit Rich, Three Feet From Gold, Outwitting the Devil,
Rich Dad Poor Dad,* and fourteen other Rich Dad books

## PART 1

# Financial Foundation

GOAL SETTING

RISK VS REWARD

UNDERSTANDING DEBT

FINANCIAL LITERACY

# CHAPTER 1

# MILLIONAIRE MAP

*Give a child a fish and you feed them for a day;*
*teach a child to fish and you feed them for a lifetime.*
—**Our version of the old Chinese proverb**

As parents and caregivers, we all aspire to provide the best life we can for our children. We carefully mold them to be caring, healthy, happy, and educated. But how often do we focus on their financial education? When we teach adults about money, one of the most common refrains we hear is "I wish I would have learned this when I was a kid." Usually, the next question is, "Why don't they teach this stuff in school?" This is a tough question to answer because it's one we've asked ourselves over and over. It just doesn't make sense that a topic that touches your life in some way or another nearly every day isn't even addressed by the school system. In the rare instances when it is, the language is so vague and the coverage so shallow that it probably creates more confusion and fear in students than it does understanding. Fixing this issue is a long-term goal for us, but until then, the only answer, parents, is that you must teach your kids about money at home. When we recommend this to parents, the reply we usually hear is, "We don't even know where to start." Even parents who have some money expertise don't know when to teach what. Recognizing which financial concepts should be introduced at which ages is a challenging endeavor. So often, we've heard the plea "I wish there was a checklist that would teach me what my child needs to know about money and when I should teach it." These questions and that plea are why we wrote this book.

This book is about the methods that we—both millionaire parents—used with our kids and recommend that you use to make your kids millionaires. Our stories and how we built our wealth are very different. Our circumstances and family situations were also very different. Consequently, sometimes the two of us offer different ideas for how you can make your kids millionaires. While you read the book, expect similarities and differences in our approaches to creating wealth and teaching your kids how to become millionaires. As you read along, consider which path makes more sense for you and your child based on your beliefs and your situation. In some areas you may gravitate toward one set of processes and views rather than the other. This is OK. The point is that you choose your path and make a plan. Then you take action. This book will serve as a map or handbook to this process, complete with checklists and actionable, specific, age-by-age guidance on how two millionaire parents are making their kids millionaires and how you can too!

The intent of this book is not to create an exhaustive encyclopedia of every financial concept. Doing so would take thousands of pages and put all of us to sleep. Instead, our intent is to set the foundation of financial curiosity and what Loral calls "Living out loud!," establishing an open conversation about money that will drive a **Choose a path and make a plan.** lifetime of financial learning. Our experience has taught us that raising kids who are smart about money is not only possible but practically guaranteed if you do it thoughtfully and consistently. This book provides the guidance to help you, but in the end, you must put forth the effort. You don't have to be financially educated or a millionaire yourself to make your kids millionaires. You just have to put in the work and follow the guidance in this book. It isn't an overnight process. This book is intended to be used as an 18-year guide on how to put in that work. As a result, although we've strived to make our recommendations universal, it is possible that some things may become outdated over the course of that 18 years. It's also possible that many things we don't mention in this book will become mainstream over the next 18 years. For example, we don't really discuss technologies like block-

**This book is an 18-year guide.**

chain, cryptocurrency, NFTs, or the metaverse in this book even though they are already being adopted and we believe they will be a large part of our future. In fact, we're one of the early adopters of using some of these new technologies, including our use of NFTs to help sell this book. The reason we don't mention these technologies is partly because we believe in teaching the basics to children first and foremost, and partly because the ever-changing landscape for these technologies means that we don't know exactly how they will look in 18 years. To ensure you have the latest information, we'll provide updates on MakeYourKidsMillionaires.com when the need arises.

While there is a considerable amount of financial education in this book, you shouldn't construe its contents as investment advice, which can only be given by a certified financial advisor, which we are not. It's also worth noting that, although we're American and use terminology from the United States, the principles in this book are universal and can be applied worldwide; you may just have to substitute some terms used in your country. For years, we've been successfully teaching these financial concepts to students from all over the world. In fact, Loral's first book, *The Millionaire Maker*, has been distributed in dozens of countries, and Loral has traveled to six continents to teach these prin-cipals. Many of the concepts discussed in this book have been more extensively discussed in her five previous *New York Times* bestselling books. Parents are highly encouraged to read those books if they want to get a deeper understanding of her teachings.

If you bought this book thinking you could shove it in your kid's face and be absolved from the responsibility of helping them, then you have purchased the wrong book. This book was written to teach you, the parent, and be a reference to guide your child's financial education and journey. Similarly, if you bought this book hoping you could cram the information down your child's throat in a week and then mark it off your to-do checklist, then you will be disappointed. Properly using this book and teaching your child requires a long-term commitment to training them and doing things differently than the masses who live paycheck to paycheck. This book can provide the tools and motivation to make that commitment. Finally, reading this book will be not like waving a wand that magically and instantly creates millionaire kids. This book can help you raise kids who will eventually become millionaires, but it won't happen overnight or even by any established timeline. Your child's speed toward millionaire status depends on a myriad of factors. The most important is how well you can lead them on their journey. Congratulations on purchasing this book and committing to take that first step!

# THE PATH AND PLAN OF TWO MILLIONAIRES

## Loral's Story

Let me (Kyle) introduce you to my coauthor, Loral Langemeier. She's a money expert, sought-after speaker, entrepreneurial thought leader, and author of five *New York Times* bestselling books who is on a relentless mission to change the conversation about money and empower people around the world to become millionaires.

Loral's straight talk electrifies audiences and inspires powerful action from live stages and television programs ranging from CNN, CNBC, The Street TV, Fox News Channel, Fox Business's *America's Nightly Scoreboard*, *Dr. Phil*, *The View*, and *The Circle* in Australia. She is a regular guest host on, and has been featured in articles in *USA Today*, the *Wall Street Journal*, the *New York Times*, and *Forbes* magazine. She was the breakout star in the film *The Secret*.

It was a long road to becoming a millionaire for Loral as a farm girl who grew up in Nebraska. Like most people, Loral's parents didn't talk about liabilities, assets, or net worth. They taught her the value of a good work ethic and responsibility. Based on this foundation, Loral learned what it takes to reach your goals.

By age 17 Loral began asking herself, how can I make more money? Then she met Dennis Waitley, who gave her the book *Think and Grow Rich*. This book became a life-defining gift. It sparked curiosity within Loral that eventually led her to start asking the question, "Why are there so few millionaires?" Loral started studying financially successful people to see what set them apart.

At this point in her life Loral, who had been planning to become a lawyer, decided to change her focus and get a degree in business and finance. She then proceeded to get a master's in exercise physiology. It was a natural field of study for Loral as she had always been an athlete and enjoyed working out. To pay for college, she decided to use her growing knowledge to start her first business as a personal trainer, training individuals as well as teaching aerobic classes.

One of the first lessons Loral learned in running her business was the concept of leverage. As her personal training business quickly grew, she realized she needed to figure out a way to serve all of the personal training clients she was attracting. After thinking through her situation, Loral realized that she needed a team of trainers to not only help her train the clients she had committed to helping, but also free up her time to grow the business. This allowed her to create and offer corporate wellness solutions, helping employers create spaces where employees could work out, and led to opportunities that would take her career even further.

Loral worked for a number of manufacturing clients who wanted to promote wellness for their employees, and this eventually led to her applying for a contract to work with Chevron corporation. Chevron wanted someone to help build fitness centers for workers on offshore oil rigs as well as manage the project. Loral thought it would be an incredible opportunity and eventually won the contract to build 272 fitness centers.

This was one of those moments in Loral's life that she calls a YES! moment. This is when you say "YES!" to an opportunity and then figure out how to do it. By working with other companies, contractors, and interns, Loral was able to put a team together to fulfill the work and create the multiple fitness centers. The success she realized from that project then landed her additional work with Chevron. Whether it was creating fitness centers on oil rigs or in refining or manufacturing facilities, Loral had grown a simple personal training business into a significant and literally global organization.

In 1996 when her relationship with Chevron changed, Loral was introduced to Robert Kiyosaki and Sharon Lechter by Bob Proctor, whom she had met through a leadership conference. She started her relationship with Bob Proctor as a mentee and eventually developed a business partnership. She was sitting at Sharon Lechter's kitchen table when she was first introduced to Kyosaki's book *Rich Dad Poor Dad* and his board game, Cashflow. She enthralled with what she learned and ended up becoming *the* master distributor of the game. Loral's experience in the *Rich Dad Poor Dad* organization gave her the insight that started her journey toward educating people about financial literacy.

Years later, in January of 1999, Loral called her mentor and said, "It's time. I'm ready to get super serious." She had just learned she was pregnant and immediately knew that she wanted to become a financially free single parent in under nine months. There was no longer any doubt on her underlying motivation for reaching her big goals. She had a *big* "why" that she was committed to.

Her mentor said, "You have to do everything I say and do it on time. Most people do this too casually." Loral replied, "I have to become a millionaire in nine months." Her mentor asked, "Why nine months?" Loral said, "Because I'm going to have a baby and I'm going to be a single mom."

Loral's mentor then proceeded to teach her how to raise capital and put it to work in the Oklahoma real estate market. They bought and rehabbed single-family homes and apartments. Sometimes they would buy all the real estate on entire streets! Loral and her partner did a lot of flipping projects to create money, and then used it to make even more. The key to success was raising the money and then using it as good debt and putting it to work. By Loral's thirty-fourth birthday, in only six months, she had become a net worth millionaire. It was a monumental year because she also began her life as a single mom when her son, Logan, was born. Several years later her daughter, Tristin, joined the family. It was one of the happiest times of her life.

Loral is presently owner and operator of several businesses including Integratedwealthsystems.com, a financial educational company, where she shares her advice without hesitation or apology. She has created, nurtured, and perfected a three-to-five-year strategy to make millions for the average person.

In the process of buying and selling hundreds of companies, she has taught her children the concept of money and how to make it grow. As a former single mother of two children, she is redefining the possibility for women to have it all and raise their children in an entrepreneurial and financially literate environment. In 2016 Loral married Jason, her hot Canadian, and joined families with his daughters Sierra and Kaylee. They are now raising a blended, multinational family and partnering in new real estate deals and other ventures.

In this book, we will give you the tools to help create a future for your children and teach them financial freedom, and how they, too, can become millionaires. Here's specifically how Loral did it. Each of the following steps will be explained in detail throughout the book.

First and foremost, parents need to have their own business. This allows for uncapped earning potential, which is key for building wealth. The business needs to be incorporated so the parents can enjoy and utilize the 80,000 pages of the US tax code to their advantage. This is called living the corporate lifestyle, and you will learn more about it in the book.

Once the business has been incorporated, it needs to employ the child so that the child can earn verified income. Paying the child verified income opens up the opportunity to create tax-advantaged accounts that you can use to grow money tax-free. The parent should then open up various savings-type accounts under the child's name like Roth IRA accounts, investment accounts, educational savings accounts, and cash accounts. This will provide diversified ways to grow the child's money.

Once all of these accounts have been created, the parent needs to create additional financial vehicles to help protect what has been established. This includes a will and trust. Finally, the parents need to obtain additional proper life insurance, which not only provides cash in the event of an unforeseen tragedy, but also acts as a means of wealth transfer. Once all of this infrastructure has been created, both the parent's job and the child's job is to contribute as much money as possible to the accounts through entrepreneurial ventures. Once the child turns 10, the parent creates another savings account that Loral calls the "car account" that will eventually be used to purchase the child's first car. Depending on your financial situation and what you have decided about who will pay for education or training after high school, this might also be a time for your child to begin saving for that as well.

This book outlines the steps necessary to accomplish all of these tasks on an age-by-age basis. With sound investing and by contributing to the accounts as much as possible, your child will also be capable of achieving millionaire status. Therein lies the millionaire plan. When you make money, you put it away as fast as you can. Good luck with your path and plan.

## Kyle's Story

Let me (Loral) introduce you to my coauthor, Kyle Boeckman. He's a retired lieutenant colonel with 25 years of service as a fighter pilot and instructor pilot in the United States Air Force. He's also a self-made millionaire by age 37, despite never having had a huge income. In the Air Force, his financial acumen helped him manage military projects valued at $100 million in both the Middle East and East Asia and oversee a $200 million dollar airspace program. It also aided him in serving as director of a base safety department that was responsible for the safety of 2,500 military and civilian personnel. Finally, he was privileged with the opportunity to fly $12 million fighter jets, teach over a thousand young pilots from eight different countries to do the same, and lead other instructor pilots under his supervision to teach thousands more. Kyle is grateful for the incredible experiences he had in the Air Force and the opportunities he had to teach and lead young people in the protection of freedom, but now he's excited to pivot toward teaching parents how to lead their children to a different type of freedom—financial freedom.

Kyle also grew up in a small town in middle America. For Kyle, it was a town of about 5,000 people named Perry, Oklahoma. In Perry he participated in typical small-town activities like high school football, wrestling, and baseball, worked on a farm in the summers, fished when he could, and tried, mostly successfully, to stay out of trouble. Kyle's parents came from humble means and worked incredibly hard to maintain a middle-class lifestyle for their family. He is forever grateful for the sacrifice and example they provided. They did an amazing job at teaching Kyle about integrity, work ethic, and money discipline. As a result, he was able to attain a full-ride scholarship for college, so when it came time to leave the house after high school, Kyle was pretty much on his own financially.

Kyle's journey to becoming a millionaire didn't take six or nine months. It took much longer. However, it never required a huge amount of income. Kyle likens his wealth to the inevitability of a snowball rolling down a steep mountain picking up size and speed as it rolls until it's eventually an avalanche, with its own massive inertia. It's tough to define when a journey like this starts. Though Kyle did have some small money-making entrepreneurial endeavors in junior high and high school, his first real job was as a farmhand and tractor driver on a cattle and wheat farm making $2.50 an hour at age 14 and eventually progressing to the kingly wage of $4.25 an hour at age 17. Though he spent some of the money he earned to buy a car, the rest he saved and later invested.

After high school Kyle received a congressional nomination and was accepted into and attended the United States Air Force Academy in Colorado Springs, Colorado. Though his college education at the Air Force Academy was grueling and challenging, the education was excellent. Furthermore, all attendees were given a full scholarship in exchange for committing at least six years to the military after graduation. When he completed college, Kyle was excited to put his modest lieutenant salary to work and start investing right away.

The first mutual fund Kyle invested in was the top performing mutual fund in the United States the first year Kyle owned it. Investing seemed easy. Sadly, over the next three years the same fund was one of the worst and lost all the gains from the first year and then some. Kyle learned quickly that the investing experience is not without ups and downs. It was clear that he needed to learn more so he didn't need to depend on others to manage his money. Despite this tough lesson, Kyle, then a first lieutenant in the Air Force, kept living frugally, saving nearly half his income, then shelling it into investments to let the power of time work for him. He kept adding to the snowball.

In addition to adding to the snowball, he was also adding to other areas of his life. Along the way, he married his beautiful wife, Tracy, who somehow put up with his crazy work hours and constant relocation from base to base. Soon after, he added two new members to his family in his beloved sons Bryce and later Bret. Together, Kyle's family forms the foundation that is more valuable than any amount of money he could ever possess. As a young Air Force officer and pilot, Kyle worked 12-hour days and then, after spending some precious family time at home, had to study flying material or prepare for his flights for up to four hours more nearly every night. Still, he would find a way to squeeze in research on financial and investing topics whenever he had the chance. Eventually he learned enough to not have to depend on others to manage his money and investments. The more he practiced and studied about money, the better his investing results became. Methodically, year after year, he learned about investing, saved, invested, and stayed patient and disciplined. Though he did tend to take some risks by buying primarily fast-growing technology companies, his investing and millionaire strategy was pretty basic: put in the time and work to learn about money, save aggressively, make great investments for the long term, and let compound interest work for you. In other words, keep adding to the snowball and let it keep rolling down the mountain and gaining size.

After sticking with stocks at the beginning, Kyle eventually began studying real estate and even attained an inactive Oklahoma real estate license, which helped him be better educated for his next step. After considerable research and due diligence, Kyle and Tracy began purchasing, renovating, and managing single-family rental properties. After years of property managing their own houses, Tracy eventually went on to also get her real estate license and together, she and Kyle started their own real estate business. As they accumulated more houses, these properties slowly but surely added to their income and net worth as they appreciated.

As Kyle progressed in rank to captain, then major, and eventually lieutenant colonel, his salary increased, but his spending increased much less. Along with their rental income, this allowed him and Tracy to continue to put approximately 50 percent of their income into investments most years—a practice they continue to this day. Kyle's naturally thrifty nature didn't stop his family from enjoying life and traveling. He and Tracy take multiple trips every year, and Kyle has been lucky enough to travel to 22 countries all over the globe, many of these with his family.

Eventually Kyle diversified into a variety of additional nontraditional investments that also have grown and produce income. As a result, despite never having what would be considered a high salary, Kyle was able to grow his snowball more and more each year. Thanks to that and compound interest, he became a millionaire at age 37.

When Kyle retired from the Air Force at age 43, he was completely financially free and had enough passive income from his investments to live off and support a family of four for the rest of his life, even if he didn't have a military pension. This is the avalanche that feeds itself as it rolls down the mountain. Though Kyle did steepen the slope of the mountain by improving his investment returns through intense study of finances, he's a strong believer that it doesn't take a genius to become a millionaire. It mostly just takes discipline, hard work, and time. If the mountain is high enough and you do your part adding to the snowball as it rolls, the avalanche is inevitable.

It took Kyle thousands of hours of research, hard work, and discipline to achieve the financial literacy and wealth he has today. Kyle's never-ending quest for greater financial knowledge continues to this day, but he's impassioned to share and condense the secrets he learned over a lifetime of education to help others become financially literate and wealthy as well. He is constantly striving to find better ways to teach people about money. Kyle is relatively new to the financial education business, but he's been instructing young people for over 15 years. He also received a bachelor's degree in human factors from the United States Air Force Academy and a master's in engineering psychology from the University of Illinois. These degrees helped give him insight into the way people learn and think.

Although he is an entrepreneur at heart and has businesses now, Kyle's journey to follow his passion and become an Air Force fighter pilot necessitated he become an employee of the government. Although being a fighter pilot isn't generally considered a traditional job, it is traditional in the sense that he was an employee with a fixed income and not a business owner. Having a set salary meant he had to focus more on managing his expenses and learning everything he could about investing. This pursuit of financial education has helped him achieve over 25 years of consistently outperforming the market in his stock and real estate investments as well as other nontraditional investments.

As a 25-year veteran of the military, Kyle is living proof that reaching financial freedom doesn't take an incredibly high-paying job or even an inheritance, a trust fund, or any version of being born with a silver spoon. What it does take to achieve financial freedom is persistence and a plan. Although Kyle never needed to work again, he knew it was his duty to continue to serve society by resuming his passion for instruction and teaching others the plan and path he followed.

After instructing young people for over 15 years how to fly high-performance jets in support of freedom, Kyle's passion for teaching has evolved into helping people all over the world learn his secrets for acquiring financial freedom at an early age. His program, Flight To Financial Freedom, leads people down their own flight path to the wealth they desire and deserve. Kyle uses his background as a flight instructor in the United States Air Force to teach people with a system similar to the one the world's premier air force has been employing in pilot training for over 60 years. He also incorporates his education in engineering psychology to help people understand their own psychology and the math needed to reach their goals. If you complete the education, conversations, exercises, and actions in this book, Kyle is confident your child will be well on their way to being financially literate and accelerating in their own Flight To Financial Freedom and millionaire status. Step into the cockpit and get ready for takeoff!

## HOW TO USE THIS BOOK

Given the stories you just read, you can see that we all have different paths in our walk to financial freedom. Our challenge to you, the parent, is that you use this book to choose your path and make a plan. Are you a single parent like Loral, or part of a traditional family like Kyle's? Will you be an entrepreneur nearly all your life, or will you spend most of it as an employee with perhaps some side hustle businesses that later become bigger businesses? Do you plan to make most of your wealth in more traditional assets like stocks and real estate, or will you create your riches by buying primarily businesses and off–Wall Street assets? Do you intend to leave a large financial legacy to your children, or do you prefer to mostly let your kids create their own financial freedom?

Some financial concepts are universal. We'll discuss these concepts in the next two chapters, titled "Millionaire Mindset" and "Millionaire Actions." We'll reference these concepts throughout the book, so feel free to refer back to them whenever necessary. We'll also point out some areas where we have differing opinions on how to create a plan. Furthermore, we'll explain the reasons for these varying opinions and the objectives at the heart of these differences so you can make your own decision on which path you would like to take. We were both able to become millionaires in our thirties, so neither way of doing things is right or wrong, but you may prefer a particular method for you and your child. After evaluating the two perspectives, all you have to do is pick a path and make a plan. In the end, we want the same thing you want: to help your children understand and master money so it can be a conduit toward helping them reach their dreams, rather than an obstacle.

We worked hard to create specific actions, examples, and talking points in this book. It would be easy to read through the entire book in a relatively short period of time. However, that is not the best way to use this book. Our intent is that this book be used as a reference to guide your money conversations with your children. It shouldn't be given away after one read. You will want to refer to it for each age group and throughout your child's life to ensure their money mastery is on track. As we mentioned before, this book is intended to be an 18-year read. By the time your child has left the nest, this book should have been referenced dozens of times and be worn, highlighted, and filled with handwritten annotations or sticky notes.

The book is broken down into age-based chapters, as well as sections within each chapter. We would recommend that everyone start by carefully reading Chapters 1 through 3. These chapters set the foundation for the rest of the book, and it's important that you know the concepts well so you can teach them to your child. After that, we recommend reading, or at least skimming, through the rest of the book to get a sense for topics we will cover in future chapters. This will help you become familiar with the destination of the flight we are taking you on and may help explain why we do or do not cover certain topics at earlier ages. In a perfect world, parents would get the book when their child is born and follow along as they grow up. However, you may already have children at varying ages. If your child is older than five,

**If your child is older than five, we strongly recommend that you read through all the chapters for age groups younger than your child up to the chapter for your child's current age. If you skip chapters, you will miss out on teaching many of the foundational concepts your child needs to understand.**

we strongly recommend that you read through all the chapters for age groups younger than your child up to the chapter for your child's current age. If you skip chapters, you will miss out on teaching many of the foundational concepts your child needs to understand. If there is something you have not taught your child or accomplished, then ensure you cover it. The goal is to make sure that at some point you have thoroughly educated your child on all the concepts we discuss in the book.

Once you reach a section on a topic you haven't taught your child, we recommend that you focus on only that topic, or maybe a few others at most, following the guidance or talking points in that section. If you don't feel like you grasp the material enough to teach it, you may need to work on getting educated on the topic for yourself first. We highly discourage you from taking the easy route and just skipping that section. Teaching your kids about money, business, and investing is one of the most important and enduring things you can do for them, and it will make a huge difference in their life. Very little is taught at school, so if you skip an important topic then nobody else is likely to fill in the gaps. You *must* teach these concepts at home. We believe it is your responsibility as a parent. (To clarify, when we use the term "parent" we are referring to not only biological parents but anyone who is a caregiver of a child, including nonbiological parents, grandparents, and guardians.)

Once you are confident you fully understand the topic in a given section, spend several weeks making sure you incorporate the example conversations or actions into your daily life. Whenever possible, try to keep it fun or incorporate games so your child will always associate money and learning about money with positive emotions. Learning is much more effective if it's entertaining and not a drudgery. Try to make sure you bring up each topic at least three times before you move on. Don't give up. We have several resources and options for getting help on MakeYourKidsMillionaires.com. Even after moving on, commit to incorporating the new money concept or action you introduced into regular conversations with your child about money. Usually, the best teaching examples are not the ones you repeat from a book but the new organic conversations that happen unexpectedly in daily life, which may be inspired by ideas from this book. Remember, the point of this book is to motivate you to learn more about money and to instill that motivation in your child, so feel free to get creative! Additionally, you should talk

**You *must* teach these concepts at home. We believe it is your responsibility as a parent.**

to your kids about money at a level higher than what you think they'll understand. With the foundation they will get from the teachings in this book, you'll be amazed at how much they can comprehend. Even if they don't fully get it, when they see the concept again it will make more sense to them. Remember, the best way to teach is ultimately by example. Let them see you make smart, planned money decisions, and describe how you are making those decisions when they happen. Be willing to explain and let them learn from your failures as well, so they don't have to learn the lesson themselves.

After you feel like your child has a full grasp on the content in the section you have focused on, move on to the next section. Some sections may discuss content you have already fully covered through your own parenting. Congratulations! If you are confident this is the case, then feel free to move on the next section. Just make certain your child is exposed to all the content and has done the recommended actions. You can use the Millionaire Kids Checklist at the beginning of the book to help you ensure you cover all the topics. If your child is advanced, you may be able to begin introducing concepts from the chapter associated with the next age group. That's great, but be very careful to avoid working too far ahead and turning the learning process into a frustrating chore for your child.

Go to our website, MakeYourKidsMillionaires.com, for further resources on the topics discussed here and to take a quiz to see what your financial needs and behavior indicate. We will continue to release additional materials to supplement the book, so be sure to check back on the website often.

We also suggest that you reference the Recommended Reading list at the end of this book. You can begin with Loral's first three books:

*The Millionaire Maker, The Millionaire Maker's Guide to Wealth Cycle Investing,* and *The Millionaire Maker's Guide to Creating a Cash Machine for Life.* The bonus of you having to teach the financial material in this book to your kids is that this will help you cement the concepts for yourself as well. The best way to fully absorb a concept is to learn it to the level that you can teach it. Nobody said parenting would be easy. Parenting a millionaire is even harder, but we think this book will help make the flight more navigable.

## THE LORAL LANGEMEIER TEACHING PHILOSOPHY: YES! STRATEGY AND CONCURRENT LEARNING

My whole life as a single mom and entrepreneur has been about saying yes and figuring it out. These are called YES! moments, and it is important to define what they are. YES! moments are those instances when you have the choice to make a decision to say YES! to a challenge and then figure out how you will monetize that opportunity. A key to taking full advantage of YES! moments is saying YES! and then figuring out who you can add to your team to help you accomplish that goal. This allows you to have the time to deliver on that goal as well as take on more projects.

In the teaching style of YES! Energy, I refer to the YES! Energy equation, which shows you how to create more YES! Energy in your life. The mentality, the psychology, that lens that you look through in life, has to be YES!, and I would challenge you to do a self-assessment. Do you look through the lens of optimism and YES!, and what's possible, or do you live life through a lens of no, hesitation, or caution and miss opportunities all the time because of it?

That is your opportunity to generate YES! Energy in your life. In my book *The Millionaire Maker,* we introduced wealth builders to the Gap Analysis, which is a method of assessing and mapping the distance from where you are to where you want to be. This is the first step in a systematic approach to generating wealth that we call Sequencing. Once you grasp the importance of engaging in a sequential process, you will increase your capacity to make, keep, and invest money through leadership of your team. This is how we teach people to become millionaires and create generational wealth.

The challenge with teaching people about investing is that nearly everything they have ever been exposed to is stock or real estate training. What people don't see is how to invest off of Wall Street. How do you lead your own wealth, your own investing, and your own investing teams? My model of teaching is modeling others and adult learning theory. This approach not only encourages but supports modeling.

When I started, I would take people out of the classroom and into the street. I would take people on real estate tours, gas and oil well tours, hemp facility tours, franchises, or whatever the asset class might be. Whatever the business is, modeling the actions and following someone who has already walked the path is clearly the simplest, most proficient and effective use of anyone's time.

Between having YES! Energy, having a millionaire plan, having a millionaire matrix sequenced properly, and modeled by those who have walked the path and become multimillionaires, my style of learning is more organic than a systematic learning brain processing style. If you want to be a millionaire, you need to actively spend time with people who are either already millionaires or actively working to become one. Your first step toward becoming a millionaire is to visit https://integratedwealthsystems.com and take the financial personality quiz to see what your path toward becoming a millionaire looks like.

## THE KYLE BOECKMAN TEACHING PHILOSOPHY: THE PILOT TRAINING MODEL

Why is it that society tells us money is more forbidden as a topic than even religion, politics, or sex? We all have to use money in our lives, so why not talk about it? Not teaching or talking to your kids about money before they go off into the world is like kicking them out of the nest and hoping they will instinctively fly and not go crashing to the ground. The problem is that humans don't have any more instincts about money than they do about flying. It must be taught. In my model I actually teach people to fly to their financial freedom. The model is time-tested and effective. It's about learning by doing. It's the same model I used to teach pilot trainees how to fly in Air Force pilot training. Here's how it works.

## 1. Academics
The first step for all pilot training students is academics. Trainees have to pass through academics, sometimes called ground school, and learn the academic knowledge needed to fly the airplane. This includes an array of information about everything from aircraft systems and aeronautical engineering concepts to airspace structures and even basic meteorology.

## 2. Simulation
Once students demonstrate proficiency in the academic phase, they move on to the aircraft simulators, which let the students experience the visual and hands-on feel of flying but in a safe environment. This is an important step for a couple reasons. First, it allows for part-task training. This allows the student to focus on one thing until they get it right and helps prevent them from feeling overwhelmed. Second, it allows them to build confidence in an environment where their mistakes are not fatal. This confidence is essential to the student's success.

## 3. Demonstration
After proving their effectiveness in a simulator, students are finally able to physically get in the jet. However, before they are given an opportunity to fly or try a specific task, they receive an expert demonstration on what it should properly look like from their instructor. It's extremely important that instructors provide an excellent demo because students will often copy what they saw the instructor do more than what their instructor tells them. Demonstration is also given during

the simulation phase, making the order of steps 2 and 3 sometimes interchangeable.

## 4. Supervision

Now that the student has seen a demonstration of how it should be done, they are finally ready to take the controls and give it a try. Even when the students do begin to fly, the instructor supervises them in the same aircraft and has his own set of flight controls with the ability to take over and override the student pilot when necessary. Under the watchful eye of their instructor, slowly but surely, the students are permitted to fly more and more of the time.

## 5. Solo

Eventually, after the instructor has witnessed proficiency in all the necessary skills, the student is finally deemed proficient enough to fly solo. This is a huge day for the young pilot. It's like the freedom and exhilaration you felt when you first drove a car by yourself. Though the student knows the learning isn't over, they can take great pride in their accomplishment.

The model above is the one I encourage for teaching your child about money, and it's a model we'll reference several times in this book. In pilot training this system is repeated not only for the broad phases of training but over and over for various tasks and skill sets. While one skill is reaching proficiency, another may still be in the academic stage. Sometimes the student may even need to take a step back and repeat steps to better solidify the muscle memory and habits necessary to make a skill permanent. The same will be true of your child's learning about finances. Throughout the book we will methodically help you walk your child through these phases, starting with the academics and simulation of adult aspects of money. In later years you will show them how you handle money. Then you will begin letting your child assume their money controls more and more. All the while you will still be able to "take over the controls" if necessary. By the time they leave the nest they will be ready to fly solo on their own Flight To Financial Freedom. Doesn't this make a lot more sense than just pushing them out of the nest with no training and hoping they get lucky?

Let's look at how the Pilot Training Model applies to just one of the broad financial concepts we discuss in this book—credit. In Chapter 5, when children are ages six to eight, we advise that you discuss the very basic academics of credit in the section "Basics of Credit Cards, Debit Cards, Checks, Etc." When your child is 9 to 11, we help you expound on this subject in the section "Good Debt Versus Bad Debt." Even more academics is recommended in Chapter 7 at ages 12 to 15 when we cover the section "Credit and the Credit Score." Meanwhile, the simulation phase is also begun at this age in the sections "Get Your Child an Authorized User Credit Card" and "The High Cost of Borrowing." When you get your child an authorized user credit card, you will simultaneously give them a demonstration of how you use and pay off your credit card. Although the authorized user credit card also allows you to provide the oversight necessary in the supervision phase of the pilot training model, the most advanced supervision comes in Chapter 8 when they are ages 16 and 17. In the section "Advanced Credit Cards—Friend or Foe?" we recommend more academics for your child, along with a more realistic simulation and supervision phase. Additional academics comes at this age in the form of the section "College Prep and Student Loans." Finally, the solo phase of the Pilot Training Model for credit occurs in Chapter 9 when they are ages 18 and beyond. Here we show them the reason why credit is so important in the section "Help Them Buy Their First Real Estate Investment." These steps discuss only the credit aspect of money. Throughout the book, we discuss all the other major financial concepts as well. When one concept has reached the supervision stage, another may still be in the academics stage. Just as your child begins to reach proficiency in one aspect of money, they will begin the model again to learn more advanced financial concepts. The more phases of the Pilot Training Model you can complete for each concept, the more cemented and ingrained will those concepts be for your child.

# WHAT'S THE BEST STRATEGY?

As you can see, we even have different strategies and teaching styles. Kyle is more of a logical thinker and is very methodical. His style is often appreciated by kids who like structure. Loral's strategy, on the other hand, is more free-form and based on taking decisive action. What is best for you may be dependent not just on your personality but also on the personality of your child. We'll reference both viewpoints so you can choose your path.

Before proceeding, we'd like to make one final point of emphasis. Whichever teaching strategy you use, true learning requires integrating the concepts from this book into your everyday life over the long term. No matter how quickly you read this book or how aggressively you teach the concepts, you can't turn your child into a millionaire in a week. It takes time. In his bestselling book titled *First Things First*, Stephen Covey refers to "the law of the farm." He describes that true change and learning can't be rushed. Covey explains that even though you could cram knowledge in the short term, it won't make a life-changing and lasting impact unless you abide by the law of the farm. He relates how silly it would be to think you could forget to plant the crops in the spring, do nothing all summer, then think you could quickly cram in the cultivating, planting, and watering in just one day and hope to have a bountiful harvest the next day. It just doesn't work that way.

Because we both grew up working on farms, we can relate. You should talk to your child about money all the time, not just via occasional lectures. Show and explain to them how money is a part of everyday life, and let them know it's not a forbidden topic. Take the time now and for the rest of their childhood to slowly but surely sow and cultivate your child's knowledge of money, and it will indeed yield a bountiful harvest that will be capable of feeding them for a lifetime.

# CHAPTER 2

# MILLIONAIRE MINDSET

*Money comes easily and frequently.*

—Loral Langemeier in acclaimed documentary film *The Secret*

In this chapter and the next one we will be teaching you, the parent, the concepts we think are important to give you the foundation you need to teach your child about money. To help you appreciate our perspective, it's important that we get you thinking like a millionaire first. Then we can be on the same page toward getting your child to have a millionaire mindset. Let us reiterate that point. This chapter and the following chapter are written with the parent in mind and are not materials we recommend teaching to your child right away. Chapters 4 through 9 include a chronological checklist of materials for your child, and they will refer back to these chapters when appropriate.

Some of the concepts we will teach in these chapters may be foreign or uncomfortable to you. We even introduce some basic math. If you end up feeling lost or frustrated, please be patient and don't give up. Take your time and follow along, and the concepts will eventually become second nature to you. We encourage you to approach these concepts with an open mind. Try not to read them and immediately question their validity. Generally, when people digest information either by hearing or reading it, they listen in a judgmental mode of either affirming "Yes, I believe that" or "No, I don't believe that." However, the only way we can truly learn is to understand that there may be other perspectives or ways of doing things. In order to open our mind to learning these new perspectives we must try to avoid listening and thinking "That isn't true" every time we hear something that doesn't fit our paradigm of beliefs. Instead, we would challenge you to think "What if that were true?" Doing so will give you a much more open mind to learning.

Welcome to what, for many of you, may be a whole new way of thinking about money. Some of the things we teach are different than what you may have heard before, but this is how the wealthy think and act. We call this way of thinking the "millionaire mindset."

**KYLE SAYS: When referring to the idea of absorbing new ideas and mindsets rather than judging them, I like to say that you should "try to be a sponge and not a filter."**

**LORAL SAYS: These are not suggestions. It is the truth of how millionaires are made.**

## FINANCIAL FREEDOM OVER RETIREMENT

Congratulations on committing to making your child a millionaire and financially free. Financial freedom is the fundamental concept that we talk about in our teaching. But what do the terms "millionaire" and "financial freedom" even mean? The millionaire part seems pretty easy to define if you are American—1 million US dollars in net worth. But what if you live elsewhere? Loral teaches and owns companies in South Africa, where the South African rand is only worth one-fifteenth of a dollar (as of this writing). It would be much easier to be a rand millionaire. What if you live in South Korea, as Kyle and his family did for a year during a remote military tour? The South Korean won to US dollar conversion rate stands at over 1,000 won to 1 dollar (as of this writing). That means with only 1,000 US dollars you have over 1 million won! Some of your kids are won millionaires already! (Don't worry, that's not how we plan on making your child a millionaire.)

With the guidance you learn in this book and the action you will help inspire, your child should easily be able to be worth $1 million in US dollars in their lifetime, if not at a relatively young age. The problem is that inflation will make $1,000,000 have much less purchasing power in the future than it does now. Who is to say what it will take for your child to be truly wealthy like we hope they will be? That's why, even though the millionaire term is catchier and more recognizable, we feel a much more important goal is to make your child financially free.

But what does financial freedom look like? How do we define it? Does it mean we are retired? According to Merriam-Webster, a few definitions of retire are "to withdraw from action" or "to go to bed." A synonym is "to recede." As Loral has said for years, "Retirement is an agricultural word that means to put cattle to pasture to die." None of those definitions sound like much of a goal we would want to aspire to reach at any age, much less an early age. So, retirement in the traditional sense isn't the answer. Financial freedom is the answer, and you can have it at any age. Can you imagine your kids being financially free in their twenties?

If you do an internet search for the term "financial freedom," you will get various definitions ranging from "able to make life decisions without being stressed about money" or "having enough money to do what you really want in life." The problem with these definitions is they are not very measurable. We'll talk much more about goal setting in a future chapter, but one of the rules is that goals should be measurable. If they aren't measurable, how do we know we've achieved them? The answer is as easy as PI$\geq$E. It's pronounced like the tasty dessert pie and even more appealing. Our belief is that financial freedom centers around creating passive income. Passive income is just a fancy way of saying money that comes in automatically, with little to no effort required to achieve it. This will almost always come from assets and investments. We'll discuss this more later. Having financial freedom means that you have enough passive income to cover all your future expenses. At last, we have a definition that is measurable. With his mathematical background and military affinity for acronyms, Kyle even created an easy-to-remember formula: Financial Freedom is PI≥E. In other words, we reach Financial Freedom when our passive income is greater than or equal to (represented by the ≥ sign) our expenses. Here's the formula:

$$\text{Passive Income} \geq \text{Expenses}$$

If we replace Passive Income with "PI" and Expenses with "E" we get:

$$\text{Financial Freedom} = PI \geq E$$

We don't propose to know what your child's expenses will be later in life, but as they grow older and wiser, they should be able to figure it out. We'll even show them in this book how to begin forecasting their expenses at an early age so they will be practiced when they are ready to reach financial freedom.

The beautiful thing about reaching PI≥E or your Freedom Day using this definition is that it means you never have to work again. That's not to say you wouldn't stay active and do something. You might even choose to continue working. You just won't *have* to. We aren't retiring and going to bed after all. It just means you have the freedom to do whatever you want. Recall the metaphorical story of the investment snowball rolling down the mountain. Once the snowball gets large enough, it picks up speed and becomes an avalanche and has its own massive inertia to keep it rolling down the mountain even without your work or contributions. This is the essence of financial freedom. To learn more about Freedom Day, read

**KYLE SAYS: I like to say that when people have finally reached the point of their passive income exceeding their future expenses and achieved my definition for financial freedom that they have been able to "Pass the PI≥E."**

**LORAL SAYS: When people finally achieve their long-term money goals, I refer to it as their Freedom Day. Financial freedom is one of the most important of the goals one could set for Freedom Day.**

*The Millionaire Maker* (get a free copy at MakeYourKidsMillionaires.com).

Having the freedom to do whatever you want with your life is an incredible feeling. You no longer need to worry about working to meet your needs—your income comes passively. No longer would you have to feel the

KYLE SAYS: I like to refer to the Confusion, Uncertainty, Frustration, and Fear about money as CUFF. The goal is to get "off the CUFF."

stress about money that so many people must endure.

Now imagine you could give your child the ultimate gift of financial freedom and help them eliminate stress about money forever. That's what financial freedom can provide!

## THE SIMPLEST WAY TO ACHIEVE FINANCIAL FREEDOM

English philosopher William of Ockham stated in his law of parsimony that "Entities should not be multiplied without necessity." This has often been paraphrased as "The simplest solution is most likely the right one." The next formula we are about to provide is so incredibly simple that we risk offending you by even talking about it. However, as William Ockham knew, simple things can be elegant. Also, you'll hopefully be teaching your child this formula once they are old enough, so it's best that it be simple enough for them to understand at an early age. Doing so will create the mindset they need and provide the foundation for building wealth. The most basic equation for how to start is that you must first keep your income greater than your expenses. This can be depicted with the equation where I = income and E = expenses:

**Income > Expenses**

or

**I > E**

If you get this backwards and E is greater than I, you deplete your bank account and eventually go into debt. If I is greater than E, you can invest the difference to grow your wealth. Eventually these investments can provide you passive income (PI), which allows you to achieve financial freedom, or PI≥E. This cycle is described as the Wealth Cycle in *The Millionaire Maker's Guide to Wealth Cycle Investing*. We'll get into this concept more in the next chapter.

We warned you it would be simple. Yet despite its simplicity, many people around the world just can't seem to follow it. They consistently spend more than they make and go further and further into debt. We like to say it's not difficult, it's different. To have a millionaire mindset and build true wealth you must ensure that you and your child follow this formula unfailingly. In fact, the quickest way to financial freedom is to make the income not just slightly greater than the expenses, but much greater. Here's where the elegance comes in, and where some of our differences emerge. There are two ways to make income much greater than expenses. It makes sense because the equation has two sides. Let's look at the equation again.

$$I > E$$

The first way to make the income much larger than the expenses is to raise the income to a very high level. The second is to lower the expenses to a very low level. Either way works, and both require commitment. While Kyle was building his wealth, he tended to focus most on lowering his expenses. Loral focused more on raising her income. If you are thinking ahead, you've probably considered that in a perfect world you could "Pass the PI≥E" or reach your Freedom Day the quickest by doing both simultaneously. In fact, we both endorse doing that as much as possible. It should be obvious that if your expenses go up just as much as your income does, then you aren't making any progress. Likewise, all the expense reductions in the world won't help you if you don't have some income. You or your child's individual situation may make one side of the equation easier to work on than the other.

## The E Side: Expenses

Kyle, for example, chose early in his life to commit to being an Air Force pilot. As a pilot he worked 12-hour days most of his 20-year career, sometimes including weekends, and was at times deployed. This left him very little time to stoke his entrepreneurial fire and increase his income. As a military member, he also never had a huge salary. Despite this, he was able to acquire and renovate several rental properties and a large portfolio of stocks that grew in value and generated some income. However, he wasn't able to use a business to really ramp up his income until the last few years of his career. As a result, he increased his assets and wealth mostly by focusing on lowering his expenses, especially while he was young. By being frugal, he was able to invest a very large percentage of his income so that, by age 43, he had enough passive income being generated by his investments that he and his wife didn't need to work at all. As a result, although Kyle is now a business owner, he emphasizes the "E" (expenses) side of the equation in his teaching a bit more than Loral.

## The I Side: Income

Loral, on the other hand, has been a single mom entrepreneur her whole life. She did plenty of travel, lots of long hours of her own, and built an expert team. She was able to use her knowledge of money to grow that business and ramp up her income significantly at a young age. Her first education company made $1.7 million by year two. Although she is aware of her spending and minds her cash flow, rather than being frugal like Kyle, she would just make more money to invest in assets to grow her wealth. Thus, her teaching tends to emphasize the "I" (income) side of the equation a bit more than Kyle.

## Both Sides

Neither of us could have made it to millionaire status or financial freedom without being mindful of both income and expenses, but our different paths prove that there is more than one route that can be followed to reach wealth. We've both learned valuable lessons along our journey to Freedom Day, or PI≥E, and have chosen to give back by passing these lessons on to the world. Fortunately for you, the reader, you'll get to learn from both our perspectives, and you can use those lessons to teach your children how to find their own path to millionaire status and financial freedom.

## ENTREPRENEUR MINDSET

A common theme in this book is the value of teaching your kids the mindset of an entrepreneur. Even though we both spent time as employees (Loral for only a few years), we both feel it's required that you teach your kids about being an entrepreneur.

There are three key reasons we believe people should be entrepreneurs. First, being a business owner means your income is totally uncapped. It's one of the few income-producing endeavors where there is no limit to how much you can make if you work hard (and smart) enough to grow your business. In fact, the ability to use entrepreneurism to raise one's economic standing is one of the pivotal advantages of capitalistic economies.

We'll discuss this more in a moment, but suffice it to say, the benefits of having your own business are numerous. Second, being an entrepreneur allows you to create additional income even if you already have employment in a job (sometimes referred to as "W-2 income" due to the IRS Form W-2 given to employees). Many huge companies today were started as "side hustles." For example, Steve Jobs was working at Atari when he built the first Apple computer. Twitter, Craigslist, and Khan Academy are just a few of the other companies that were started as side hustles to their founders' jobs. Even if you don't want to grow your business to be

> **LORAL SAYS:** Teaching people to be an entrepreneur is what I'm known for. I've been teaching for years that "Christopher Columbus didn't come to America so he could get a job."

the next Apple, creating a side hustle can allow you to pursue and create income from your passion while still having the consistent and reliable income of a job. Third, even if your child never aspires to become an entrepreneur, knowing the mindset of businesses and how they work is a vital skill. People who are familiar with business concepts will often perform better even outside of their own business because they realize how to make their organization more money. The leadership and innovative thinking that successful entrepreneurs possess are skill sets sought after in all aspects of life. Additionally, experience and knowledge as an entrepreneur makes people better investors.

Most investing, whether it be real estate, venture capital, or stock investing, requires a good knowledge of business. After all, stocks are merely small stakes in the ownership of a business. If you can grasp the fundamentals of business, your stock investing prowess will be much better.

Earlier we mentioned the advantages of being an entrepreneur. Loral teaches eight key differences between how wealthy entrepreneurs deal with money versus how employees do. Table 2.1 is a good summary of these differences. In fact, it's why so many people have a hard time being an entrepreneur. We are traditionally only taught the left column.

> **KYLE SAYS: Even though I was an employee for over 20 years while in the Air Force, I credit my passion for understanding the way businesses operate with helping me achieve market-beating investment returns.**

**Table 2.1** Key Differences Between How Entrepreneurs and Employees
Deal with Money

| | EMPLOYEE | ENTREPRENEUR |
|---|---|---|
| 1 | Employee makes the money | Your business makes the money |
| 2 | Boss controls your hours | You control your hours |
| 3 | Expenses are paid after tax | Expenses are paid pretax |
| 4 | Take vacations | Take business trips |
| 5 | 401(k) | Solo 401(k) |
| 6 | Debt and credit cards = bad | Debt and credit cards = critical |
| 7 | Retirement | Financial freedom/Freedom Day |
| 8 | Fixed tax filing date | Variable year-end filing date |

1. As mentioned earlier, the biggest advantage of being an entrepreneur is that your income is virtually uncapped. If you work hard and do well in your business, it will translate directly into more income for your business—no blaming it on your boss or coworkers if you don't make enough money. This income goes directly into the business and makes the business (which you own) more money. The employee has a relatively fixed income, and when you do better it's your employer who reaps the benefits and not you the employee. If you are an entrepreneur, you can also turn up the spigot on sales if you decide you need more income and are willing to invest the capital and time. Simply said, companies make money. Individuals get taxed.

2. The principal reason most people start their own business is because they want the freedom to control what they do for a living. However, the freedom provided by being a business owner goes beyond that. While many business owners put in more overall hours than their employee counterparts,

the beauty is in the freedom of *when* to work. Want to take
a business trip or spend more time with your kids? You have
the power.

3. Owning your own business allows you to pay expenses related
to your business before tax. In other words, if your business
needs a new tool, you can buy it with pretax dollars and then
expense/deduct it from your business profits, which will lower
your tax bill. There are over 80,000 pages of tax code that deal
with businesses and help entrepreneurs get tax deductions. As
an employee there are almost no deductions.

4. One of the many expenses you can deduct as an entrepreneur
is the cost of business trips. Savvy entrepreneurs don't take
vacations. They take business trips instead. Want to go to
Florida? As long as you have a legitimate business reason to go
there, and follow IRS guidelines, you can expense the trip. You
obviously still have to do actual business while you are there,
but you don't have to do business all day. As always, make sure
to get guidance from your accountant to make certain your
trip qualifies.

5. Most people are familiar with 401(k) accounts. A 401(k) is
a work-related retirement account in which your employer
allows you to put some of your salary ($20,500 for 2022 with
an additional $6,500 in "catch-up" contributions if you are 50
or older, equaling up to $27,000) directly into a tax-advantaged
investment account. In many cases the employer will match
a percentage of the employee's contribution. A solo 401(k) is
very similar except that it is for small business owners with
no full-time employees. As the business owner, you get to
choose how much you match. Instead of matching only a few
thousand, you can actually choose to max out the employer
contribution ($40,500 for 2022). This means that if you are
under age 50 you could contribute up to $61,000 into a tax-
advantaged account in one year. If you are age 50 or older, you
could actually contribute $67,500. This is an enormous benefit.

Amounts may change, so do a search for "contribution limits" on the irs.gov website to get updated numbers.

6. Another difference between business owners and employees is that business owners realize that debt isn't necessarily bad. In fact, using other people's money to help you make more money is critical, and is how you can grow your business at a much greater rate than could be possible if you had to fund all the capital for the business out of your own accounts. This will be discussed much more later in the book and is a pivotal concept toward becoming a millionaire.

> **LORAL SAYS: One of the phrases I like to teach my students is that "debt is just the cost of money."**

7. Business owners, and the wealthy in general, also think about the term *retirement* in different ways. In a 1905 valedictory address to Johns Hopkins Hospital, the physician William Osler expressed the commonly held viewpoint of the early 1900s regarding retirement. He stated that after age 60 the average worker was useless and should be put out to pasture. Though this view has changed some in recent years, it is still not uncommon for workers to be "pushed out" after age 65. As a business owner, you can be as active as you want for as long as you want. You can also choose to hire employees and take a passive role whenever you want, especially if you've reached financial freedom. Thus, you can still continue to enjoy the income of the business.

8. As an employee, your tax filing date is limited to the calendar year, typically April 15. This limits your flexibility on when you can take deductions and use expenses. As a business owner, however, you can adjust your filing dates of your business or businesses. In the United States it often becomes September or October. This allows you to potentially pull forward or push

back expenses or income into a different personal filing year so that you can maximize your tax savings.

As you can see, the advantages of being an entrepreneur far outweigh being an employee. If you want to remain an employee, you should at least get a side-hustle so you can take advantage of these benefits.

## INVESTOR MINDSET: COMPOUND INTEREST

It's important to get your child to think with the mindset of an investor. An investor is always thinking about how their wealth can compound and grow over time.

**KYLE SAYS: One of my favorite financial lessons that I enjoy teaching students involves an example similar to one I learned in second grade from one of my most influential teachers.**

This lesson on compound interest starts with a simple quiz.

### The Rich Neighbor Example

*Your rich neighbor offers you a one-year contract to take care of his yard each week. He offers two compensation choices:*

1. $20,000 weekly
2. A single penny the first week with your salary doubled weekly

This particular contract is binding for the entire year. You must tend to his yard each week for the entire year, and he must pay you for the entire year. Which would you choose? Before moving on, take a moment to review the problem and decide.

Now let's review the math to figure out which option would produce the most income. Table 2.2 shows the math for the first 13 weeks. Note that, for the column depicting the doubling penny option, the numbers displayed don't appear to exactly double every week. This is because the numbers listed are the cumulative amount earned by that week. For example, in week 2 you earned $.02, but that added with your week 1 income of $.01 equals a cumulative salary of $.03.

**Table 2.2** The Rich Neighbor Example After 13 Weeks

| WEEK | OPTION 1:<br>$20K PER WEEK | OPTION 2:<br>ONE PENNY DOUBLED PER WEEK |
|:---:|:---:|:---:|
| 1 | $20,000 | $0.01 |
| 2 | $40,000 | $0.03 |
| 3 | $60,000 | $0.07 |
| 4 | $80,000 | $0.15 |
| 5 | $100,000 | $0.31 |
| 6 | $120,000 | $0.63 |
| 7 | $140,000 | $1.27 |
| 8 | $160,000 | $2.55 |
| 9 | $180,000 | $5.11 |
| 10 | $200,000 | $10.23 |
| 11 | $220,000 | $20.47 |
| 12 | $240,000 | $40.95 |
| 13 | $260,000 | $81.91 |

Through week 13 (one-quarter of the year) those of you who chose the first option of $20,000 per week are probably feeling pretty confident since you would have $260,000 and the people who chose option 2 would only have $81.91 so far. Let's see what the next 13 weeks look like. In Table 2.3 you'll see that after 26 weeks, half way through the year, the game has changed considerably.

**Table 2.3** The Rich Neighbor Example After 26 Weeks

| WEEK | OPTION 1:<br>$20K PER WEEK | OPTION 2:<br>ONE PENNY DOUBLED PER WEEK |
|---|---|---|
| 14 | $280,000 | $163.83 |
| 15 | $300,000 | $327.67 |
| 16 | $320,000 | $655.35 |
| 17 | $340,000 | $1,310.71 |
| 18 | $360,000 | $2,621.43 |
| 19 | $380,000 | $5,242.87 |
| 20 | $400,000 | $10,485.75 |
| 21 | $420,000 | $20,971.51 |
| 22 | $440,000 | $41,943.03 |
| 23 | $460,000 | $83,886.07 |
| 24 | $480,000 | $167,772.15 |
| 25 | $500,000 | $335,544.31 |
| 26 | $520,000 | $671,088.63 |

As Table 2.3 shows, on week 26 the option of choosing the penny the first week (doubling weekly) has now surpassed the income you would make by choosing $20,000 per week. Incredible, right? The power of compound interest wins again. If you chose option 2 and accepted only one penny for the first week, give yourself a hand—even if you only chose it because it seemed like a trick because option 1 seemed to be obviously better. But we're not done compounding yet. We still have 26 more weeks before this contract is complete.

So how much higher will the compounding option grow? What will be the total income at the conclusion of the entire year? Before proceeding, take a moment to look at the numbers above and venture a guess. Now let's look at Table 2.4 to see the results for the final 26 weeks.

**Table 2.4** The Rich Neighbor Example Weeks 27 Through 52

| WEEK | OPTION 1:<br>$20K PER WEEK | OPTION 2:<br>ONE PENNY DOUBLED PER WEEK |
|---|---|---|
| 27 | $540,000 | $1,342,177.27 |
| 28 | $560,000 | $2,684,354.55 |
| 29 | $580,000 | $5,368,709.11 |
| 30 | $600,000 | $10,737,418.23 |
| 31 | $620,000 | $21,474,836.47 |
| 32 | $640,000 | $42,949,672.95 |
| 33 | $660,000 | $85,899,345.91 |
| 34 | $680,000 | $171,798,691.83 |
| 35 | $700,000 | $343,597,383.67 |
| 36 | $720,000 | $687,194,767.35 |
| 37 | $740,000 | $1,374,389,534.71 |
| 38 | $760,000 | $2,748,779,069.43 |
| 39 | $780,000 | $5,497,558,138.87 |
| 40 | $800,000 | $10,995,116,277.75 |
| 41 | $820,000 | $21,990,232,555.51 |
| 42 | $840,000 | $43,980,465,111.03 |
| 43 | $860,000 | $87,960,930,222.07 |
| 44 | $880,000 | $175,921,860,444.15 |
| 45 | $900,000 | $351,843,720,888.31 |
| 46 | $920,000 | $703,687,441,776.63 |
| 47 | $940,000 | $1,407,374,883,553.27 |
| 48 | $960,000 | $2,814,749,767,106.55 |
| 49 | $980,000 | $5,629,499,534,213.11 |
| 50 | $1,000,000 | $11,258,999,068,426.20 |
| 51 | $1,020,000 | $22,517,998,136,852.50 |
| 52 | $1,040,000 | $45,035,996,273,705.00 |

If you couldn't quite make out the total for the doubling option due to all the numbers and commas it is $45,035,996,273,705, otherwise known as over $45 *trillion*! That's not a typo. We said trillion, not million or even billion. Run the math through your own spreadsheet if you don't believe it. It's true. We just gave you a trillion-dollar idea! Now you just need to find somebody gullible enough (and rich enough) to agree to pay you a single penny the first week, doubled every week for a year. If you find that person, we'll accept a meager 1 percent royalty!

What can we learn from this exercise? The first lesson is the incredible power of compound interest. It's no wonder that Albert Einstein stated, "Compound interest is the eighth wonder of the world. He who understands it, earns it . . . he who doesn't . . . pays it. Compound interest is the most powerful force in the universe." When you guessed what you thought the total would be for option 2 in the example, what number did you guess? Most guess in the millions.

This leads us to the second point of the exercise. Our brains aren't wired for calculating exponential growth. Until we see an example like this one, we just don't truly appreciate it. But exponential growth is exactly what can happen with your investments or, sadly, your lifestyle debt if you let it. That's why Einstein said you either earn interest if you understand it or you pay it if you don't. Wouldn't you like to be on the side of those who understand it?

**KYLE SAYS: In my years of teaching the Rich Neighbor Example I've never had a single person even guess as high as a trillion, even after seeing the first 26 weeks.**

In the example above, your income doubled every week. You'll be hard pressed to find an investment that does that. As a result, you obviously won't see the same incredible growth from this example. But that doesn't mean your investment returns can't still be incredible in their own right. Let's look at a few more realistic examples of compound interest, and some tools you can use to estimate compound interest in your daily life. The point of these tools is to help you make more informed decisions about what to do with your money. See our site MakeYourKidsMillionaires.com for more financial tools.

## The Rule of 72

The rule of 72 is a commonly used tool to approximate the number of years it would take for an investment to double, given a known investment return. The formula is this:

**72/(investment return %) = years to double**

Here's an example. The historical return of the US stock market is approximately 10 percent. If we plug this number into the equation, we can see that, historically speaking (historical returns do not guarantee future returns), it should take about 7.2 years to double our money. For this reason, 7 years is commonly used as an estimate of how long it should take to double the value of your investment in the stock market, sometimes referred to as an investment double. The problem with the rule of 72 or even the 7-year approximation is that, over a long investment time horizon (like for your kids), it still takes some mental math to figure out how many doubles you can expect. A better tool was required.

## The 10X Tactic

We introduce to you the 10X Tactic. With 10 percent returns (the approximate historical return of the stock market), it takes just under 25 years for your investment to be approximately 10 times larger, a 10X return. In other words, if you can assume 10 percent returns, in 25 years you can simply add a zero to the end to estimate what the investment will become. Let's look at an example:

*At 10% returns, in 25 years the $6,000 in an IRA becomes $60,000.*

**KYLE SAYS: The 10X, 100X, and 1,000X Tactics described in the next few sections were created by me and my son Bryce. To be fair, they were mostly created by Bryce. They are the simplest and quickest way I've ever seen to approximate long-term growth of an investment in your head, and to help you appreciate the incredible power of compound interest.**

Note that we simply added a zero to the $6,000 to reach $60,000. This works for any investment amount. The other interesting part of the math is that the years required to 10X are proportional to the return percentage. In other words, if you can double your investment return to 20 percent, it will take half as long, approximately 12.5 years, to get a 10X return. Conversely, if you can achieve only 5 percent returns (half of 10 percent) on your money, then it will take twice as long, or 50 years, to get your 10X. Thus, the ratio of your expected return relative to 10 percent will have the reciprocal ratio relative to the 25 years. Achieving 3 times 10 percent returns (30 percent returns), would require one-third of 25 years, or approximately 8.3 years, to 10X your money.

**KYLE SAYS: When Bryce and I discovered these tactics, we were flying back from an investment education event that Loral hosted called the Big Table, at which I had been a guest instructor. I was using a spreadsheet to show Bryce the incredible power of long-term compound interest. As we reviewed the numbers, Bryce noticed that even though the numbers were exponential, there were some consistent patterns in the numbers. The rules that resulted from us investigating these patterns are described in the following sections.**

If your child is willing to keep their money invested even longer, they can expect their investment to continue to grow at this rate. Since your money 10X every 25 years (at 10 percent returns) it stands to reason that an additional 25 years would also result in an additional 10X, making a total of 100X (adding two zeros) if you kept the single investment earning 10 percent for 50 years. All of these calculations are only approximately correct, but since we've already demonstrated how poorly people estimate compound interest, they get you close enough to have a better sense of how your money can compound than you could guess without them.

## The 100X Tactic

Though the 10X Tactic is great for calculating a one-time investment, it isn't very helpful for figuring out future values when an investor contributes annual contributions (as we highly recommend). Though the 10X Tactic allows you to 100X your money after 50 years, a much quicker path exists to help your child 100X their money. This path is achieved through annual contributions. One can approximate future value for annual contributions by using an equally easy calculation, the 100X Tactic. The 100X Tactic states that with 10 percent investment returns on annual contributions, it will take 25 years to achieve 100X returns. In other words, after 25 years you can approximate the future value (at 10 percent returns) by adding two zeros to the end. For example:

> *At 10% returns, in 25 years, $6,000 in annual contributions to an IRA becomes $600,000.*

As you can see, although not as eye-watering as the Rich Neighbor compound interest example, we've still been able to build a healthy nest egg through the magic of compound interest. Unfortunately, because of the annual contribution value, unlike the 10X Tactic, the 100X Tactic doesn't abide by the same math ratios that allow different investment return percentages to be easily calculated. Consequently, it's best used for approximating 10 percent returns. However, it's still quite useful because 10 percent is the standard baseline investment return that is often used when comparing alternative investments. In the IRA example above, we've used compound interest and annual IRA contributions to reach over halfway to our goal of making our kid a millionaire. How do we reach the rest of the way?

## The 1,000X Tactic

You guessed it. We would now like to introduce the 1,000X Tactic. We wanted to see what happened if we could really build money for the long term, so we extended the time frame of the previous rules to come up with the 1,000X Tactic. The 1,000X Tactic is nearly identical to the

100X Tactic; it just takes more time. The 1,000X Tactic states that with 10 percent investment returns on annual contributions, it will take approximately 50 years (closer to 47.5 years) to achieve 1,000X returns. In other words, after about 50 years you can approximate the future value of annual contributions (at 10 percent returns) by adding three zeros to the end. Interestingly, you can actually still achieve 1,000X returns in less than 50 years (approximately 48.5 years) without making any annual contributions after the first 25 years. This is due to the 10X Tactic, which allows one-time investments to 10X and add a zero after 25 years (assuming 10 percent returns). Because of the incredible power of time and compound interest, the last 25 years of annual contributions only get you to 1,000X returns about one year quicker than if you only made annual contributions for the first 25 years. Let's look again at our IRA example:

> At 10% returns, in 50 years, $6,000 in annual contributions to an IRA becomes **$6,000,000**.

We've finally eclipsed our $1 million goal! In fact, with $6 million we are well into multimillionaire territory. Even if you had only put $1,000 per year you would still eclipse 1 million. Although 50 years may seem like a long time, it isn't that long if you get your child started investing in their IRA right away (as recommended in Chapter 4). Also, if your child follows the tips in this book, they should eventually be able to put away much more than $6,000 and achieve higher returns than 10 percent. This would allow them to reach $1 million much quicker!

As we said before, the purpose of the 10X, 100X, and 1,000X Tactics is not to predict exact future values of investments. Since we can't predict with certainty what our investment returns will be, they will only give you approximations. Instead, the point is to guide spending and investment decisions. For instance, let's suppose your 16-year-old child has earned some cash and is faced with a decision whether to buy a $12,000 car or a less expensive one that is only $7,000. Using the 10X Tactic, you could quickly calculate that the future value of the $5,000 they could save by buying the less expensive car would be approximately $50,000 in 25 years when they were 41—potentially a down payment on a house. Alternatively, in 50 years when they were 66, that same choice alone (choosing the less expensive car) could provide them $500,000 and a large chunk of the money they would need for financial freedom.

Children don't always make forward-thinking decisions in their youth (nor do adults), and they may still choose the expensive car, but at least they would be making an informed decision with full awareness of what they would be giving up in the future by making that purchase today. This knowledge alone can help them make decisions that are in better alignment with their long-term financial goals. The consideration of what alternative things they could use their money for and the awareness that choosing one way to use their money means it isn't available for other things is called opportunity cost. We discuss this concept more in Chapters 4 and 7.

## INVESTOR MINDSET: TAX-ADVANTAGED ACCOUNTS

Although understanding the growth of your investments through compound interest is probably the most important factor in the investor mindset, a close second would be knowing how to keep as much of that growth as possible. One of the best ways to keep more of your investment money is through paying less taxes via tax-advantaged accounts.

So just what is a tax-advantaged account? For the purposes of this discussion, a tax-advantaged account is an account that is exempt from taxes for contributions or withdrawals or both. We will address several of these types of accounts in the Chapter 4 sections titled "Open a Roth IRA for Your Child" and "Set Up a Tax-Advantaged Education Account." Now we'll discuss the general concept of tax-advantaged accounts and how they work.

Whether it be the United States or any other country in the world, governments need taxes to operate, and they usually find a way to get those taxes one way or another. Taxes on investments are no different. They usually either tax you on the front end by taxing your income or on the back end by taxing your investment gains. If you don't have your money in a tax-advantaged account, then the government will actually tax you on both. Tax-advantaged accounts are categorized based on whether they fall into the front-end tax or back-end tax. The three basic categories are tax-deferred, tax-exempt, or completely tax free.

## Tax-Deferred

Tax-deferred accounts include traditional IRAs, traditional 401(k)s, traditional solo 401(k)s, traditional SEP IRAs, and the Thrift Savings Plan (TSP). These accounts are often considered "traditional" because they were the only type of widely used tax-advantaged account until the Taxpayer Relief Act of 1997, which established the Roth IRA. These accounts provide an immediate tax savings in the year of the contribution, but future withdrawals will be taxed at your ordinary income tax rate. In other words, they are taxed on the back end but not the front end. For example, if your income for the current year was $50,000 but you contributed $5,000 into a traditional IRA, your taxable income for that year would be only $45,000. This would effectively lower your current tax bill, but you would still have to pay taxes on your withdrawals when you were ready to remove the money from the account and use it. It's also worth pointing out that tax-deferred accounts pay no annual taxes on interest, dividends, or capital gains. As the name implies, all these taxes are deferred until the end. For regular accounts, annual taxes on these factors serve to erode your investment balance and reduce the money available to compound each year. Depending on what you are invested in, this could lead tax-advantaged accounts to grow at a much faster rate than non-tax-advantaged, regular accounts. In general, contributing to tax-deferred accounts is preferable when you think your tax rate in later years will be less than your current tax rate.

## Tax-Exempt

The second type of tax-advantaged account is tax-exempt accounts. Some of the more commonly used tax-exempt accounts include Roth IRAs, Roth 401(k)s, Roth Solo 401(k)s, 529 College Savings Plans, and Coverdell Education Savings Accounts. Tax-exempt accounts aren't really completely exempt of taxes because they provide no immediate tax benefits. However, the withdrawals are exempt from taxes. Thus, they are taxed on the front end but not on the back end. For example, if your income for the current year was $50,000 but you contributed $5,000 into a Roth IRA, your taxable income for that year would still be $50,000. However, you would pay no taxes on the withdrawal. Like tax-deferred accounts, tax-exempt accounts also have the advantage of avoiding annual taxes on interest, dividends, and capital gains. This boosts their growth rates in a similar way. If you think your tax rate will be higher after age 59.5 when you can pull out your funds than it is when you make the contribution, you would probably be best served with a tax-exempt (sometimes called a Roth-style, after the Roth IRA) account.

## Fully Tax-Free

The final type of tax-advantaged account is the fully tax-free account. This account is free of taxation on the front end and the back end—for contributions and withdrawals. Since the government generally likes to take its share on one side or the other, this type of account is very rare and often has limitations. One example is the Health Savings Account (HSA). Money is contributed to an HSA before taxes, just like a tax-deferred account. This money then grows without the requirement to pay tax on the earnings. Additionally, as long as the HSA is used to pay for qualified medical expenses, withdrawals aren't taxed. It's the best of both worlds. HSAs do have special requirements, including having a high-deductible health insurance plan, so you'll need to do your research and talk to your accountant to see if you qualify. If you do, and you anticipate having medical bills that aren't covered by your insurance, it can be a great way to legally pay less in taxes. Another type of account that can be completely tax-free is the Flexible Spending

Account (FSA). There are health, dependent care, and limited purpose FSAs. These accounts must be set up by your employer, and they allow you to set aside pretax dollars for purchases related to one of the three categories associated with your FSA. Similar to an HSA, the money is not taxed upon withdrawal. However, unlike HSAs, FSAs must be used in the same year they are contributed, meaning they can't compound over time like the HSA can. This "use it or lose it" status means you have to carefully forecast your expenditures. Also, they may disqualify you from using an HSA or from taking certain tax credits, like in the case of the Dependent Care FSA. As always, seek counsel from a tax professional.

Depending on your income level, some tax-deferred or tax-exempt accounts may end up being tax-free or at least close to it. If your income is very low (like for most kids), you may be effectively paying zero tax or nearly so. Therefore, even contributions to a tax-exempt account wouldn't really be getting taxed on the front end—making this an obvious scenario where choosing a tax-exempt account would be best. Likewise, if your income when you make your withdrawals is very low, then your effective tax rate may be nearly zero then as well. Also, some states give exemptions or partial exemptions on contributions to even tax-exempt accounts, reducing the tax even on the front end for these accounts.

## Which Tax-Advantaged Account to Choose?

Table 2.5 shows when the different tax-advantaged accounts are taxed.

**Table 2.5** When Various Tax-Advantaged Accounts Are Taxed

| TYPE OF TAX-ADVANTAGED ACCOUNT | TAXED ON FRONT END? | TAXED ON BACK END? |
|---|---|---|
| Tax-deferred | No | Yes |
| Tax-exempt | Yes | No |
| Fully tax-free | No | No |

The problem with a non-tax-advantaged account, or regular account, is that it doesn't have the advantages of either of the previously listed accounts. You end up paying tax on your investment twice. First, you pay tax on your income. Therefore, anything left over that you can commit to a regular investment account is with after-tax dollars. Second, in a regular account, you also pay tax on any withdrawals from the account. This double taxation can really add up.

Since this is a book about your kid, let's look at an example for which type of tax-advantaged account would be best for your child. For this example, assume your child is 12 years old and earns $6,000. They want to invest all of the money for the long term. If they invest that $6,000 in a tax-deferred traditional IRA and achieve 10 percent returns until they are age 70, that single investment would become a significant amount of money. How significant? Well, if we assume they will have to pay 32 percent tax on their withdrawal at age 70 (probably more), then they will have an after-tax withdrawal of $1,026,682. That single investment made them a millionaire! Not bad. But what if they had instead invested in a tax-exempt Roth IRA. We'll use the same 10 percent returns until age 70. Since their tax rate at age 12 was probably effectively zero (we'll discuss taxes more in Chapter 6), the front-end tax savings of the previous traditional IRA didn't help them, but the back-end tax savings of a Roth IRA did. Now their withdrawal amount would be $1,509,826. They were able to keep nearly $500,000 more. We don't know about you, but half a million dollars seems pretty significant to us. In Chapter 4 we'll explain a technique that will allow your child to start investing well before age 12 and with annual investments. This will allow them to achieve millionaire status well before the age of 70.

In almost all cases, young people would best be served by investing their money in a Roth IRA. The tax savings on the back end are much more significant for them. If you are an adult and trying to decide which account to choose, be aware that if you are in your peak earning and tax-paying years, and you expect to be in a lower tax bracket after age 59.5, the traditional IRA might be better suited for you due to the front-end tax savings. Every person's situation is different. To find out what is best for you, we recommend making some assumptions about your current and anticipated future tax rates and throwing them into a spreadsheet or online calculator. As mentioned before, we will have resources at MakeYourKidsMillionaires.com that can help with these calculations. If your head is spinning over all the numbers, don't get discouraged. Look at the scale of the numbers. Even the worst scenario made your child a millionaire. The most important thing you and your kids can do is to start investing right now and get that money compounding and working for you.

## LIFESTYLE CYCLE VERSUS WEALTH CYCLE

The next key theme that is discussed throughout the book is the concept of Lifestyle Cycle versus Wealth Cycle.

If we handed you $10,000 right now and you did not understand how to put it into the Wealth Cycle Process, then you would be no closer to generating wealth than you were before you had it. That's because most people grew up living in a Lifestyle Cycle. In the Lifestyle Cycle, wealth can never be built because money that comes in goes right out again to support perishable, one-time-use consumption. And in many Lifestyle Cycles, money is spent, thanks to credit cards, even before and at a greater rate than it's earned. This would be reflected by an equation where $I < E$—never a good thing. Conversely, in the Wealth Cycle, money coming in supports and buys assets. Assets are money-making

**LORAL SAYS: The following sections on Lifestyle Cycle and Wealth Cycle are summaries of a portion of my content from my *New York Times* bestseller *The Millionaire Maker*. These concepts are also discussed in depth in my other bestseller, *The Millionaire Maker's Guide to Wealth Cycle Investing*. I recommend you read them to get a more detailed appreciation of my teachings.**

resources that will generate cash flow and create wealth. Note the differences between the Wealth Cycle on the left and the Lifestyle Cycle on the right in Figure 2.1. An income statement (to be discussed more later) would show primarily income for those in the Wealth Cycle but mostly expenses for those in the Lifestyle Cycle. The balance sheet (also to be discussed later) would show primarily assets in the Wealth Cycle but liabilities in the Lifestyle Cycle. Liabilities are the opposite of assets. They are things you owe that take away from your wealth. Also note the flow of money in the chart. In the Wealth Cycle income buys more assets, which generate more income to buy more assets. In the Lifestyle Cycle expenses result in liabilities, which create more expenses and liabilities. If you aren't following the terminology, it's quite possible that you are living in the Lifestyle Cycle. We'll explain all these concepts in this book so you can ensure that you and your child can stay out of the Lifestyle Cycle and in the Wealth Cycle. These powerful cycles can work either for you or against you.

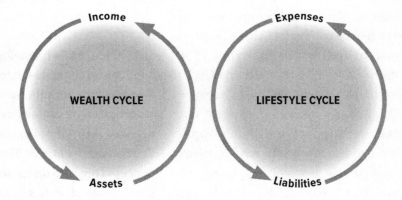

**Figure 2.1** Wealth Cycle Versus Lifestyle Cycle

The difference between having wealth and not having wealth is the difference between living in a Lifestyle Cycle and living in a Wealth Cycle. As crazy as it sounds, a person earning $14,000 a year who understands the concept of a Wealth Cycle has a much better chance of building and sustaining wealth than a person who makes $1 million a year and lives in a Lifestyle Cycle. Thus, although it would be nice of us to hand you $10,000, it's better if we teach you about the Wealth Cycle Process. As the saying goes, it's better if we teach you to fish than if we give you a fish. The Wealth Cycle Process shows you how to continually make money by increasing your assets, thus creating a Cash Machine to feed those assets, and steadily building your passive income so you can expand your wealth. Now that you are familiar with the Wealth Cycle mindset, we'll explain in the next chapter the millionaire actions you can take to energize your child's Wealth Cycle.

## CONDITIONING FOR A MILLIONAIRE MINDSET

The fundamental premise of the millionaire mindset is that you are already a millionaire; you just haven't attained it yet. The problem is that it's natural to get caught up in your subconscious programming that tells you that you aren't a millionaire. The programming and paradigms you have about money are your conditioning. Conditioning is one of the most important concepts in *The Millionaire Maker*. The book explains how important it is to recognize that any limit to your thinking exists only in the paradigms ingrained in you, not in your ability to create a big vision. We encourage you to establish a vision that's unencumbered by your past paradigms. Let's talk about paradigms. How would you finish the phrase "Money is . . ."?

Much like our views about people, food, or health, our beliefs about money came from our parents, our teachers, and other adults in our lives. These adults' beliefs were influenced by the circumstances through which they lived, or what they learned from their parents. You could even say it goes back to what those parents learned from their parents, and so on. These beliefs are ingrained, and because they're usually subconscious, the cycles are continuous until someone breaks them. It's not their fault if your parents taught you limiting and restrictive beliefs about money. They were only repeating the cycle of what they had been taught and what society reflected. Consider some of the following paradigms you may have been taught:

**Money is scarce.** Some of us have parents or grandparents who lived through the Great Depression, an era that rooted an entire generation in a scarcity mindset. Others experienced great hardship during the Great Recession of 2008. In the future, some people may have scarcity mindsets based on the financial downturn of 2020. These people passed on to their children the idea that money was in short supply and that, when it did surface, it had to be squirreled away. Even banks were considered untrustworthy. If the phrases "We can't afford it" or "Money doesn't grow on trees" resonate with you, you may suffer from a fearful relationship with money.

**Money is evil, dirty, or bad.** Several of us have parents or grandparents who believe that the road to bad places is lined with green. They've only ever seen the drawbacks of the money chase, and the audacity and indulgence of those with too much money. Some even believe that wealthy people are bad people. Novels and films often highlight the idea that it's the crooked ones who make the money. If the phrase "The meek shall inherit the earth" sounds accurate to you, then you may have a hostile relationship with money.

**Money comes monthly.** The most common way to make a living is to be employed, either with a company or as a skilled professional, with a weekly wage or an annual salary. Historically, this provided the safe, sure thing required by heads of household. Yet, that level of risk was usually balanced with an equal level of reward—low. For most, even those who do very well, working for a company or as a skilled professional is a constrained opportunity. Most employees, even well-paid ones, have only a small increase in salary during their lifetimes. These slow and small increases in salary may have been acceptable back when pensions were common, but with the virtual death of pensions in modern society these small pay increases make it difficult to generate wealth. "Slow and steady wins the race" may have helped the turtle, but if it reflects your relationship with money, then you may have a cautious relationship with money.

**Money is for others and not me.** Some people feel that they don't deserve to be wealthy or that there is only so much of the millionaire pie to go around. The reality is that creating wealth and financial freedom is available to everyone. It is our right to be wealthy, and our hope is that people take their space and know they deserve it. By making money, you are not taking it from someone else. It's more like the concept that a rising tide lifts all boats. By making money, you create a greater capacity to contribute to society, and it's your duty to do this. If you struggle with this concept and you've ever thought "Wealth is for others" or "I'll never have money," then you may have a defeated relationship with money.

**Money is a man thing.** There was a time when men alone made and managed the household money. That time was not so long ago. Some of you may have grown up with such conditioning. Although there are gender tendencies with money management, they are a result of years of conditioning. Women and men need to understand that money knows no gender. One of Loral's programs that really resonates with wealth builders is "Wealth Diva: A Man Is Not a Plan." If you ever thought "Let him bring home the bacon," then you may suffer from an apathetic relationship with money.

**Money is medicine.** For some people, retail therapy goes a long way; there's no difficulty a new pair of pants can't cure. We live in a culture of consumerism. Many of us use money to fill the unsatisfying holes in our lives. Some people grew up with a sense of entitlement about money, assuming their parents or a trust fund would always pay for everything. In the process, they became careless about what they had. This is a vicious and unproductive cycle. The new car gets old, the closet fills up with clothes, and the toys pile up in the playroom. This is not to say there aren't wonderful things to buy and spend our money on; after all, money should be fun. But as with overeating, too much spending on the wrong things can get any of us feeling sluggish and sad. If you love the saying "Shop 'til you drop," then your relationship with money may be disrespectful and nonchalant.

**Money is always a menace.** For too many people, money is always viewed as a problem. Bills are a hassle. Keeping up with the Joneses is exhausting. Being an entrepreneur sounds like too much work. Some people may even think getting rich would be a burden and make these things worse due to all the paperwork and responsibility. These views of money create a perspective that money is a problem, not a solution. If you've ever thought "It's hard enough just to survive, let alone thrive" or "More money, more problems," then you probably have a negative and pessimistic relationship with money.

**Money talk is taboo.** Many of us have been brought up to believe that conversations about money are in bad taste. Money and financial success, and failures, are considered personal subjects that shouldn't be discussed and certainly shouldn't be taught. Few of us talked with our parents about how much money they made. Incredibly, some people don't even know their spouse's salary. This approach has unintended consequences and has created a world where very few people are having real conversations about money and finances, the very conversations they need to learn and succeed. If your parents ever told you "Money is not discussed in polite society," then you may have a withdrawn and uninformed relationship with money.

In each of these examples, it's clear that unless your parents made a conscious choice to think and act differently, they conditioned you to have the same mindset they did. There is no doubt they had your best interests at heart and did the best they could, most likely having learned these beliefs from a culture that dictated commonly held and subconsciously acknowledged agreements about money. If you decide to break this cycle, you will have the opportunity to teach your children to have more productive beliefs and a more profitable relationship to money. As you become aware of the limiting beliefs you hold, you can work to change them. With the help of this book and mentors and respected friends, you can change your paradigms and those of your child. By sharing your desire for new beliefs and asking your mentors and respected friends to help you spot the subconscious limitations you may be putting on yourself, you will teach your brain to follow your behavior. Begin now by restating your beliefs. For example, if you've discovered that you hold any of the above examples as beliefs, you will:

1. Change "money is scarce" to "money is abundant" and support an optimistic relationship with money.
2. Change "money is evil, dirty, or bad" to "money is good and acceptable" and create a friendly relationship with money.
3. Change "money comes monthly" to "money comes constantly and from a range of sources" and create an opportunistic relationship with money.
4. Change "money is for others and not me" to "who better than me for money to come to?" and create an empowered relationship with money.
5. Change "money is a man thing" to "money is for everyone to know about and understand" and create a thoughtful relationship with money.
6. Change "money is medicine" to "money is a tool to improve my life for the long term" and create a respectful and responsible relationship with money.
7. Change "money is a menace" to "money is a solution" and create a constructive relationship with money.
8. Change "money talk is taboo" to "money talk is vital" and create a communicative and educated relationship with money.

You can see how much better it is to be optimistic, friendly, opportunistic, empowered, thoughtful, respectful, responsible, constructive, communicative, and educated than to be fearful, hostile, cautious, defeated, apathetic, disrespectful, nonchalant, negative, pessimistic, withdrawn, and uninformed. With practice, you can ensure that you and your child have the right positive paradigms and attitudes about money. How do you do so? Reconsider the phrases in your brain. Play to win, not to lose. Be decisive, not tentative. Increase and expand your money, rather than guarding, preserving, and squirreling it away. Be excited and enthusiastic, not fearful or overly cautious. Wealthy people are proactive and create the lives they want to live.

Consider your language. The vocabulary you choose not only reflects, but actually affects your thinking and that of your children. For example, the word "if" is conditional, while the word "when" is definitive. From this point on, your dreams and goals, along with those of your child, are when, not if. Do not let "if" pass your lips in relation to this pursuit. You will get there, there's no doubt—it's only a matter of when. Begin now: "When I become a millionaire, I will . . ." Have your child repeat the phrase. When you become more affirmative, your child will follow your lead.

You must reset your mind and psychology to reinforce what it is you want, instead of supporting the very thing from which you would like to move away. You can start by restating your beliefs to reverse that financial conditioning. Take the statements you've summarized about the preconceived notions you culled from childhood, such as "Money is difficult to earn and even more difficult to keep," and flip that around. In this example, that would restate to "Money comes freely to me; money is easy to keep and multiply." Repeat these phrases out loud and around your kids. It may seem trite, but it's anything but. Experts will support the fact that something tangible occurs when you, and others, hear you verbalize your beliefs. When you restate your beliefs, you are announcing your dreams to yourself, which is the first step in making those dreams come true. When others hear your dream, loud and clear, they begin to understand the real you better and can help direct you, through referrals or resources, toward your goal. It's a prosperous cycle that starts with you, what you believe, and just as important, what you say. Once you've begun to master your own language and affirmations, help your child do the same. Don't let the negative conditioning you may have received in the past carry on to any more generations of your family.

It's time to conceive a new perspective for both you and your child. Most people do not have a clear direction or vision of what they want their life to look like when they have great wealth. Though no official ceremony takes place, too many people have said "I do" to their current reality, making a lifetime commitment to something that really doesn't satisfy them. Don't let this continue for yourself, and definitely don't let this happen to your child. Make no mistake about it. Even after you commit to a new vision for wealth in your life, the little voice in your head is going to mess with your plan. There's no getting around it; there is a lot of noise in your brain. The ingredients that make up this recipe of noise include excuses, blaming, confusion, uncertainty, fear, frustration, disjointed conversations, rationalizing, procrastinating, distraction, and lack of focus. They need no introduction and no explanation. We know them all too well. As you move forward, you must turn off the negative noise of your brain.

The next mistake you must avoid if you want to condition yourself and your child with a millionaire mindset is you must avoid getting stuck in your own story. The stories we contrive in our heads started with the results we observed, usually those of adults around us, and continue with the results we create, usually very similar to the ones we observed as kids. This is a vicious cycle. Our story is created from our experiences. Each time we have an experience, we filter it through our feeling and reason to either confirm or deny the truths we believe. For example, if you invest in a real estate deal and it fails and you lose your money, you can choose either to learn from the experience by taking the lesson and building a new experience, or to get stuck in the drama of your story. If you do not recognize your truths, you will continue to affirm negative truths.

**LORAL SAYS: I like to tell my clients and students, "Don't get stuck; get it done."**

If you have stated new truths, then you can reflect on each experience in a new light and spiral up into a better story. A self-fulfilling prophecy is better when the prophecy is positive. If you want to help your child become a millionaire, then you have to take charge of your own story and take responsibility for your own actions. Thankfully, our children don't have a long and tragic story holding them back. If you are willing to be the leader of your own life, you can set the positive example they need to create the effective story and life of abundance and financial freedom that they deserve.

You created your current financial situation based on your beliefs. It's OK if you don't yet believe the new possibilities for your financial future. It takes action to reconstruct and then reinforce thought. Those who do it the opposite way, waiting for the belief in order to create the action, have a long wait. Instead, you will program your brain the way it was programmed in the first place, by letting it learn from your actions. By acting first, the reaction is visceral, as it was when the notions were first imbedded. This will create a more enduring change, because you're not painting over old paint but stripping the walls and starting over. You will be uncomfortable, and maybe even frustrated. That's because you're growing. As you change your financial situation, this will reprogram your brain to a new and progressive set of beliefs. It took you years to be conditioned the way you are. That conditioning did not come from lectures and thought exercises; it came from behavior and practices. Behavior and actions will turn your brain around. As your brain is being redesigned you will be able to create this new design for your child as well, ensuring a legacy of wealth and success that can endure well past when you are gone. The action begins!

# CHAPTER 3

# MILLIONAIRE ACTIONS

*The path to success is to take massive, determined action.*
—Tony Robbins, self-help and motivational speaker

In the last chapter we talked about the millionaire mindset and how we are often weighed down by the scarcity mindset that was taught to us in our childhood. It's important not to pass this mentality on to our children if we want them to be truly wealthy. To be successful they need to think of money as being abundant. It's funny that the common saying among those who have a scarcity money mindset is "Money doesn't grow on trees." When people say this, they mean that money doesn't come easily.

We remember being children and arguing that even though money doesn't grow on trees, fruit does, and you can sell that fruit for money. We both grew up in families that had fruit trees. What most people probably don't realize about fruit trees is that they require a lot of work. They require watering, pruning, spraying for pests, harvesting, and cleaning up fallen pits, just to name a few. We remember dreading having to help our parents with the fruit trees. It was backbreaking work, but we're glad our parents taught us that lesson. We didn't have an abundance of money growing up, but we did have an abundance of home-grown fruit. It's just that it took a lot of work to grow that abundance. Money is no different. It's quite abundant—you just have to work for it. Perhaps the reality is that the opposite phrase, "Money does grow on trees," is accurate. Money is abundant, and it continues growing and producing as long as you put in the work and take the actions necessary to achieve it. The millionaire mindset is important, but it's nothing without millionaire actions.

## MONEY MUSCLES

Money muscles transition us from a millionaire mindset to millionaire actions. They can be thought of as the habits we have about money that lead us to action. These habits are born out of the thoughts we have about money and the paradigms we've set for ourselves. Let's talk about the way our body's muscles work. When pushed to their limits through uncomfortable exercise, the muscle fibers undergo trauma and break down. Our body repairs these fibers by fusing them, which increases their mass and size. The next time we work out, the muscle is stronger and can take on more workload. Our money muscles work the same. As our new money habits become engrained, we get stronger and better able to take on more challenging financial situations. The actions of talking about money, making money, forecasting money, and investing money become easier. As we flex these new money muscles, we will gain confidence. This confidence will motivate us to even more action. Just like with regular muscles, building our money muscles will involve some soreness and discomfort along the way. It's that discomfort that lets us know our money muscles are growing.

Everyone has money muscles—for some they're just a bit atrophied. If you had a dream to run a marathon, your first steps would most likely be to get some running shoes, stretch out the kinks, and jog a few miles. Similarly, if you dream of being a millionaire, you need to start with the building blocks that will help you go the distance. Becoming a millionaire requires getting into financial shape, and that means building your money muscles.

Prompted in part by consumer product companies and the entertainment industry, many of us are obsessed with our health and fitness. It's also pervaded our conversation, sparked by articles and journals.

Many of us have become proficient in fitness studies, diets, medical procedures, and scientific terminology. People have no problem revealing the most intimate details of their health to perfect strangers.

As health and fitness govern our physical lives, money and finances affect our economic lives. Money may not be the most important thing in life, but it can probably have the most impact. Money may not bring us happiness, but having it in abundance can remove one of the largest causes of unhappiness and stress in our lives and marriages. Whether right or wrong, it seems that more people measure themselves by the yardstick of their wealth than by their health, and yet money and finance conversations rarely take place. If the conversation does occur, it usually covers general issues like Wall Street or the nation's credit card debt, not anything personal or specific, like our own portfolio or bad debt.

If you want to become a millionaire, it's time to get in shape, build your money muscles, and run the race toward wealth. As with all exercise programs, the first days are the most difficult; you'll be a little sore at first. Not only will it take your brain a while to adjust to this new behavior of focusing on your finances and committing to a positive perception of money, but it will also require a time commitment. This means that you will have to build this program into your schedule. This too, will seem second nature after a while—much like taking an hour to jog, or to watch a favorite TV show, or to meditate. As those things eventually fit into your day, so will this. It will make each day of your life more important and significant. Time and again, we've found that when we put substance into our schedule, the unsubstantial moves off. As you progress and get financially conditioned, the process will become more fun and exciting, and it will get easier and easier. You won't believe you haven't been doing it your entire life.

## WEALTH CYCLE ACTIONS

In the last chapter, we introduced the concept of the Wealth Cycle and how important it is to change your thought process from one of a Lifestyle Cycle to a Wealth Cycle. Now we will describe the actions required to accomplish that. Just as every person's life is particular to them, so must each person's Wealth Cycle plan be tailored to the individual. In her book *The Millionaire Maker*, Loral explains that the Wealth Cycle Process is based on 12 building blocks that you will employ in your own fashion, depending on your specific requirements and objectives (Figure 3.1).

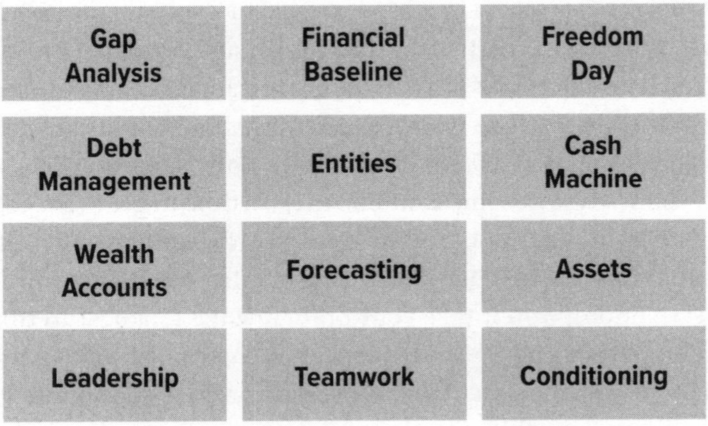

| Gap Analysis | Financial Baseline | Freedom Day |
|---|---|---|
| Debt Management | Entities | Cash Machine |
| Wealth Accounts | Forecasting | Assets |
| Leadership | Teamwork | Conditioning |

**Figure 3.1** The 12 building blocks of the Wealth Cycle

We'll discuss many of these building blocks in more detail throughout the book, so don't get too bogged down by them now or try to memorize them. Some are more applicable for adults than children, so we will focus on those blocks your child needs to learn the most. The blocks are briefly defined as follows:

1. **Gap Analysis:** An innovative financial model that will create a map from where you are to where you want to go.
2. **Financial Baseline:** An overview of your current financial situation in the form of an income statement that includes revenue and expenses and a balance sheet that includes assets and liabilities.

3. **Freedom Day:** The realization of each goal, starting with 120-day objectives and accelerating beyond millionaire status.
4. **Debt Management:** A five-step debt elimination plan that erases consumer debt, the greatest barrier to wealth building.
5. **Entities:** The organization of trusts, partnerships, and corporations that hold and service wealth and take advantage of the tax strategies devised by Congress and state legislatures to protect companies and help businesses grow.
6. **Cash Machine:** The fuel that accelerates the Wealth Cycle, which comes from your capacity to create more income from a legitimate business venture. You must learn to earn.
7. **Wealth Accounts:** The accounts where you consistently pay yourself first, out of your earnings. This account is specifically earmarked for purchasing investments. The assets you buy with the Wealth Account will eventually replace your earned income with passive income.
8. **Forecasting:** A projection of your revenue, expenses, assets, and liabilities and how to direct those numbers into companies that make full use of the tax code.
9. **Assets:** Direct and diversified asset allocation, which is essential to create passive income to feed the Wealth Cycle.
10. **Leadership:** You must learn to "lead your wealth." Though you may, and should, choose to delegate your wealth building, no one can drive the Wealth Cycle process like you can.
11. **Teamwork:** You must build and direct a team of professionals to help you develop and execute your strategies and reach your goals. Wealth building is a team sport.
12. **Conditioning:** Adopting a financial way of thinking. As you accumulate the experience that gets results and gain the confidence to commit even more significantly to your wealth plan, you will develop a positive and healthy relationship with money. We discussed this in Chapter 2.

Now that we've introduced these concepts, let's break them down and talk about how these actions work toward achieving wealth and financial freedom.

## Gap Analysis, Financial Baseline, and Freedom Day

All wealth plans begin with the first three blocks: Gap Analysis, Financial Baseline, and Freedom Day. These three blocks are tools for uncovering where you are and where you need to go.

The first Wealth Cycle block is the Gap Analysis. The Gap Analysis uncovers the financial gap between where you are now and where you want to be—between your current financial situation and your long-range goals. Specifically, you will understand how much money it takes, and what you must do, day-to-day, for you to reach those goals. Of course, to complete the Gap Analysis we must first know where we are now.

The Financial Baseline involves figuring out where you are currently with your finances. This could be considered the starting line. To measure this, you will use the balance sheet to figure out your assets and liabilities as well as an income statement to know your revenue and expenses. Revenue is similar to income, and we will sometimes use the terms interchangeably in this book. However, revenue in the context of a business and accounting tools like income statements is the more correct term to describe the money that comes into a business before any costs or expenses have been accounted for. Your child will learn about balance sheets and income statements in the Chapter 7 sections titled "The Balance Sheet" and "The Income Statement."

In order to complete our Gap Analysis we next need to figure out where we are going. What are our goals? These specific financial goals are what Loral calls the Freedom Day. The long-term goal might be financial freedom, or as Kyle calls it PI≥E, or something different or short-term, but we need to define the specifics of that goal. Your child will learn about goal setting in the Chapter 5 section titled "Your Child's Money Goals." This is an opportunity for you and your child to clarify your purpose and create a vision to step toward making it happen.

As you consider the Gap Analysis, realize that the gap between your Financial Baseline and your Freedom Day goals may be small, but for most of us with a big healthy vision, it's usually a large gap. We can assure you, this is good news. This gap is not a threat to your ambition. It is, in fact, a necessary element to fueling that very ambition. It should be a motivator. It should drive you to take immediate massive action in order to change your situation and move forward. When combined, the first three blocks are continuously revised and adjusted throughout the process.

## Debt Management, Entities, Cash Machine, Wealth Accounts, Forecasting, and Assets

The six building blocks of Debt Management, Entities, Cash Machine, Wealth Accounts, Forecasting, and Assets are core strategies that ensure money making and wealth building. These middle building blocks of the Wealth Cycle, though engaged simultaneously, are used in different sequences and with different emphasis, depending on the needs and wants of the individual wealth builder.

The first building block in the middle section of the Wealth Cycle building blocks is Debt Management. Although we won't go into the specific debt management tactics discussed in *The Millionaire Maker*, we do talk about debt extensively in several sections of this book, including "Good Debt Versus Bad Debt" "College Prep and Student Loans," and the sections on credit and credit cards. Our passionate hope and belief is that this book will ensure that your child never gets stuck in the vicious Lifestyle Cycle that can create massive consumer debt.

The next building block is Entities. Although entities are perceived as advanced for kids, they can still be taught to them at an early age, and they are absolutely essential for adults who own a business and are worth learning about for kids as well because they may eventually need them for their business as well. The entities we are referring to in the Wealth Cycle are technically just legally established companies or organizations that are separate and distinct from their owner. They are almost like a fictitious person that is created only on paper. In the section "Entrepreneur Mindset" in Chapter 2 we discussed several advantages of businesses over individuals. Many of these advantages exist because of the entities that own your business and the substantial tax and liability advantages afforded these entities. Under the US tax code, assets held in some entities are treated differently than an individual's personal assets. This can save taxes and, consequently, increase cash flow. Other entities protect the individual owning them from liability associated with that entity or protect assets in the entity from the personal liability of the owner. This can save you money if you get sued, and it can even prevent litigation because the assets are either hidden or owned by an entity and not the individual. We both have an assortment of entities to protect our assets. Knowing which entity to use can be complicated, but that's one major reason we are such advocates of having lawyers and accountants on your team.

The Cash Machine is the legitimate business venture you create to bring in revenue. It is where you "learn to earn." By bringing in multiple streams of revenue you can accelerate the Wealth Cycle much faster than if you just had a fixed-income job or relied on the growth of the assets alone. The Cash Machine and assets are discussed at length throughout this book. They are the jet fuel for your airplane. Without them, your aircraft isn't going anywhere. With enough of them, you can fly on your Flight To Financial Freedom as fast as you want to go.

The Wealth Account is the Wealth Cycle building block that is like traditional saving. The difference is that the Wealth Account is specifically allocated for investing. It should be an interest-bearing account that allows you to pay yourself first until you have enough to invest in assets that can provide passive income. As the Wealth Account grows you can buy more and more assets. The idea of the Wealth Account is crucial for building wealth. As such, we will be discussing it in several chapters in this book.

Forecasting involves projecting what your future revenue, expenses, assets, and liabilities will be. It's similar to what most people know as "budgeting" but without the negative connotation. In Chapter 7 we'll provide more information in the "Forecasting" section.

Assets are the things you own that have value and provide the passive income necessary to reach financial freedom and "pass the PI≥E." As your assets grow, they will provide more income, which will allow you to buy more assets. This cycle of turning income into assets, and assets into income, is the key to building sustainable wealth. The money works for you, not you for it, so you can focus your attention on maximizing your rates of return.

## Leadership, Teamwork, and Conditioning

The last three blocks we'll discuss are the bottom three foundational blocks of Leadership, Teamwork, and Conditioning. These blocks are the core competencies which drive the actions of the previous blocks.

As the pilot of your own Flight To Financial Freedom, you must lead yourself and your team to the financial destination you desire. You have to make certain that everyone is aware of your flight plans and coordinating their efforts to accomplish the mission—your financial goals. Without leadership, your team would be flying blind. In Chapter 5 we'll talk more about leadership in the section "Leadership Is Vital."

As we will discuss in Chapter 5, teamwork is fundamental. It's impossible to be an expert at everything. Even when he was the pilot of the vaunted Fairchild Republic A-10 Thunderbolt "Warthog" aircraft, which only has one seat, Kyle knew he needed a team to complete the mission. Even fighter pilots usually employ wingmen to provide mutual support. He also had team member support on the ground from crew chiefs, maintenance personnel, air traffic controllers, intelligence officers, medical personnel, security forces, comptrollers, and a host of other support personnel. Without the teamwork of all these specialists his flights could never happen. Similarly, to build great wealth you need your own team of professionals: accountants, lawyers, bookkeepers, mentors, brokers, professional advisors, and investment partners, just to name a few. Having that team in place allows you to focus on what you do best. An African proverb states, "If you want to go fast, go alone. If you want to go far, go together." Our goal is to help you go far. We'll talk more about teamwork in Chapter 5 in the section "Teamwork Is Fundamental."

We already discussed Conditioning at length in the previous "Millionaire Mindset" chapter. Conditioning involves changing not just the way we think, but also the way we act. It is discussed and trained throughout the rest of this book. We will be teaching you to condition your child to think and, more important, act like a future millionaire. An important aspect of this conditioning is getting your child to understand the importance of leadership and teamwork.

# BEYOND THE BUILDING BLOCKS: SEQUENCING

Proper sequencing is essential to bringing it all together and making the Wealth Cycle work. Sequencing could be succinctly described as doing the right thing at the right time. The most common mistake we see in wealth building is people doing the right thing but at the wrong time. One example would be paying down low-interest existing debt on assets (like your home) before beginning to build wealth through assets that provide you income. Another might be focusing on your Cash Machine before you've done a Gap Analysis to establish your goals.

When you begin the Wealth Cycle process, you engage each and every building block; they are codependent and indivisible. You will always keep track of a Gap Analysis that will tell you how to get from where you are—your Financial Baseline—to where you want to go— your Freedom Day. You will always employ Debt Management, and if you have or create consumer debt, you will always make it a priority to eliminate it immediately while simultaneously building your wealth. You will always have Entities (legally established companies), which means you'll always run your life like a business. And that means you'll always have a business, a Cash Machine, that will create more money for your Wealth Cycle. You will always run the right expenses through the right entities, which means you will always be Forecasting. You will always be prioritizing a portion of your money into a Wealth Account used only for investing. You will always be investing in assets, and those assets will create more assets, and more assets. You will always support these activities with leadership and teamwork and be mindful of your financial way of thinking, or Conditioning.

Now that we've provided a foundation for you as the parent to comprehend the framework of the millionaire mindset and millionaire actions, it's time to get to work teaching your child. The rest of the book will follow along with your child's progression, becoming more comprehensive and challenging chapter after chapter as the child grows older. Similar to the five-step pilot training model, it will often start with the academics of a concept that will later be simulated, then demonstrated and supervised, then finally accomplished solo by your child. We will give you specific recommendations for things to teach, stories of how we taught our children, and models for actions you should have them perform. We will also give some examples of things you should do on behalf of your child to set them up for success. The book will serve as a guide to steer your money conversations with your child, but you still have to be the one to lead them. The journey won't be easy, but it will be rewarding. That sentiment you'll feel when you gently nudge them out of the nest will be confidence that you've given them all the tools they need to fly to their own financial freedom and fulfill their phenomenal potential for wealth. The journey starts now!

## PART 2

# Age-Specific Guide

GOAL SETTING

RISK VS REWARD

UNDERSTANDING DEBT

FINANCIAL LITERACY

# CHAPTER 4

# BIRTH TO AGE FIVE

*The best time to plant a tree was 20 years ago.*
*The second-best time is now.*
—Chinese proverb

**W**e can hear the objections already: Are these people crazy? Two-year-old kids don't even realize the world doesn't revolve around them. They can barely talk. They can't be taught about money. Well, we disagree. If there is anything we've learned from parenting, it's that kids can learn more than you think. Even if they can barely talk, they can still listen . . . and learn. How else could they repeat at the worst possible moment that embarrassing curse word you accidentally let slip just once?

Many of the concepts we recommend teaching at this age may seem obvious. Clearly nobody makes it to adulthood without understanding that money buys things. Why worry about teaching this concept when people obviously figure this out eventually? The reason we recommend consciously committing to teaching these concepts very early is that doing so puts your child a leg up on others whose parents don't make such a commitment. With the basic concepts and academics firmly grasped, thanks to your early teaching, your kids can move on to more advanced concepts while others are still trying to pick up the basics. They can also start simulating and trying out the financial actions you teach them about at an early age. This allows them to start becoming an investor and entrepreneur much earlier than their peers. Faster learning equals more time earning—for both your child and their investments. We also have several tasks in this chapter for you, the parent, to accomplish. Many of these steps can be accomplished right after birth or, in the case of the first one, even before. *Don't let these tasks overwhelm you.* We front-load many of the tasks in this chapter to ensure that you have the opportunity to take advantage of the compounding effects of time. Once you get these tasks done, they are much easier to maintain throughout your child's life. Again, the sooner these steps are accomplished, the better off your child will be.

## DECIDE ON A LEGACY PLAN

Perhaps even before you have a child, you should consider what it is that you want for that child. Obviously, you want to provide them everything you can to give them a happy, successful, fulfilling, and loving life. But what about money? What kind of financial legacy do you want to leave?

Based on the fact that you are reading this book, we can assume you want to leave a legacy of financial literacy for your children—but what is your plan for your actual money? If you don't have any money to give your child, then the point is obviously moot, but if you are a parent reading this book then you potentially have years to build wealth and reach a point financially where you too will be faced with this important decision. Will you be giving your child all your wealth, or do you want them to make their own way? Perhaps a little of both? The choices you make about your legacy are important because they will frame the way you approach many of the recommendations and actions in this book. Neither approach is wrong. There are positives and negatives to both.

Let's discuss first the idea of planning to leave your child a large legacy of money. The positive for giving them money is that it can keep them from having to stress about money. It can empower them to accomplish their dreams and have the things they want. The negative is that being able to have whatever they want can often lead to entitled and spoiled kids who eventually become entitled and spoiled adults who lose all the money you worked so hard for. It's been said that 70 percent of all wealthy families lose their wealth by the second generation. A stunning 90 percent lose it by the third generation. By the third generation, the kids are often so spoiled that they no longer have the work ethic displayed by the first generation that created the wealth. It doesn't have to be this way, of course. If you teach your child how to manage money and raise them to be financially responsible, your hard work and wealth can be a legacy for many generations to come.

This is a reason why parents may not want to leave their kids a large legacy of money. Those who have to work hard for their money have a strong sense of accomplishment and pride associated with that money. The fact that they earned it themselves can often be a large boost to self-esteem and a sense of fulfillment. Additionally, the hard work required to build wealth often fosters other positive character traits. By not leaving your child a large

**LORAL SAYS: I believe strongly in leaving a large financial legacy for not just my children, but also several generations. Some of the actions that I took regarding legacy are described in my story in Chapter 1. You will read more details about many of the steps I took in some of the upcoming sections and throughout the book. These steps are the building blocks for leaving a legacy.**

**KYLE SAYS: I'm not as big of a believer in leaving my kids a financial windfall. I believe the pride my kids will feel from attaining their own wealth will outweigh any financial benefits of having a large financial legacy given to them. Future sections of this book will discuss examples of situations where I chose to encourage my kids to be happy with and earn the things they have, to teach them about hard work and financial discipline.**

legacy of wealth you may actually be helping them achieve the happy and fulfilling life you desire for them.

The negative to not giving your child a large legacy of money is that your child will have to work hard and face the stress and uncertainty of not knowing if they will have the financial means to fulfill their desires and dreams. They may miss out on some of the joys of life because they are spending so much time making money. Again, it doesn't have to be this way even if you decide not to give them money or you don't have the financial means to give them money. If you follow the guidance in this book, your child will be well equipped to lead a life of wealth and prosperity that will allow them to fulfill their dreams and desires while still enjoying the joys of life.

The idea of legacy is one where we as authors have differing viewpoints. Though we both grew up without much money and weren't given any sort of money legacy, our conclusions on what is best for our children are somewhat different.

Take note of how we communicated the reasons for doing what we did with our children. Although we have different opinions on the importance of legacy, the dichotomy between us is never as simple or absolute as it seems. Loral does have several measures in place to ensure her kids have ownership and get a sense of accomplishment in their wealth, so she is not on the far end of the pro-legacy spectrum. Similarly, Kyle isn't completely on the anti-legacy end of the spectrum. He isn't going to leave his kids destitute, and he does have a plan that could give financial incentives to help his kids create their own wealth. Above all, we both believe strongly that the most important legacy we can leave our children is the legacy of financial literacy and the skill set to create their own wealth. We also both believe in the legacy of creating responsible, hardworking children who contribute to society and do something with their lives. Regardless of what you decide to do with your financial legacy, it's important that you give it much thought. The sooner you can decide, the more quickly you can take action on the steps necessary to set your child's financial future in motion.

# START A BUSINESS AND
# GET INCORPORATED

If you haven't already, now is the time for you as the parent to start your own business. We discussed many of the reasons for starting a business in Chapter 2 in the section "Entrepreneur Mindset." If it's been a while since you read that section, we recommend that you review it now. We won't reiterate all the advantages listed in that section, but the primary benefits revolve around taxes and income. The tax benefit is the ability to control your business tax deductions. The income benefit is the ability to control how much you can increase your income—to effectively grow the "I" in the I > E equation. As we mentioned before, the faster you can grow your "I," the faster you can put the difference into investments and assets that will feed the Wealth Cycle and bring you more income and wealth. Perhaps equally important as the tax and income reasons for starting your own business is the fact that it will make it easier to model the strategies we teach. In this book we will be recommending that you teach and help your child to become an entrepreneur. It's not impossible to do this without being one yourself, but it is necessary that you have a good understanding of business and entrepreneurship. The best way to learn is to do it yourself so you can then teach your child.

Some of you reading this are already entrepreneurs, and that's great. Others are saying, "There is no way I have the time or desire to start a business." Perhaps you even have restrictions from participating in other jobs and businesses at your main place of work. Still others may have such a lucrative or enjoyable job that you don't feel the need to ever quit your job or do anything else. We get it. However, even for you naysayers we would still recommend that you get what we referred to in Chapter 2 as a "side hustle."

A side hustle doesn't have to be full-time. It doesn't have to even take up much time at all. If you purchase real estate and help in the management of it, you have a business. You just may not have called it one yet. If you buy into a direct sales or multilevel marketing company, you are an entrepreneur as well. If you occasionally sell quilts at the church, as mentioned in *The Millionaire Maker*, that can become a business as well. Having a business allows you to take advantage of all the tax breaks and benefits that the rich have been taking advantage of for centuries. Then you can teach those benefits to your kids. In the meantime, you need to employ your kids with your business. Not only does this give you a chance to teach them valuable skills, but it also allows them to start taking advantage of some incredible tax benefits and investment vehicles for themselves. We'll talk about this much more in the upcoming section "Open a Roth IRA for Your Child." In order to take advantage of this benefit and many of the tax benefits from having a business, you do need to take some steps to formally become a business.

Once you become an entrepreneur and your business (no matter how part-time) begins to grow, you need to strongly consider getting incorporated. We talked about incorporation in the Chapter 2 section "Entrepreneur Mindset" and again in Chapter 3 in the discussion of Entities, which is one of the 12 building blocks of the Wealth Cycle Process. Getting incorporated creates a separate business structure or entity that is distinct from the individuals that own the business. Although sole proprietorships and partnerships are business entities that have specific purposes, we don't recommend them for most circumstances. For the purpose of this discussion, we will primarily be discussing the limited liability company (LLC) and corporations due to their superior liability and tax treatment.

We've already talked about many of the advantages of having a business. In addition to the parenting reason of being able to employ your child, there are four main reasons to take your side hustle a step further and incorporate that business: liability, credit, credibility, and taxes.

### Four Main Reasons to Incorporate

1. Liability
2. Credit
3. Credibility
4. Taxes

The first reason to become incorporated is to provide liability protection. For example, a properly structured and maintained entity protects your personal assets from creditors and court judgments against the business. It could also protect your business from creditors and lawsuits against you personally. Additionally, getting incorporated allows the business itself to develop its own business credit and receive loans, credit cards, or lines of credit on behalf of the business. Similarly, businesses that are incorporated often get more credibility from lenders, partners, and even customers. Finally, incorporation can potentially provide tax benefits if structured correctly. The mere fact of being incorporated opens up deductions and expenses that wouldn't be allowed if you didn't incorporate and remained a sole proprietor.

If you as the parent have your own business or even side hustle, you should get incorporated. Which type of corporate structure to choose is a very personalized decision based on numerous factors. Different entities have different advantages. Some provide better tax advantages but little liability protection. Others provide liability protection but may have no tax advantages, or even tax disadvantages. This is where the concept of building a team to handle your wealth comes in. You need to get advice from a lawyer and accountant to help balance the liability and tax consequences of your personal situation. The laws regarding taxes and estate planning are constantly changing, so you need a professional to guarantee you have the plan that's right for you. Failing to do so is just asking for trouble, particularly if you have a large fortune to pass to your heirs.

Another situation where incorporation should be considered is if you own real estate or other assets or investments that may be subject to litigation. Having these assets in their own corporate structure separates them and their liability from your personal assets. For example, if a tenant of your rental property sued you, a suitable entity could prevent them from being able to take your personal accounts and assets. Having your assets in a properly structured corporation can also create an organized entity that will be easier to pass on to your kids in the future if you choose to do so. Additionally, because the corporation would have several years to season and develop its own credit history and credibility, your child would be able to immediately have access to credit and the other benefits that come from having an established history as a credible business.

So far, we've discussed all the advantages to getting incorporated, but we would be remiss if we didn't mention it comes with a little extra work. To provide the liability protection for which they are intended, corporations and LLCs must be operated as a separate entity from their owners. This means they require separate bank accounts and accounting, among other things. Additionally, even LLCs, which are known for requiring less corporate hassle, still require administrative paperwork to guarantee a court would uphold their separation from the personal assets of their owners. These additional administrative duties need to be handled by either you or your lawyers and accountants. Either way, it is your responsibility to make certain they get done. Being a millionaire isn't always easy. However, the more assets you accumulate and wealth you acquire, the more the advantages outweigh the disadvantages. If you want a life of abundance and wealth for you and your child, it sometimes takes a bit more paperwork. This is what millionaires do.

> **LORAL SAYS: I teach my clients "Do paperwork or be poor."**

We can't overemphasize the importance of not making these decisions on your own without the advice of a professional. Lawyers and accountants spend their whole life studying the intricacies of corporate liability and tax law so you don't have to. With the help of a professional, you can create a corporate structure that meets your needs and can provide the perfect mechanism toward helping you build and keep your family's fortune.

## EMPLOY YOUR CHILD

Put your child to work! We know this sounds radical, but your child can do "age-appropriate" work immediately following birth. While your newborn probably can't do your taxes (you wish!), they can do jobs such as modeling shoots and be paid for it. We're not trying to convince you to turn your child into an international supermodel. Do you have an incorporated business as we recommended in the last section? If so, you can employ your child. Whether it be a family picture or an individual picture, your child can be paid for promotional pictures that might be used on the website or social media advertising for that business. As long as the pay is reasonable and the job is real and age-appropriate (talk to your accountant for specifics on what is appropriate), it is legal for your child to make an income working for your own business.

We have a friend who made calendars for his business that he sent out to all his customers. The calendar featured pictures of the cutest person he knew—his daughter. The cutest baby in the world can't be expected to work for free, can she? Loral did the same thing for her children when they were born. Her children also worked in her business in their first five years while traveling the world with her. They appeared in her promotional videos. They picked up trash and handed out programs. They helped count the

**LORAL SAYS:** I remember a time in Oklahoma when I was working with my four-year-old son, Logan, on an apartment building I had purchased. The bonus for his day's work was to go swimming in the apartment pool. Some of the apartment kids came by and jumped in the pool with him and asked if he was new to the apartments. Logan quickly answered, "Nope, I own this place." This goes to show that kids are watching and listening and absorbing everything you do and say. Start them young.

**KYLE SAYS:** Unfortunately, I didn't have a business until my kids were a little older, but as soon as I did, my children worked for the business as well. As your child gets older, they can do more and more. My kids graduated from picking up sticks or nails at a rental property renovation to painting and demolition, then mowing, tiling, and even basic bookkeeping and video editing when they were teenagers.

attendees and even the money earned during educational events she held. Her kids also picked up tools and painted inside the apartments she was renovating.

In the process, you the parent get to teach your child about hard work and even a skill that they can later use as their own business. We're both confident our kids will know how to buy and renovate their own rental properties someday since they have participated in nearly every stage of the process. We haven't even spoken about the life skills you can teach your employee child about many of the topics we'll discuss later in this book like the value of hard work, goal setting, and teamwork. Although teaching your child life and work skills is very important, perhaps an equally important reason to employ and create income for your child is so you can start their IRA. We'll talk about this little-known millionaire strategy in the next section.

> **LORAL SAYS: This is an example when you should use the YES! Energy philosophy and commit to doing it. "Say YES! and figure it out later."**

## OPEN A ROTH IRA FOR YOUR CHILD

An IRA for your baby? That's right. As long as they have verifiable income from age-appropriate work, your baby can begin taking advantage of the tax-exempt benefits of Roth IRAs by saving for their golden years. If they are under 18 you can even make the contributions yourself if you choose to. The child just needs to have the income, not necessarily be the one to make the contribution.

Starting an IRA for your child is one of the best ways to help secure their financial future. Why would you start an IRA for your new child? There are two huge reasons. First, the sooner your child starts, the sooner they can begin putting compound interest to work for them. Review the compound interest example from the section "Investor

Mindset: Compound Interest" in Chapter 2 now to see why this is important. Having them start saving for their future financial freedom now versus when they are 25 or older can give your kid an extra 25-year period for their money to 100X than if they had waited until age 25. Recall the investment snowball example from Kyle's story. The higher the mountain, the longer that investment snowball has to grow larger and pick up momentum as it rolls down. Let's look at a fictional but realistic example of two children and how compound interest can play out with an IRA in the real world.

## Odette's Story

Odette was born to a mother and father who had a real estate business. They didn't have much money, but they knew they could employ Odette right away and open a Roth IRA for her as soon as she had income. Before she was a year old, she was in several photo shoots along with her family that were used to promote her parents' real estate website. These pictures were updated every few months to keep the content fresh. Her parents' real estate business paid Odette $300 total in modeling fees for six sessions that year. Odette continued working for the business for the next 18 years. When Odette was older, she was able to help the business with office cleanup, photography, and eventually bookkeeping.

For 18 years the business paid Odette every year, and her parents put just $300 into her Roth IRA each year. This money was put into investments that averaged 10 percent returns per year. After she was 18, Odette went off to join the Peace Corps and chose to ignore her parents' advice to put more money away (you can lead them to water, but you can't make them drink). At age 65 she hadn't contributed a single penny to her IRA beyond what her parents had contributed through age 18. The account, however, had continued to garner 10 percent returns over its history. All told, only $5,400 total had been contributed to her account. What do you think the value of Odette's account was at age 65? Any guesses? We'll reveal the amount in a moment.

## Aisha's Story

Aisha was born to wealthy doctors. They made great money and were smart, but they didn't know much about financial matters and never learned they could start a Roth IRA for their child. As a result, Aisha was never taught about the importance of starting an IRA. After attending medical school and paying off most of her debt, Aisha finally decided she needed to open a Roth IRA at age 30. She had a good income, so she was able to contribute and invest $4,200 every year from age 30 to 65. All told, she made 35 contributions of $4,200 for a grand total of $147,000 in contributions. Just like Odette's account, Aisha's account garnered 10 percent returns over its entire history. What do you think the value of Aisha's account was at age 65? Any guesses? Let's look at the numbers.

| NAME | AGE BEGUN | YEARS OF CONTRIBUTIONS | CONTRIBUTION PER YEAR | TOTAL CONTRIBUTIONS | ACCOUNT VALUE AT AGE 65 |
|------|-----------|------------------------|-----------------------|---------------------|-------------------------|
| Odette | < 1 | 18 | $300 | $5,400 | **$1,327,196** |
| Aisha | 30 | 35 | $4,200 | $147,000 | **$1,252,133** |

The good news is that due to their contributions into their Roth IRAs, both Odette and Aisha are millionaires! Since they both used Roth IRAs, all the funds in their accounts can be withdrawn tax free. The astonishing part is that even though Aisha contributed 27 times more money into her account, she still ended up with less money than Odette, who contributed much less and never contributed a penny of her own money after age 18. Even though Odette was less responsible with her saving than Aisha, Odette's parents' foresight and the extra years of compounding for her account proved incredibly important. By contributing less than a dollar a day to Odette's account during her childhood, her parents had made her a millionaire! Let that sink in. *You can make your kid a millionaire by investing less than a dollar a day on their behalf during their childhood!*

Hopefully you are now beginning to fathom the enormous advantage compound interest provides when time is on your side. The second huge reason you should start an IRA for your young child right away is because of the vast benefit of tax-advantaged accounts and the contribution limits toward these types of accounts. Refer again to the "Investor Mindset: Tax-Advantaged Accounts" section in Chapter 2 for a discussion of how important tax-advantaged accounts can be. The incredible tax savings they provide is remarkable. The problem is that, as good as IRAs are, they have contribution limits ($6,000 for 2022—$7,000 if age 50 or older). Unless you start at a very early age, it is difficult to put enough money into IRA accounts to make a significant contribution toward reaching your financial freedom. That's why we recommend starting these accounts for your child as early as possible.

When you create an account for your child who is under the age of 18, it will be considered a custodial IRA. A custodial IRA is managed by the custodian (generally the parent) until the child turns 18 or 21, depending on the state. As mentioned before, the contributions can be made by either the custodian or the child, as long as the child has at least that much verifiable income. It's up to you to decide which route you would prefer. One of our favorite options is to have older children be offered a matching contribution. We match every dollar they contribute to their IRA up to a certain value so as not to exceed their allowable contribution. This incentivizes them to invest into the IRA while still making sure they have some skin in the game. If you are the custodian, it is up to you to make the investment decisions. As your child approaches the age where they will take over the account, you can slowly begin giving them some say in the investments for the account. We recommend using the pilot training model to slowly teach your child about, then supervise their investing decisions in the account. That way, when they take it over and go solo, they will have already demonstrated proficiency in managing money and it won't be overwhelming for them. We'll talk more about how you can use the five-step pilot training model to teach your child about investing throughout the book.

Now that you recognize that you truly do need to start an IRA for your child (and yourself if you haven't already), what investments will you hold inside that IRA? The answer to this question depends on a few factors. The first factor is what type of financial institution you choose to manage your account. Technically, non-licensed individuals cannot buy stocks directly on the stock exchange. They must do so through an intermediary at a licensed financial institution. There are four primary types of institutions that can do this: mutual fund companies, full-service brokerages, discount brokerages, and self-directed brokerages. A full description of these types of institutions is beyond the scope of this book, but Table 4.1 highlights some of the basic differences between these institutions.

**Table 4.1** Differences Between Stock Management Companies

|  | MUTUAL FUND COMPANY | FULL-SERVICE BROKERAGE | DISCOUNT BROKERAGE | SELF-DIRECTED BROKERAGE |
|---|---|---|---|---|
| **Fees** | Medium | Medium to high | Low or zero | Very high |
| **Flexibility** | Low | Low | High | Very high |
| **Guidance** | None—automatic | Medium to high | Low or none | None |

Note that we didn't reference performance in the chart. The performance of each investment depends on the individual company (or you in the latter two), so it can't be generalized across types of institutions. In general, we like discount brokers because of their high flexibility and low fees. With practice and experience your child will be able to at least match, if not beat the performance of most mutual funds and full-service brokers without having to pay their high fees.

A quick internet search for discount brokers will bring up a list of the more popular ones. We recommend doing your own research to decide which one fits you best. Most now offer free trades. Some provide educational tools imbedded in the platform to help you be a better investor. Others allow the purchase of fractional shares. Fractional shares allow investors with small accounts to buy less than one share (a fraction of a share) of stocks that may cost thousands of dollars that they would otherwise not be able to purchase. These new features of discount brokerages have made the world of investing much easier and more accessible to everyone. Setting up one of these accounts often only takes about 30 minutes or so of your time, so there is no good excuse not to do so today.

New financial technology (fintech) companies are constantly improving the individual investor's landscape. One company we particularly like in the brokerage realm is iFlip. Although iFlip isn't a brokerage itself, it makes software that integrates with a discount broker to provide the same sort of algorithmic trading technology and artificial intelligence that is used by the pros. Although the premium version of its software does have a subscription fee, you can get started with its basic version for free. The advantage of the software is that it uses artificial intelligence and technical factors similar to those used by expensive hedge funds to reduce risk by getting you out of the market before it crashes. It's particularly useful for people who don't want to be constantly checking their stock portfolio or who have a low tolerance for risk but still want to participate in the market's upside. To learn more, check out the following link: https://MakeYourKidsMillionaires .com/iflip.

Another factor to consider when deciding what financial institution you want to use is the type of investment you will purchase. If you are in anything other than a self-directed IRA, your choices will generally be limited to mutual funds, ETFs, or stocks. A mutual fund is a basket of stocks chosen by a mutual fund manager. The advantage of mutual funds is that they are professionally managed and have built-in diversification because they generally own a large assortment of stocks. The problem with mutual funds is that most underperform the overall market and charge fees that can be up to 2 percent of the funds invested. These fees can quickly eat into your returns. To combat the fee problem, a special type of mutual fund was created.

Former Vanguard chairman John Bogle is credited for creating the index fund. Rather than paying a mutual fund manager an exorbitant salary to manage a mutual fund, it sought to mathematically and automatically match a segment, or index, of the stock market like the S&P 500 or Dow Jones Industrial Average. Because an index fund is mathematically calculated and doesn't have a fund manager in the traditional sense, it can charge much lower fees. The only problem with index funds was that they still had some of the disadvantages of mutual funds relative to stocks. They still had minimum investment requirements, generated capital gains (albeit very small amounts compared to mutual funds), and weren't as liquid as stocks because they traded only at the end of the day.

Some of the issues associated with index funds were solved with the creation of the first US Exchange Traded Fund (ETF). The ETF works like an index fund by tracking the same potential indexes or segments of the market, but it is traded as a stock instead of a fund. This reduces the minimum investment problem, lowers (slightly) the already low index fund fees, provides slightly better tax efficiency, and affords much greater liquidity by even offering the ability to trade it throughout the day (not that you generally should). The ETF is an excellent option for providing diversification without having to pay the fees associated with mutual funds.

### What Would We Do?

If we were stock beginners, we would start investing in your child's discount brokerage by putting their money in ETFs that match one of the major indexes like the S&P 500 index, Dow Jones Industrial Average, or Nasdaq composite or an artificial intelligence software like iFlip. After getting our feet wet with ETFs, if we had the time and inclination to try investing in individual stocks, we would put a small percentage of our account in a few individual stocks. As our portfolio grew, we could slowly begin increasing our number of individual stocks, but keep the percentage relatively low. We wouldn't want our child to get discouraged if they lose a significant amount of their investment because one company went down in price. In other words, we wouldn't put too many of our eggs in one basket.

If we decided to dedicate a larger percentage of our portfolio toward individual stocks, we'd only do so after we gained knowledge and experience and had a proven track record of consistently beating the ETF performance. If we did have the talent and inclination to invest in individual stocks, the IRA we created for our child would eventually be a great account to start slowly letting our child "take the controls" on their own investing flight. We'll talk more about surrendering this control in Chapter 7 in the section "Begin Relinquishing Control of Their Stock Investments." Until then, we as parents will have to do most of the IRA flying.

## SET UP A TAX-ADVANTAGED EDUCATION ACCOUNT

Though it certainly won't be the first expense associated with having a child, paying for college could easily be the biggest. With tuition rates increasing well beyond inflation, the costs of college tuition are becoming more and more cumbersome. Although we foresee a time when colleges are structured much differently and aren't seen as "mandatory" as they currently are, the reality is that attending college does still have a positive correlation toward increased income for your child, whether they are an entrepreneur or a W-2 employee. We talk more about the investment of college and student loans in the Chapter 8 section titled "College Prep and Student Loans."

Whether you wish to pay for your child's college education or not is a matter of personal preference. Some parents feel that paying for college is an extension of their childhood and that doing so will best set them up for success later in life. Others feel that college is a time for children to transition into being adults and that making them pay for their own college education helps them appreciate it more and be more apt to take it seriously. As your child begins to make their own money (as advised later in this book), it might even make sense to have your child set aside part of their own earnings to place in their education account.

One can also encourage relatives to give money into the account as gifts instead of buying a toy or gadget that will only provide short-term use. What better gift for a grandparent to give than to help provide for the education of their grandchild? Rather than sending a birthday or Christmas card with cash they could send a deposit into the education account. It may not seem as personal a gift, but it helps fight the notion that life is about possessions and instead teaches the child to put away money for life experiences and investments in their own education. Additionally, the powerful effect of compound interest (as discussed in Chapter 2) will make that gift much more valuable than its original denomination. In fact, many of the education savings vehicles we discuss here can actually be passed on to your grandchildren (sometimes with certain restrictions) if your kid ends up not needing to use all the money for college. If this occurs, the money will have even longer to compound and can be part of a legacy that may last several generations.

A totally different and advanced strategy for paying for your child's education is potentially available if your child is an employee of your company. If your child needs an education to fulfill their role in the company, then in certain circumstances that company can pay for the education. There are specific requirements to take advantage of this strategy, so make sure you consult a licensed and qualified accountant before planning to do so.

In a perfect world, your child would acquire scholarships or perhaps grants to help fund their college expenses. Unfortunately, this isn't always the case. We both have been fortunate so far in that our children have received considerable scholarship money. Vast resources exist for tapping into scholarship money and, incredibly, much of it goes unused. Therefore, you shouldn't despair if you don't have money to set aside for your child's education. Neither of us was given money by our parents for college. Our parents told us early on that money wasn't available to help us pay for college. As a result, each of us worked hard to ensure that we received scholarships to fund our own education. As long as you set the expectations for your child early on, they can take the necessary actions to be prepared.

If you decide that you do want to help pay for your child's education, it is important that you get started right away so your investments have time to grow and compound. What investments you choose for inside your education account will depend on your investment experience and expertise. We discussed a few of these options in the previous section "Open a Roth IRA for Your Child." Regardless of what you invest in, you want to do it in the most economical way. This would generally be the way that saves the most in taxes. If you haven't already, now would be a good time to read or review the section "Investor Mindset: Tax-Advantaged Accounts" in Chapter 2. That section discusses the tax implications of different types of tax-advantaged accounts. Five primary options exist for saving toward your child's education, and all have some form of tax advantage. These options include:

### Five Options for College Savings

529 College savings plan
Coverdell Education Savings Account (CESA)
Individual Retirement Account (IRA)
Uniform Gifts to Minors Act (UGMA)
Uniform Transfers to Minors Act (UTMA)

Knowing which account is best for your situation depends on several factors, including the current and anticipated future income, net worth, and tax bracket for both the parent and the child. These aren't always easy to know with certainty, so you'll just have to make a few assumptions and go with it. Several resources are available online that cover this topic, but to ensure you make the best decision for your situation it is best to discuss this important financial obligation with your accountant or financial advisor.

The Coverdell and 529 plan are the most commonly used vessels for college savings. They were created specifically for college savings and have the best tax savings for most situations. Both plans also offer the ability to have people other than the original creators of the account provide funding. For example, grandparents or aunts and uncles can contribute to the 529 plan or Coverdell account, even if the parents are the ones who set it up. Encouraging relatives to give to the account rather than spoiling the kids with toys they will quickly outgrow is an important tip, particularly for parents with limited funds to establish these types of accounts. Also, as we've said many times, the sooner you can contribute to these accounts, the longer that money can compound and potentially pay for a larger portion of the schooling. You can find out more about these accounts at MakeYourKidsMillionaires.com.

## CREATE A WILL AND ADVANCE DIRECTIVE

If you have a child, then you need a will. It's that simple. Nobody wants to think about their own mortality, but the fact remains that all of us will eventually die. For a few of us, it will happen unexpectedly and at a much younger age than we would hope. If you are one of these unfortunate few, wouldn't you want your child to be taken care of according to your wishes, and not those of the state? A last will and testament, often referred to simply as a will, is a legal document that dictates how your debt should be handled, who will have custody of dependents, and how assets shall be divided, including those with sentimental value. A trust takes it a step further and will ensure your estate doesn't go into probate at all. We'll discuss trusts in the next section.

If you don't have a will (or trust), then the distribution of many of your assets and care of your dependents could ultimately be decided by the probate court of your state. This can cost your heirs thousands to tens of thousands of dollars, depending on the size of your estate, and can drag on for weeks or sometimes even years. Do you really want the state to decide what to do with everything you've worked for? Worse yet, do you want the state to decide who gets to take care of your children? A will can spell out your desires. With a well-written and valid will, the probate process can be much quicker, cheaper, and less stressful for your heirs and family. More important, it lets you decide how your assets will be distributed.

The great news about wills is that they don't have to be complicated or expensive. What they do need to be, however, is accurate and complete. If you choose this route, make sure to do your own extensive research. Begin to learn the probate rules associated with your state so that you will know with certainty that the will you eventually have is valid. To guarantee legitimacy of your will, we highly recommend you instead consult a trusted attorney to create a customized solution that will be certain to hold up in probate court. If you have a will that is deemed to be invalid it will be effectively ignored, and the distribution of your assets and care of your dependents will again be back in the hands of the state. This is a situation in which paying an attorney now could save your heirs tenfold those costs after you die.

What if you don't die but become incapacitated and can no longer communicate your wishes? This is the realm of the advanced directive.

The advanced directive, also known as a living will, is a legal document that provides instructions regarding the financial or medical care a person wishes to receive if they become incapacitated or seriously ill and cannot communicate their preferences themselves. In some states there are two types of advance directives—medical and financial. The medical advanced directive will answer questions such as whether you want to be resuscitated, what life-sustaining treatments you desire, whether you wish to donate organs, and who will make medical decisions on your behalf. It will often include a healthcare power of attorney to legally appoint that decision maker.

The financial advanced directives will determine who will handle your finances if you are incapacitated. This will usually fall in line with your trust documents. Advanced directives are important because, like a will, they allow you to communicate your preferences when you can't speak for yourself. When you set up your will, the attorney will often recommend you set up an advance directive at the same time. We highly recommend you take this advice and set one up. The combination of the will and the advance directive will make sure your family is taken care of, your assets are properly distributed, and your desires are achieved even when you can no longer communicate them.

# CREATE A TRUST

Trusts sometimes get a bad rap in popular culture. The stigma of the spoiled trust-fund baby is one that most of us have seen in movies or TV shows. Unfortunately, the caricature of an entitled elitist is sometimes true—but it doesn't have to be. It is possible to set up trusts for your children, raise them responsibly, and leave a legacy for your family without creating spoiled brats. In a moment we'll discuss numerous reasons you should probably set up a trust. First, let's discuss some reasons you probably should not.

If you have no aspiration to acquire any assets or wealth, then you probably don't need a trust. If you are reading this book, that's probably not you. Likewise, if you do plan to eventually acquire assets but currently don't have any, you probably don't need a trust—yet. Costs and maintenance time are required to set up a trust. Nonetheless, for anybody who intends to achieve wealth and has already begun to acquire some assets, a trust can be worth its weight in gold. A trust is the foundation for setting up generational wealth. Given the high rate of divorce, single-parent families, and blended families, a trust can help clarify how your estate will be divided among heirs. This can prevent the infighting that can occur between heirs if everything is not formally spelled out.

Here are some specific reasons you may need or want a trust:

1. To control what happens to your assets when you die
2. To avoid probate court and provide privacy of assets
3. To protect trust assets from creditors
4. To plan for business succession
5. To shelter assets from estate and transfer taxes
6. To protect beneficiaries from their own poor judgment
7. To control future charitable giving from your estate
8. To aid a special-needs family member

If you want to accomplish any of the items above, the trust may be the best vehicle to accomplish it. These reasons don't necessitate that you have a giant fortune. They just require that you have some assets that you would like to control and protect.

Trusts can be revocable or irrevocable. Revocable trusts, often called living trusts, are estate planning tools that can be changed by the grantor until their death, upon which they become irrevocable. Irrevocable trusts, on the other hand, cannot be modified, amended, or terminated without the permission of the grantor's named beneficiary or beneficiaries. Each type has its own advantages and disadvantages. The irrevocable trust provides potentially better tax advantages and protection from creditors but allows less flexibility since it can't generally be revoked or changed. The revocable trust allows the malleability to change its conditions while still providing probate protections. However, this malleability comes with a price. The fact that it can be changed means it can be more easily targeted by creditors. Ultimately, the best type of trust for you and your family is a personal choice and involves many factors. We highly recommend using an attorney who specializes in estate planning. Especially when it comes to trusts, it's better not to be "penny wise but pound foolish."

If you already have a trust or have decided to open a trust, you may think you don't need a will. You would be mistaken. Even if you have a trust, you still need a will for two main reasons:

1. A trust won't include everything you own.
2. A will can do some things a trust can't.

For a trust to protect a possession, it must have been formally and legally transferred into the trust. Very few people take the time to transfer every single item they own. Additionally, what if you bought something new right before you died? It wouldn't be covered by the trust. A will can formally dictate what should happen with those possessions that don't get entered into the trust.

A will can also do other things a trust cannot cover. For example, a will can dictate what will happen regarding the custody of minor children. This

**Tomorrow isn't promised for any of us.**

won't generally be covered by a trust. A will can also include special requests like forgiveness of debt or other personal requests that won't be included in a trust. The good news is that if you do have a trust, the will might not need to be as comprehensive as if you did not.

In the end, legacy planning should include at least a will, an advance directive, and for most people, a trust. For some people, legacy planning would include a host of other things like corporations, life insurance, and a durable power of attorney. We'll talk about a few of these things in the upcoming sections. Don't put off the important actions of taking care of the estate planning for your child. Tomorrow isn't promised for any of us.

## PURCHASE LIFE INSURANCE

You most likely need life insurance to cover the multitude of expenses your family would face if you were to die. Once you have a nest egg to cover all these expenses, you may not need life insurance, but you might still want it. There are two primary types of life insurance: term life insurance and whole life insurance. With term life insurance you pay a set insurance premium for a specified time period and the insurance guarantees payment of a death benefit if it occurs during that time period, or term. Whole life insurance, sometimes called permanent life insurance, can take various forms and names depending on the policy. It generally requires the payment of insurance premiums for a set period of time but provides a death benefit for life. Whole life insurance is much more expensive on a per-year basis than term insurance. A benefit to whole life insurance is that it provides a policy cash value that grows as you contribute to it. This cash value is usually invested on your behalf to help it

**LORAL SAYS: Because I am interested in leaving a legacy of generational wealth, I'm a big proponent of whole life insurance. The liability protection and tax benefits to my heirs make it an integral part of my estate planning.**

grow even more. Another benefit of whole life insurance is that the cash value is usually protected from creditors, which helps estate planning. Many people choose term insurance because it is simpler, cheaper, and they aren't familiar with the advantages of whole life insurance.

For some people, whole life insurance can make a lot of sense because of the associated tax advantages. Some withdrawals, as well as the death benefit paid to beneficiaries, are tax-free. Similar to the tax-exempt accounts we discussed in the Chapter 2 section "Investor Mindset: Tax-Advantaged Accounts," this can be a substantial advantage to people whose family will be in a significantly higher tax bracket later in life than when the contributions are made or people who plan to leave their children a considerable fortune. Some strategies for using whole life insurance also include a component of borrowing from the cash value. Since you are borrowing from yourself, this can effectively produce a tax-free income source later in life. Particularly for people in high tax brackets, this can be a powerful tool not only to reduce taxes, but to effectively be your own bank by providing a source of capital for your expenses or even investments.

For people who plan on being wealthy, whole life insurance is certainly something worth investigating. As always, we recommend talking to your accountant and a licensed insurance agent to get the specifics. It's especially important with whole life insurance that you dig into the details of due diligence and beware of hidden fees that might override any tax advantages you receive. You also need to make certain you use a reputable insurance company that will still be around when your policy pays out. Although whole life insurance may not be for everyone, in the right circumstances it can be an important tool toward building generational wealth.

## MONEY BUYS THINGS

Although many people avoid talking about money at all with a child this age, setting a good foundation right away is pivotal to the child's development. It seems obvious, but perhaps the most basic concept of money they can learn is simply that money buys things. It's hard to imagine, but there was a time when even you weren't aware of this concept. When your one-year-old or two-year-old sees you grabbing things at the store, they don't understand you aren't just taking those things. It must be explained to them that you are purchasing those things in exchange for money. Let them see you making a small cash purchase of something they can relate to, like food or juice purchased for them. Using actual bills or coins is important at the beginning to simplify the concept. A grocery store purchase is perfect for this since they can relate to food and know that it is something people need to have. As you hand the money to the cashier, point out to them that "Mommy is buying the juice you like with money. We trade the money for the juice."

Remember, as with everything we teach in this book, repetition is key. You may have to point out this transaction several times. A key concept to convey to your child is that when you have money, you can trade it for things you need. It's important that they begin to grasp the fact that money isn't an end, of and by itself, but rather a means to an end. At age two or three, after you give the money to the cashier, point out that the store owners can now go and trade the money for something they want. When your child reaches ages four and five, you can explain that the cashier doesn't keep the money, the money goes to the store to buy more product and the cashier gets paid to work for the store. This can lead to great conversations with your child when they ask the standard four-year-old question, "Why?"

One way to think of the purpose of money is to think of the idea of water—our most basic of human needs. We all need water to live. The pipes that run through our cities and houses are necessary tools to bring that water to us, but the water is what we really need. In the same way that a pipe can help water flow from one place of need to another, money can be thought of as the pipe, or conduit, from one person's needs to another's. The idea of money as a mere conduit is an important one to begin conveying early. Just like the water pipes, it's a tool to get what we need and want, but it's only a tool. Later in life you'll teach your child how to use that tool.

# COUNTING MONEY

Use money to help your child count. If your child would rather taste a penny than count it, you might want to hold off on this lesson a bit. However, once they can be trusted not to eat it, counting money with your child can be a great way to introduce both counting and basic math. Start with pennies and have them count a handful of coins. While counting, point out that "This money is valuable and can help us buy things, so make sure you don't lose it (or eat it)." Once your child grasps the idea of counting pennies, you can explain subtraction by removing pennies from their hand. As they get older, you can try introducing the concept that different coins have different values. If you teach your child to count nickels or dimes, it will help them learn to count by fives or tens. Eventually you can even introduce quarters into the mix. If they've mastered addition and subtraction, then the different denominations can also help them begin to fathom the concept of multiplication.

Another example of a type of currency that your child will eventually want to learn about and count is cryptocurrency. Although cryptocurrency's digital nature doesn't lend itself toward counting at this age, that doesn't mean you shouldn't teach your kids about it, since it will likely play a role in their future. This is probably

**KYLE SAYS: I remember sitting at the dinner table with my kids with several piles of different coins. Once they mastered counting the number of coins I would make stacks of five pennies and explain that the value was the same as a nickel. After my kids mastered this concept, I added additional stacks of five more pennies to equal the value of a dime, and later a quarter. Eventually, I made it a game to have my kids figure out different ways to make equal stacks of money using different coins.**

a lesson you should teach them a few years later than this chapter, but if they do ask you about it you can simply describe it with the pipes analogy from the previous section. At its core, cryptocurrency is like any other currency in that it is a conduit that allows people with needs to trade with other people who need something. As long as there are people who will abide to the agreement that it holds value and can be used for trading things, it will continue to be viable. When your children are several years older you can begin to explain the differences between normal currency and cryptocurrency. For now, it's best to focus on something tangible that they can actually touch and count.

LORAL SAYS: I also remember teaching my kids about counting, as well as sorting different currencies from around the world. We would talk about how some currencies were paper and others were coins, but they all represented money that buys things wherever you are in the world. As they became older, the tooth fairy would frequently use different currencies that my kids would have to sort and count. In this way, I was able to explain the transactional nature of money and the fact that it was universal, even if the type of currency wasn't.

You might even let your child win rewards for passing certain counting or sorting milestones. What rewards would they win? How about rewarding them some of the coins they just counted? To cement the point that the coins have value, consider letting them use their newfound wealth to buy a treat or small toy, or perhaps address the idea of saving the money. As they near the end of this age range, you can even use shopping trips as opportunities to count money. Have them compare price tags of different items in the store. Pick out a cheap item and tell them how much it costs. See if they can count out the coins necessary to buy it. Yes, this will slow down your shopping, and these lessons are best accomplished in the

Many people miss out on the variety of teaching opportunities that everyday tasks like shopping can provide for children.

actual store and not online! For some of you, this may be painful. It will be worth it someday when they are capable of paying for both of your groceries because you've given them such a firm understanding of money. Many people miss out on the variety of teaching opportunities that everyday tasks like shopping can provide for children. What teaching opportunities can you find for your child?

# GOAL SETTING FOUNDATIONS

Goal setting is integral to a child's success in life. It's so important that we will discuss it in four different sections of this book. If you follow our guidance, your child will be an expert at setting and achieving goals by the time they are an adult. Of course, your child isn't an adult yet, just a very young child. But that doesn't mean it's too early to begin laying the foundation for what will eventually become goal setting. At its most basic level a goal is just something we want to do. Even your two-year-old can understand that. Goals at this age should be of short duration and relatively easy to attain. The point is to create a habit of setting small goals and achieving the satisfaction of reaching them. If your child is learning to count pennies like we discussed in the last section, they can have a goal. You might say, "Great job counting to five, Tristin! Now let's see if you can count even higher. Let's set a goal to count to seven!"

Equally as important as setting the goal is celebrating children's victory when they reach the goal. This is the time to heap praise on them and let them know how proud you are of them for reaching their goal. Using the term "goal" when you talk about this will help them associate positive feelings with goals and help them work to set and achieve new goals. It becomes a positive feedback loop of setting then achieving goals, then continuously setting and achieving goals. Remember to never forget the feedback. Even at this age you can look back and reflect with your child how they did. You might say, "Tristin, I'm so proud of you. When we started today you could only count to five but now you met your goal of counting to seven! We practiced and practiced and now you did it!" In the next chapter we'll provide some specifics on how to set well-defined goals. For now, we're just introducing the concept and the terminology and using the term *goal* rather loosely. As your child gets older you can begin challenging them with more difficult goals, and those that might take a longer duration to complete. Until then, just work on the repetition of setting, achieving, then reflecting on the goals.

Although most of the goals you set for your child should be short-term at this point, you can also begin to plant the seed of long-range goals. Loral created a unique way to talk about longer-term goals with her children that blended the idea of Christmas and New Year's resolutions. During the holidays, starting at age two, she would get together with each of her children and talk about the year that had passed and the one that was about to begin. To make it fun, Loral would outline the shape of a stocking and draw a line down the center of it with the current year at the top of one side and the upcoming year at the top of the other. On the left side, the child would reflect and write down what they did that they enjoyed in the previous year.

When her children were toddlers, Loral had to guide most of the conversation, of course. As her children became older and reached five years of age, they were able to add more and more to the conversation and the stocking. At this age they may have written things like "won our soccer league," "became friends with Luke," or "learned to play Chopsticks on the piano." Loral would then guide the conversation to what things they would want to do in the next year. The right side of the stocking would be reserved for these goals for the upcoming year. For Loral's daughter, Tristin, this might have included goals related to her dance or basketball competitions. A year later, Loral and her children would pull out their stockings from the previous year to review and reflect how they had done toward meeting the goals they had written down.

Even though she was sometimes leading the conversation, talking about the stocking was an early stage behavior of getting her children to learn goal setting and reflection, year after year. It also provided an opportunity for her children to notice how their actions and behaviors either helped them achieve their goals or not. She found it was very important to begin managing the conversation and promote her child's realization that actions have consequences. As each child became older, Loral would encourage them to include a goal that was related to their personal development. This would include health goals, family goals, charity goals, spiritual goals, and of course financial goals.

In addition to setting the foundation for goal setting, another advantage of the stockings was that they provided a way to track her child's handwriting and development over the years. Her son, Logan, is 22 years old at the time of this writing, so she has 20 years of stocking keepsakes he created to help her travel down memory lane. These keepsakes document his goals and handwriting, including the letters of his name, which she helped him write when he was two. Her daughter, Tristin, started even younger. In fact, Loral continues the Christmas stocking tradition to this day. Loral loves how it provides a great way to track the family's progress over the years. She also feels the exercise created a great foundation for teaching her children the basics of goal setting in a purposeful yet fun way that brings the family together and creates memories.

## BASIC OPPORTUNITY COST

Webster defines opportunity cost as:

> the added cost of using resources (as for production or speculative investment) that is the difference between the actual value resulting from such use and that of an alternative (such as another use of the same resources or an investment of equal risk but greater return)

That's a mouthful. Don't worry. We're not suggesting you use the term "opportunity cost" with your five-year-old child. It might be better to phrase it as "money choices." In other words, opportunity cost is the cost of giving up the chance to buy (or do) one thing by making a choice to buy (or do) another. Since the amount of money available at a given time is limited and we should only spend what we have, we must make smart decisions about which things to buy with that money. This is the key to opportunity cost. How do we begin to introduce this concept to our children?

One way to teach this concept is to again use the grocery store as a learning tool. You might say to your child, "Bret, Mommy has five more dollars to spend on groceries. We can either buy the granola bars you like or the juice you like. We can't buy both. If we choose the granola bars, we can't get the juice. If we choose the juice, we can't get the granola bars. We must choose which one would be the best choice. Let's talk about which one we should choose and why." This links well with the previous discussion about shopping and price checking and making choices with your child. An exercise like this might seem trivial, but by doing so you teach them many lessons, not the least of which is that sometimes life comes down to choices and they need to put thought into those choices. Believe it or not, that is the beginning of getting them to be aware of opportunity cost. Later in this book we'll help you teach your child the tools to make better decisions on their money choices. For now, just focus on getting your child to appreciate that these choices exist.

## DELAYED GRATIFICATION

Sometimes good things are worth waiting for. Although we believe in living a life of abundance and doing what is necessary to create that life of abundance for yourself, it's important not to put the cart before the horse. As Loral has stated in her books, "Successful, wealthy people are those who build their assets and then they build their lifestyles." In order to do this, we must delay consumer purchases of things we want until we've created the income to afford it. It's important to make sure you teach that delayed gratification is about responsibility, not scarcity. You have to be responsible and be aware of the consequences of your money choices.

Since the attribute of delayed gratification is largely fully formed and relatively stable once your child reaches adulthood, it's up to you to teach your kids while they are young. How can we do this? Just like in the pilot training model discussed in Chapter 1, it requires not just academic teaching of the idea, but an excellent demonstration by setting a good example. Talk to them about times when you are going to delay your gratification, even if it isn't about money. If you are considering a tasty dessert, explain to them that you really want to eat it now, but you are going to wait. "Daddy loves ice cream," you might say, "but he's going to wait to eat it until after dinner."

Teaching kids that even as adults we don't always get what we want right away will help avoid creating entitled kids. The next time they whine for candy or a toy at the store, remember that even though buying it for them might help avoid a temper tantrum and personal embarrassment, it teaches them entitlement—that they should get whatever they want whenever they want it. Although we'll eventually teach our children the financial reasons they should often delay gratification, at this age it doesn't even matter if you can afford it. They don't comprehend that yet. They just see the instant gratification. Of course, we all love our kids and want to give them everything we can, but we also need to realize that giving them everything they want is training them to believe that they never need to deny themselves anything. Not only will this entitled mentality create problems for them later with debt, but it will create

**KYLE SAYS:** In my experience, I've found one's willingness to delay gratification is one of the pivotal factors that makes up a person's money psychology. It exhibits a huge correlation with a person's ability to save money, the first step in investing. Thus, it plays an enormous factor in a child's potential for wealth.

a host of other problems with health, work ethic, self-discipline, and even addiction. In fact, we believe that developing delayed gratification is a key component in teaching kids about willpower, a trait that will be vital in helping them find success in all aspects of life.

## NEVER PAY YOUR KID AN ALLOWANCE

It's important that kids begin to develop an appreciation for money at an early age by sometimes earning and spending it on their own. As your child approaches the later years of this age group and appreciates that money buys things and how to count it, they are ready to start earning it by helping around the house. Many parents have turned to an allowance as the answer for this. The general idea of an allowance is a good one because it acts as the simulation phase of the five-step pilot training model by letting kids learn about money with quantities that won't be catastrophic to them even if they make mistakes. The problem we've always experienced with an allowance is that it sets up an expectation that they will be paid the same amount every week or month, no matter what they do. Paying your kid a fixed, flat rate teaches them to be employees rather than entrepreneurs. Why pay them a fixed amount when they don't have fixed potential?

Allowances also make it difficult to police whether they do all the chores they are supposed to do, and it can sometimes breed in the child a sense that they are entitled to their allowance regardless of how well they perform. Allowances also do not take into account the fact that some tasks are more difficult, create more value, or take more time to accomplish. They often don't seem fair to the child because in weeks when children perform particularly difficult or labor-intensive jobs, they receive the same pay. Finally, occasional extra help will inevitably be needed from them, and in the allowance system there won't be a framework for the extra pay.

> **Paying your kid a fixed, flat rate teaches them to be employees rather than entrepreneurs.**

Instead of using an allowance, we prefer a different approach. This approach keeps all the money simulation benefits of an allowance but avoids the entitlement. In this strategy, certain specific chores should be required just for being a part of the family. Since the family is all working together to help each other out, these chores should not be compensated. When our kids would complain about these chores, we would remind them they had free rent and meals and we were all part of a family team. It may take some repetition, but eventually they will learn that arguing against these basic family chores is fruitless, especially when you offer a host of other chores for which they will get paid.

For the tasks that go beyond the level of basic family chores we recommend a more entrepreneurial way of doing things—pay per job. Here's how the system works. Start by sitting down with your child and creating a brainstorm list of age-appropriate tasks that they could accomplish in exchange for pay. For now, you shouldn't assign any pay to these tasks. Just write them all down. Try to be creative and come up with everything they could possibly help with. As they grow older and more mature you should continually modify the task list to keep it age appropriate. It's probably best to also modify it every quarter to keep your kids engaged and learning, since they tend to get bored and lose attention if you don't mix things up regularly. It may take a few days to even a week to ensure you have an exhaustive list. You can use the template in the Resources at the end of this book titled "Home Tasks Negotiation List" if you would like or get the digital version at MakeYourKidsMillionaires.com. For now, just write the brainstormed ideas into the "proposed home tasks" column.

Once the brainstorm list is complete, you and your child need to decide on a shortened list of 5 to 10 items, depending on their age, that you can both agree on them accomplishing. One way to do this is by rating the items on your brainstorm list by your child's rating and the parent's rating of importance. Place these ratings in the template in the appropriate columns. This is your opportunity as a parent to groom the behaviors you want to instill in your child. Good manners and hygiene-related tasks could even be part of the list when your child is young.

Use the ratings and whatever other criteria you decide on to confirm your shortened list by putting checkmarks on the far-left column of the template next to the tasks you have finalized. The shortened list you create in this step becomes the actual list of tasks your child will perform.

Although Loral's son, Logan, started home tasks when he was age four, when he was nine, he had the tasks of helping with his sister when his mom was busy, taking out the trash for the whole house, cleaning the garage, and raking the lawn. It's a good idea to create a name for this task list to differentiate it from the chores they are expected to do just for being part of the family. We like the name "Home Tasks."

Now that you have the Home Tasks list, the fun part begins. Offer your child an opportunity to bid the jobs for a reasonable price. This will ensure they feel a sense of inclusion, which will help later in keeping them motivated. The pay your child receives from Home Tasks could be called "Home Pay." This pay should generally be per task but could occasionally be per minute or hour for very open-ended tasks. You should also negotiate the frequency at which each task should be completed as well as the maximum time allowed. Document these details on the template in the appropriate columns. Imagine having the power to say, "Bret, it was your idea to agree to empty the dishwasher for 50 cents. It wasn't mine. You agreed to do it twice a week. You need to follow through on your job." Allowing your child a say in the process will also teach them to improve their negotiation and sales skills. If you don't think young children have sales skills, you've apparently never been on the receiving end of a four-year-old's diplomatic negotiation for "just one more cookie, pleeease?!?" In the end, your child will need to realize that you'll only accept reasonable bids and your say is ultimately final. Just make sure you let it be a discussion and that you do offer a fair and adequate salary.

Kyle remembers when he and his wife Tracy were painting an investment property and they enlisted their kids' help. The boys originally wanted to be paid nearly the same per hour as the professional painter. Once they were shown the huge disparity in what the painter had accomplished in an hour relative to what they had completed, they had no choice but to acquiesce. In other cases they may do better and quicker work than what is available on the marketplace, so they should be paid appropriately. Depending on what your child bids for each job, you may find yourself paying them less for some jobs than you might have otherwise agreed to and more for others, especially those they really hate. It may take some time to hammer out all the details.

The next step in the process is to come up with a behavioral agreement to make sure your child accomplishes the agreed-upon tasks in the way you intend. The behavioral agreement will provide the expectations you have for your child's work. If you don't set expectations up front you are setting yourself up for problems and arguments down the road. This is true whether you are working with adults or small children. The behavioral agreement should include the standard necessary for a task to be considered accomplished, as well as the time frame. Write the behavioral agreement details in the "additional notes" section of the template. When they first start and are young it will probably take your child some prompting to build the habit of doing their tasks on time. Eventually, as they get older, they shouldn't be prompted at all. If they don't accomplish their tasks, then they shouldn't get paid. When they no longer have money to buy the things they want, they will learn they have to work to get paid. It sounds a lot like adult life, right? The entire process is three steps:

1. Create a brainstormed list of age-appropriate tasks.
2. Create a prioritized Home Task list with pay for each task.
3. Create a behavioral agreement.

All that is left is the follow-through. The follow-through includes keeping track of the Home Tasks your child accomplishes on a monthly basis. We have included a template titled "Home Tasks Invoice" for this purpose (see Resources). When your child is young you will probably have to help them fill this out and keep track of their tasks. Once they are older, it should be their responsibility to honestly fill it out and bill you. After going through all the effort to set up these Home Tasks, make sure you stick to it. If it sounds like work, it is. Don't fall into the trap of just doing everything yourself because it's easier and cheaper than explaining and monitoring the work of your kids. At the beginning it absolutely will cost you more in time and effort than if you did it yourself. Eventually, if you continue the Home Tasks throughout their childhood, they will gradually learn how to be independent and an important contributor to the household (Figure 4.1). The point is to teach them a skill, the value of hard work, and the responsibility necessary to follow through on their commitments. Additionally, it sows the seeds of entrepreneurism and creates their first opportunity to earn, save, and invest their own money—an invaluable lesson. In the next section we'll get them started on that lesson by teaching them how to pay themselves first.

**Figure 4.1** In a promotional video for *Never Pay Your Kid an Allowance,* Loral's son, Logan, describes his Home Tasks.

## PAY YOURSELF FIRST

Even though your child just started making money with their home tasks, it's never too early to begin teaching them what to do with that money and how to pay themselves first. Paying yourself first means setting money aside toward your savings goals before you spend any money. When we say "yourself" we are really referring to your future self, because that is who will receive the benefit of the investing you do with the money you paid yourself. The quote could just as easily be "Pay your future self first."

At this age your child probably has no necessary expenses at all since you as the parent are providing for them. This should make it easy for them to get into the habit of putting a portion of their money into a Wealth Account for investing it before they spend it. Recall from Chapter 3 that the wealth account is the Wealth Cycle building block that refers to an account specifically earmarked for investments. Although your child may not be thinking about investments and their future yet, they also don't have any bad spending habits yet. Therefore, it's the perfect time to create the habit of paying your future self first as a mandatory part of the process of making money. In fact, we would recommend you encourage your child to put at least 50 percent of their planned earnings into their Wealth Account. This will help them to turbocharge their Wealth Account while they have the incredible advantage of time for that account to compound and grow. Remember the incredible power of compounding we showed you in the Chapter 2 section "Investor Mindset: Compound Interest"? Paying yourself first makes those incredible compounded growth numbers possible.

Although we will recommend you open a savings account for your child in the next chapter, at this age we think it's a good idea to initially use the time-honored method of using jars for your child's savings so that they have a visual aid to help hammer home the concept. If you don't want to use jars you can use whatever other receptacle you want to hold the money. Loral's daughter, Tristin, used file folders to serve the same purpose. This technique acts as a banking simulation phase of the pilot training model we talked about in Chapter 1.

Here's how it works. In the last section we asked you to never pay your kid an allowance, but to instead give them Home Pay for Home Tasks they do in the household. Every week (or month) when your child receives their Home Pay, they should place it into at least three or four separate jars.

Jar 1 would be their Wealth Account jar. Since we pay ourselves first, this jar gets a deposit from our Home Pay no matter what their income was for that week. As we said a moment ago, we recommend they put at least 50 percent of their planned income into their Wealth Account since they basically have no required expenses. The exact percentages are up to you, but 50 percent should probably be the minimum. Since your child is putting 50 percent of their planned income into the jar, and we know from our Home Tasks list what your child is forecast to make each week, they can actually plan to put a set amount each week into their Wealth Account jar. That way, even if they didn't get their full income for the week, Jar 1 would get paid no matter what. For example, if their weekly forecasted pay was $10, then Jar 1 would always receive a minimum of $5. If they failed to complete all their Home Tasks for the week and only earned $5, then that Home Pay would all go into Jar 1 and they would have zero spending money for that week.

The next jar, Jar 2, would be their charity jar. This would include money they planned to give either to the church, charities, or perhaps could even include gifts for friends or family. It's never too early to teach your children about giving to others and helping those in need. We believe that one of the principal reasons for aspiring for money and teaching your kids to have more wealth is that the more we have, the more we can give. We recommend at least 10 percent for this jar, but again, the percentages are up to you.

**One of the principal reasons for aspiring for money and teaching your kids to have more wealth is that the more we have, the more we can give.**

Jar 3 would be the long-term spending jar. This jar is allocated for things your child wants to save up to buy in the next several months, which is long-term when you are five years old. For example, Kyle's son saved for over six months to get enough money to buy the Gameboy video console he so desperately wanted when he was just a little bit older than this age. Having this long- or mid-term goal kept him motivated to keep working and making money. We recommend Jar 3 account for about 20 percent of the Home Pay, but it would only get filled if the other two jars had already received their allocation of the Home Pay.

The final jar we recommend is Jar 4. Jar 4 is for short-term purchases. This might include snacks they get to buy on your next trip to the grocery store or the occasional small toy or game. There's a reason this jar is last. It only gets filled if the other three jars get their portions first. We recommend this jar receive 20 percent of the Home Pay as well. It's OK for your child to occasionally splurge and spend some of their money as long as that money is spent only after the more important needs have been filled. Doing so will help motivate your child to make sure they make enough to have money to put into this jar.

It's up to you and your child to set up the jar rules the way you see fit. The most important thing to drive home for the jar system is that Jar 1, the Wealth Account jar, always gets paid first and without fail. Table 4.1 shows our recommended jar saving allocations.

**Table 4.1 Recommended Jar Saving Allocations**

| JAR 1 | JAR 2 | JAR 3 | JAR 4 |
|---|---|---|---|
| Wealth Account | Charity | Long-term spending | Short-term spending |
| 50% of planned income—*paid no matter what* | 10% of planned income—paid if at all possible | 20% of planned income—if first two jars are paid | 20% of planned income—if all other jars are paid |

After accumulating for a short duration, you will eventually want to put the money from Jar 1 into investments and perhaps Jar 3 (and possibly 2) into a savings account. If you put multiple jars into a single bank account, make sure to keep records of which money is associated with which jar or, better yet, have multiple bank accounts. As we mentioned before, we'll talk more about opening a savings account for your child in the next chapter in the section titled "Set Up a Bank Account in Their Name (and Yours)." We would recommend you continue with the jar method for at least six to nine months or until you feel your child has ingrained the *pay yourself first* mentality into their psyche and habit patterns.

**Paying yourself first is one of the most important keys to becoming a millionaire.**

After that, if you would like, feel free to deposit the money into the bank without the temporary visual aid of the jars. However, never let them alter from the practice of always paying their Wealth Account first. Remember the Wealth Cycle that we first introduced in Chapter 2, "Millionaire Mindset"?

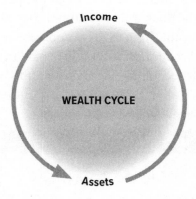

**Figure 4.2** Wealth Cycle

   In the Wealth Cycle, we pay ourselves first to buy assets, which then provide even more income, from which we pay ourselves first to continue the cycle. If you can drive this point home to them, the math of compound interest that we demonstrated in Chapter 2 will make it almost inevitable that they will eventually become millionaires. It's that important! The key is to make contributions to their Wealth Account so automatic that they believe them to be mandatory. Paying yourself first is one of the most important keys to becoming a millionaire. Their future self will thank them for it.

# SUMMARY

Take a deep breath. We covered a lot of topics in this chapter. It may seem overwhelming. Remember, many of the tasks we recommended you initiate will carry over throughout your child's life. This chapter is the foundation for the rest of the age-by-age chapters. As Bob Proctor would say, "At this age, your child is a sponge. Everything you do, they will repeat." Make sure you are modeling the behavior you want repeated.

# CHAPTER 5

# AGES SIX TO EIGHT

*If one does not know to which port one is sailing,*
*no wind is favorable.*

**—Lucius Annaeus Seneca, famous stoic philosopher**

By age six, most children have begun to be capable of expressing themselves well through words and are beginning to recognize that actions have consequences. As a result, parents can begin to teach them some more advanced concepts about money and fully embrace the academics portion of the pilot training model. This is the age where, if you began teaching them money concepts early on, they will begin to surprise you sometimes with their understanding. Ages six to eight is also the point at which they will probably begin school of some sort, so they will now be exposed to the influence of schoolteachers and classmates. Not all of these people are as enlightened about money as you are, so this is definitely not the time to let up on your teaching. Remember, the traditional school system was created to teach employees, but we want to groom future employ*ers*—leaders, entrepreneurs, and business owners. Most of the concepts discussed in this book will almost certainly not be discussed in school, so as parents we have

**Helpful reminder: Don't forget to continue teaching and doing all the things you introduced in the last chapter and expanding on them as your child's understanding improves.**

to take an active role in making sure that our children get a proper education on money. After all, it's one of the few things they will have to deal with nearly every day of their life.

# YOUR CHILD'S MONEY GOALS

Goal setting is just as important for kids as it is for adults. It's also important in flight planning as well as in goal setting to know where you are starting from.

We'll talk about your financial starting point and the Financial Baseline more in Chapter 7 in the section "Balance Sheet." However, since your kids' starting point financially is probably near zero, we'll focus for now on where they are going.

In the previous goal-related section "Goal Setting Foundations" in Chapter 4, we helped build the framework for building the goal setting habit in your child. In this section we will first ensure that you the parent recognize how we recommend that you, as an adult, set your goals. Then we'll show you how to teach your child.

We both have educational backgrounds in psychology. For years the psychological community and nearly all successful people have acknowledged the importance of goal setting. Goal setting is not just about wishing. It's about clearly defining an intention and a plan. Former first lady and esteemed diplomat and activist Eleanor Roosevelt said, "It takes as much energy to wish as it does to plan."

**KYLE SAYS: As a former pilot, I like to use an aviation-based variation on Seneca's quote at the beginning of this chapter: "It's really hard to plan a flight if you don't know where you're going." Goal setting helps you learn where you're going and discern the destination.**

**LORAL SAYS: In my teaching, your money starting point is called the Financial Baseline, and it's one of the 12 building blocks of the Wealth Cycle System that we introduced in Chapter 3.**

When we set a goal, we create a plan to make that intention come true. It's also important that we comprehend the underlying reason for our goals. One of the best ways to figure this out is what we call "The Underlying Why Test."

The Underlying Why Test gets down to the true reason for your goal. It includes stating your goal then asking why three times. Following is an example. Kyle remembers mentoring a woman who wanted to be rich but hadn't really set a goal for how she would accomplish that. We'll call her Edith. Kyle asked Edith to think for a few minutes about a specific financial goal she had for 20 years in her future. After sitting silently for a few minutes to think about it, Edith replied that her goal was to be rich. Kyle then asked her, "Why?" After some thought, Edith responded that she really wanted to quit her job. Kyle persisted and again asked her, "Why?" Taken aback a bit, Edith responded that she really hated the structure at work and wanted to do something that gave her more freedom of her time. She looked pensively at Kyle, hoping he was done interrogating her. "Why?" Kyle queried with a calm persistence. "Because I really want to spend more time with my family," she blurted. Kyle smiled as the realization swept over her. At last they had uncovered the core reason for Edith's goal and could construct a new goal that was more specific and in true alignment with her Underlying Why.

We've found some important characteristics of goals. These characteristics are the same ones that Kyle used before every flight as a fighter pilot and instructor pilot when discussing objectives for the upcoming mission.

### All Goals Should Be . . .
1. Specific
2. Measurable
3. Attainable but Ambitious

Let's talk about each of these requirements in turn. First, goals need to be specific. Broad goals like being happy or rich can't be easily defined, and it's impossible to know if they've been accomplished.

Breaking down these vague terms into more detailed and distinctive parts will help them be more easily defined.

This leads us to the second criteria, that goals should be measurable. This usually means they can be counted or otherwise quantified. Goals aren't just some nebulous star on the horizon that we dream about or hope to go toward. We want to be able to know when we've reached that destination. The only way to do this is to ensure it is measurable so that we can objectively assess and calculate our progress toward the goal. This also requires a time or duration component so that we can measure our progress on that timeline.

Finally, goals must be attainable. We could say we want to land on that distant star by next week, but if the technology doesn't exist yet, this may be a bit too lofty a goal. No matter how much we profess that we will reach that star, our brain won't truly believe it, and we won't take any action.

We found that people tend to not think big enough. Oftentimes, big goals are actually easier to meet because their big rewards inspire more action. Remember, inspiring action is the entire point of creating goals. We've also found that people tend to underestimate their ability to reach wealth. Our discussion of compound interest in the "Investor Mindset: Compound Interest" section of Chapter 2 should make it clear that real wealth is attainable for anybody. Keep those goals ambitious.

Let's revisit Edith and her goal. She stated that her goal was to be rich. This goal wasn't specific or measurable at

**KYLE SAYS: Many people make the opposite mistake and make their goals too easy to achieve. It is for this reason that I added the "but ambitious" part to the commonly used specific, measurable, and attainable criteria. Sometimes I call this new goal criteria the SMAA criteria.**

**LORAL SAYS: I use a slight variation of the SMAA criteria. I use the SMART acronym. In my acronym, the SMA is the same, but I add R for realistic and T for timely. The two acronyms are very similar and essentially mean the same thing.**

all. It's hard to even figure out whether it was attainable because there is no way of knowing when it has been reached. After going through the Underlying Why Test we found that what Edith really wanted was to spend more time with her family. One could argue that this could be attained without being rich, but let's assume the best way to accomplish her Underlying Why was to make certain she could replace her job with passive income to cover her expenses. This would allow her to dedicate the time she was previously working to be with her family instead.

The first step would be to figure out how much income she needed to replace. In this case, Edith made about $40,000 per year, and this amount could cover her expenses. There are a thousand ways Edith could replace that income with a business that would allow her to spend more time with her family, but Edith didn't want to work at all. For simplicity's sake, let's say that a wealth account that produced that $40,000 annually in a passive way would work best. To ensure Edith could grow her wealth account sufficiently to replace what was pulled out annually, we recommended a goal of $1 million. One million dollars invested in a conservative portfolio of investments would feed her $40,000 needs even if it was conservatively invested and only grew at 4 percent per year. If she was willing to let her account slowly be depleted, it would even account for increasing expenses or allow for an even more conservative portfolio. We've now established that, for Edith to achieve her Underlying Why, she should aspire to reach $1 million. This is much more specific than just "being rich," but it doesn't meet all the criteria for a good goal yet. When does she need that $1 million? If she doesn't achieve it until she's on her deathbed it wouldn't really meet the intent of her Underlying Why because it would be too late to spend time with her family. Until there is a timeline, it isn't truly measurable.

Edith would have liked to be a millionaire instantly, but this wouldn't have been attainable outside of winning the lottery. She was 28 years old and only had $50,000 in savings, so it was going to take some time, hard work, and discipline. Although she wasn't sure she could ever be a millionaire, Kyle assured her that an ambitious but attainable goal would be "to have $1 million in net worth by the age of 40." This was a goal that was specific, measurable, and attainable but ambitious. It would also lead to her achieving her Underlying Why.

The good news for Edith is that she now has a long-term, well-defined goal that will help her achieve her Underlying Why. The bad news is that her goal is so far out on the horizon that it will be difficult to take daily action toward it. To do so, we'll need to break that goal into shorter-term goals.

With a 120-day plan, now at last we have something that is short-term enough that it can guide our daily actions. This plan should include specific actions you will take to accomplish your one-year goal, and ultimately your long-term goal.

If Edith wanted to focus on her assets this year, her one-year goal might be to purchase an income-producing asset and grow it from $50,000 to $70,000. Alternatively, Edith might choose to make her one-year goal the creation of a Cash Machine business that would provide her $2,000 per month in cash flow. Her 120-day plan might be to create an online presence for that business. This could be further broken down into weekly activities to set up a website, Facebook page, and LinkedIn account for the business. Daily activities might be getting headshot photos of herself or creating a logo.

> **LORAL SAYS: In my book *The Millionaire Maker* I break down long-term goals into One-Year Freedom Day Goals. Freedom Day is one of the building blocks in the Wealth Cycle Process from Chapter 3. The one-year goal can be further broken down into a 120-day plan.**

The more granular and detailed you can be with your plan, the easier it is to follow. Think of it this way. Imagine you wanted to take a trip to a friend's house several hundred miles (or kilometers) away. If you were given a map that was taken from outer space, you would have a tough time figuring out the details of the route. The global map would be handy to give you a general direction, but you would need something more to know what to do when you reached the stop sign on Main Street. Details and specifics help us reach our destinations and our goals.

We discussed this goal-setting topic at length because even many adults haven't taken the time to set appropriate goals. Even though your kids may not think much about the future, it's important that you begin to nurture in them the habits of setting goals for the future and striving to achieve them. We would recommend that you use the exercise with Edith as an example for how you should help your child create their own goals.

In the space below or on a separate sheet of paper, write down your child's goal—for now this can be a short, intermediate, or long-term goal. For most kids we wouldn't recommend that you set the goals out too far into the future—probably no more than a year or two. The point is to get them in the habit of setting goals.

Your child's initial goal: _____

_____

Now go through the Underlying Why test to find out what they really want. Remember to follow the process of asking why three times to reach their Underlying Why. After each "Why?" write down their answer:

Why? _____

Why? _____

Why? _____

*(continued)*

Now help them come up with a goal that better suits their Underlying Why. Make sure it is Specific, Measurable, and Attainable but Ambitious (SMAA) or Specific, Measurable, Attainable, Realistic, and Timely (SMART).

Your child's revised goal: _____

_____

You might be surprised how enlightening it is to get a glimpse into what your child finds important. At the very least you'll get to know your child better. You'll also be creating a goal-setting habit that helps inspire action so your child will learn how to work toward their goal instead of just dreaming of it. Now that you've written down your child's goal here, have them write it down on a notecard, Post-it, or small piece of paper. Have them display it in a place they will see every day. Constant reminders of our goals breed constant action toward those goals and, ultimately, lead to their achievement.

Another idea that can cement a goal into our brain and bring it to life is to use pictures. One of the most successful and fun ways to engage children in goal setting and get them excited about it is to have them create a vision board.

**Constant reminders of our goals breed constant action toward those goals and, ultimately, lead to their achievement.**

To create one for your child, help them find and cut out pictures of things they'd like to purchase or achieve and have them paste these pictures onto a piece of cardboard. Remember, these don't have to be only items. The vision board is for all their goals in life. For example, they may wish to include a picture that represents your family having fun together on a special trip with their friends, or nailing a perfect performance at the dance recital. Things that cost money are only a small part of the picture of a great life! Encourage your child to be resourceful in finding pictures for their vision board. They may use magazines, catalogues, the internet, or simply draw pictures of what they want. Figures 5.1 and 5.2 show a few examples of vision boards that Tristin created when she was around seven years old.

**LORAL SAYS: Vision boards are one of my favorite goal-setting techniques for kids. I had my son, Logan, and daughter, Tristan, use these vision boards to inspire them to reach their childhood goals.**

**Figure 5.1** A vision board by Tristin at about age seven

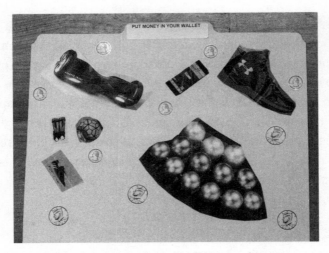

**Figure 5.2** Another vision board by Tristin at about age seven

When your child selects pictures for their board, have them explain to you why they chose them and what it will do for them once they've achieved each goal. Before gluing the items onto the vision board, ask them which things they want most and which things they want first. If their goals are things they want to buy, check that they have a realistic price for the item and add that as well. Remember the Underlying Why test. The more interactive this process is between you and your child, the stronger their connection will be with their goals and the better you'll get to know your child. If they change their mind about an item they want, they can simply paste a new picture over the previous one. It's OK to create the entire collage digitally as well, but make sure you print it out so they will have a constant reminder (Figure 5.3). Just like the written goal you created before, the vision board should be placed somewhere they will see it daily. The point is that the pictures will help them check in with their subconscious mind and envision the achievement of the goal.

**Figure 5.3** Tristin poses with her mom, Loral, as she proudly shows off her vision board folder on the set of a TV show where they discussed it.

## FAMILY FINANCIAL GOAL SETTING

Now that you've created personal goals for your child, it's time to include your child in some of your family's goals. What better way to cement the habit of goal setting in your child than to show them that your family has goals as well? Talk to your children about goals the family has set that they can relate to. They probably won't appreciate your goal of saving for your own golden years, but if you explain how you and the family are striving to save money for a trip to Disneyland, you can bet they will be interested. Including your child in the goal planning can be educational and even fun for the whole family. It will also teach them the value of goal setting and the excitement when, after hard work, you achieve that goal. We recommend having a family goal-setting session where you go through the steps described in the section "Your Child's Money Goals." This could be during Christmas, like Loral does when she has her Christmas stocking exercise, or any other time that makes sense for your family. Write down your goals here or on a separate document:

Your family's initial goal: _____

_____

Now go through the Underlying Why test to find out what your family really wants. Remember to follow the process of asking why three times to reach your Underlying Why. After each "Why?" write down your family answers:

Why? _____

Why? _____

Why? _____

Now come up with a goal that better suits your family's Underlying Why. Make sure it is Specific, Measurable, and Attainable but Ambitious (SMAA) or Specific, Measurable, Attainable, Realistic, and Timely (SMART).

Your family's revised goal: _____

_____

Just as before, learning what your child is interested in and their perspective for the family's goals can be illuminating. This would be the perfect opportunity to begin talking about the similarities and differences between your child's goals and adult goals, or those of the entire family. Consider discussing how each of you will do your part in working for the goal. This would be an ideal opportunity to show them that if they want something extra, they have to put in extra work. If a trip is the goal, tell them that if they help make extra money, they can use that money to buy extra souvenirs or special treats while on the trip. Now might be a good time to encourage an entrepreneurial endeavor like a lemonade stand, raking leaves, or shoveling snow. At the very least they should have the opportunity to make extra money through their Home Tasks as discussed in the last chapter in the section "Never Pay Your Kid an Allowance."

A carefully chosen family goal should be a motivator to inspire action in both you and your child. It can also bring you together as a family. Think of the times when you were involved in an organization that achieved a goal. Maybe this was a sports team or community organization. Remember how the hard work brought you together? Recall how incredible it felt when, after months of hard work, you finally achieved that goal. Were there times when you lifted each other up and achieved a strength greater than the sum of your parts? Even if you didn't achieve the goal, the mere act of pulling in one direction helped you come together as a team. It created bonds of camaraderie that endured well beyond the time spent working toward the goal. Take a moment to close your eyes and try to remember how you felt when you achieved that goal, and how you felt about your teammates. Isn't that the type of teamwork and emotional bond you want to cultivate with your family? Family goal setting and the requisite hard work to achieve each goal can foster that family bond.

## BREAKING THE LIFESTYLE CYCLE

Scottish professor, philosopher, and historian James Mackintosh once said, "It is right to be contented with what we have, but never with what we are." The line between staying hungry for your dreams and content with your things is a fine line to walk. We believe that big dreams are absolutely achievable, and we would never want to stifle a child's desire for grand things by saying they should be content with their current status. That's why we spent the last two sections talking about goals. In fact, we're both huge believers that money can be abundant if you have the right mindset about it.

That being said, we also believe that the incessant desire for more things is a path that will never lead to happiness. Social media and targeted advertising can now reach right into your child's phone and tell them they aren't good enough unless they have the latest toy/gadget/ game. Trying to keep up with the Joneses, as they say, is a recipe for disaster. For many, living in the Lifestyle Cycle like this will lead to a lifetime of debt where they are held like a prisoner in chains by their consumer debt—never able to achieve the independence that comes from financial freedom. This is a very difficult lesson to teach because children (and often even adults) only see the outward trappings of what they think is wealth—the fancy toys, the new car, and so on. What they don't see is the underlying debt that many people have, and the resultant shackles and stress.

One way to help your child appreciate the dangers of the Lifestyle Cycle might be to give an example from your past of an item you purchased that you thought would provide happiness, but you later learned it could not. For example, you may have bought a new vehicle or an extravagant piece of jewelry because you were feeling down and thought that purchase would make you happier. It might have worked for a week or two, but after that, the buyer's remorse set in. This is when you realized that you bought something for all the wrong reasons, and all you really did was delay your ability to reach your financial goals.

This regret almost always lasts longer than the initial joy of the purchase. Your kids may still have to experience this regret to fully learn the lesson, but warning them about it will hopefully keep them from making the mistake over and over. As with most of the lessons in this book, the other best way to teach them this concept is through leading by example. Just because you

**KYLE SAYS: I like to teach that a life pursuing your passions is far more fulfilling than filling it full of possessions. Teach your child to dream big instead of spending big and they will be well on their way to happiness.**

could afford a new car, house, boat, RV, or motorcycle doesn't mean you need to buy one. It's OK to be content with the things we have.

Conversely, the same people who have a huge appetite for things sometimes seem to have an underdeveloped hunger for pursuing their own dreams. This seems backward to us. Big dreams are what drive us and get us out of bed every day. We should always try to improve ourselves and keep dreaming and setting larger and more ambitious goals.

## SET UP A BANK ACCOUNT IN THEIR NAME (AND YOURS)

Once your child has graduated from the jar system described in the "Pay Yourself First" section in the last chapter, they are ready to move on to a more advanced and grown-up method for storing their money. Your child needs to have some place to put all that money they are making doing Home Tasks or perhaps other income-producing activities. That place is often a bank or credit union. Even if you already had a bank account in their name, this new account may be the first one that they are aware of and will participate in setting it up and contributing to it. It's OK to continue keeping small amounts of money around the house or in a traditional piggy bank, but the sooner you can teach them about financial institutions like banks the better. If you've begun playing games like Monopoly with your child, they may already be familiar with the basic concepts of a bank. One way to describe a bank to your child at this age is that it's a very safe building for keeping money. The truth is a little more complicated, and it's worth beginning to explain some of the basic academics of how a bank works. Explain to your child that banks have two main functions:

1. To provide safekeeping for money put in the bank
2. To provide loans for people who need money

Banks don't do these things as a public service or just to be nice. They are a business just like any other business. Teach your child about checking accounts, savings accounts, money market accounts, and CDs, and the differences between them. Describe how the bank will provide money in the form of interest as payment to the people willing to put their money in the bank, fulfilling function 1. The reason the banks pay people to keep their money is because that money doesn't just sit in the bank. The banks use your money so they can perform function 2, to lend to other people at a higher interest rate. The difference in interest rates, sometimes called "the spread," is how banks make money.

Here's an example you can relay to your child that may help them understand: Seven-year-old Bret was excited to earn some money. As evidenced by the picture in Figure 5.4, he worked hard to earn his cash. After spending several days helping to sand and stain the countertop and stairs at his parents' house, he was excited to make $100. He deposited this $100 into a savings account that promised to give him 1 percent interest per year. After a year his $100 grew by $1, and he then had $101 in the bank. But the bank didn't keep Bret's money in the bank the entire time. It lent $80 of it out to Sam and charged Sam 5 percent interest on the loan. As a result, Sam eventually had to pay back the entire $80 plus an additional $4 in interest. When we take the $4 the bank made from Sam and subtract the $1 it had to give back to Bret, we find out that the bank profited $3 from using Bret's money. Multiply this transaction times millions of dollars, and this is how banks can make so much money.

Obviously, the previous example was simplified. In reality, banks use leverage to lend out much more money than they receive in deposits. Still, this example should be sufficient at this age to give your child a basic appreciation of how banks work. This will be an important foundation that will help later when they learn about mortgages, promissory notes, and bonds. For this age, explain to your children that the savings account is a safe place to store money for things you need to save up for. Discuss ideas of long-term expenses they will eventually incur, such as college or a car. We don't recommend that they have to save all their money for goals that far out. Kids this age seldom have the patience for

**Figure 5.4** Bret at age seven in full safety gear,
helping sand during a home renovation

extremely long-range goals, so, as we described in the "Pay Yourself First" section, let them have midrange goals for a portion of the money. For example, they may want to earn money for a video game or gaming system like the Gameboy Bryce saved up for when he was a child. For others, their mid- or long-range goal might be saving for a new bike, or perhaps even a gift for a sibling or friend. As we mentioned before, it's never too early to teach them the value of giving.

Now that you've taught your child the basic academics of banking, and they've done the jar method as a simulation of banking, it's time for the demonstration phase of the pilot training teaching model. Reveal to your child how your bank account works. Show them a bank statement and let them see you make a deposit in your account. Tell them where your bank is, or at least where its website is, and how you access your account. If you do have online access, now might be a good time to introduce the idea of password protection and privacy. Disclose how you would write a check or use your debit card for your bank account. These functions may seem obvious and easy, but your child has never done them before so a demonstration will go a long way toward easing their anxiety and making them less fearful of banks and money in general.

With the demonstration complete you are finally ready to start the supervision phase of banking by actually opening their account. We highly recommend at this point that you put the money in an interest-earning savings account or money market account so your child can see how their money grows passively. This will be discussed more in the next section "Interest Makes Your Money Work for You." As they get older or have a business that has expenses, you will eventually open an additional checking account so they have a means of easily making payments. This will be covered in Chapter 7 in the section "Set Up a Checking Account and Debit Card for Your Child." For now, keep it simple.

It's not hard to set up an account. Just contact the bank your family uses and tell them you want to set up an account for your child. We recommend that you physically walk into the bank with your child to show them the process. Setting up the account shouldn't cost anything, and your bank will be all too happy to have another customer. We recommend that you open a few accounts for your child so they can put their wealth account (previously Jar 1) money in one and their long-term savings (previously Jar 2) in another. If not, you will still want to encourage your child to keep records of their own so they can stick to the process of keeping their virtual jars separate. You will need to be the custodian with your name on the accounts, but the bank should be able to put your child's name on them as well. When the first statements arrive (or when you check them online), show your child their name on the accounts and explain what an important step they have taken. Congratulate them on putting money away and having their own bank accounts. These accounts will form the foundation for their future saving and investing. Also, don't forget to continue to supervise their activity for the account to ensure they continue putting money away, keep track of their balances, and don't bounce any checks. Appropriate supervision will allow you to "take the controls" of their account if necessary so you can fix any bad habits before they are out on their own and have solo bank accounts.

## INTEREST MAKES YOUR MONEY WORK FOR YOU

To be truly wealthy you must learn to make your money work for you. Show your kids how interest works in the savings account or money market account you set up in the last section. Remind them that even the tiny interest they are receiving in their savings account is helping their money work for them. "But what if you could make even more interest?" you might ask. "The great thing about interest is that it grows at a compound rate."

Now is the time to use the miraculous "Rich Neighbor Example" from the section titled "Investor Mindset: Compound Interest" in Chapter 2. Don't just read the example to them. Have them take the quiz and see if they can guess the results. Then, leave plenty of time to discuss it with them afterward. The two most important takeaways they should leave with are that compound interest is amazingly powerful and that we are almost always sure to underestimate the growth it can provide.

After completing the "Rich Neighbor Example," go ahead and explain the 10X, 100X, and 1,000X Tactics. The math for these rules was intentionally made very simple so it

**KYLE SAYS: The Rich Neighbor Example usually blows the minds of even my adult students. Just think how impactful it will be for your child. I was given a similar quiz by one of my teachers when I was this age. It was so compelling for me that I remember it to this day, and it literally inspired me to a whole new perspective and appreciation of investing.**

could be calculated quickly. If your child doesn't fully get it, you can set it aside for a year or two and introduce it later.

Understanding these formulas and how to use them will make it easy to calculate compound interest and investment growth. Even better, give them some examples. When your child makes some money (not *if* but *when*), quiz them on what that money could become if invested for 25 years. If you use the 10X Tactic it's very simple. You would simply add a zero to the end of the initial amount of money. For example, $10 becomes $100 after 25 years. What about 50 years? Again, using the 10X Tactic twice you could simply add two zeros. Thus, $10 becomes $1,000 after 50 years. What if it was invested every year? Here you would use the 100X Tactic. Therefore, $10 invested every year for 25 years would become $1,000 again. The more you quiz them on this simple strategy, the better they will understand it and be able to use it in everyday life. Furthermore, the more you can ingrain the growth potential of their earnings, the more likely they will be to invest their money in the future instead of spending it on the Lifestyle Cycle.

**LORAL SAYS:** One of my mentors taught me a simple way to think about interest. Which side of the interest equation are you on? Are you paying interest, or are you receiving it? Investors receive it. People in the Lifestyle Cycle pay it.

**KYLE SAYS:** The idea is to get our money to work for us, not to work for our money. With my military background, I like to think of my money as soldiers. I want to keep my soldiers working toward the mission. The more they work, the more soldiers I get and the bigger the mission I can accomplish.

## ACTIVE INCOME VERSUS PASSIVE INCOME

Simply put, active income is money you must work for. Passive income is money that comes in automatically without you having to work for it.

Many types of income are somewhere in between and are mostly passive, but do require a little work overseeing them. We sometimes call these "pactive" income to differentiate them from income that truly requires zero work. Although pactive income isn't completely hands-off, it still generally qualifies in our minds as meeting the criteria for passing the PI≥E and giving you financial freedom. For example, a pension would be completely passive income, whereas real estate or stocks that you occasionally checked on would still qualify as passive income by most people's definition, even though we may technically call those pactive. Let's look at where some common investments would fall on the passive versus active scale (Table 5.1).

**Table 5.1** Where Common Investments Fall on the Passive Versus Active Scale

| PASSIVE | PACTIVE | ACTIVE |
| --- | --- | --- |
| Pension | Rental properties | Job |
| Annuity | Hands-off/side hustle business | Active business |
| CD | Buy-and-hold stocks/dividend stocks | Day trading |
| Money market or savings account | Network/affiliate marketing | Run a podcast or YouTube channel |
| Bonds | Write a book | Hands-on rehabbing properties |

Note that many of the passive or pactive income categories require quite a bit of work on the front end. A pension takes years of active effort to earn. As we can attest, even writing a book takes lots of active work on the front end before you can reap the passive income associated with ongoing sales. Also note that, depending on the investment, many of these could move more toward one side or the other of the scale. For example, investing in rental property can vary from fully active to fully passive depending on how much you participate in the management of the properties.

Another common example would be stocks. Even if you don't "day trade" stocks, if you are watching them throughout the day, your investment leans more to the active side. If, however, you put your money in an ETF or iFlip and check it only once a year, then your stock investment leans much more to the passive side. Speaking of stocks, if you don't own dividend stocks that provide a quarterly income, how can these be considered passive income? They really can't be considered income at all unless you sell them. However, if your total wealth in stocks grows to a point that you could easily sell off a percentage of it each year and still have enough to last your entire lifetime, we think this fits the criteria of passive income as it pertains to making you eligible to "Pass the PI≥E." The same could be true of any investment, as long as it is liquid enough that you could sell it to cover your expenses. Just make sure your assumptions don't overestimate the long-term growth of the investment, and consider the fact that investments can sometimes go down in value as well as up.

One example of money that probably wouldn't meet the criteria would be funds that are tied up in a trust or IRA that can't be accessed until you meet the dispersal requirements or reach a certain age. In this case, you would need some way of bridging the gap until those funds became available. Table 5.1 lists only a few of the ways to create income. In reality, there are dozens of variations on these options, and thousands of other income-generating options we didn't mention.

Now that your child is working for active income and also generating some passive income in their bank account, it's time to show them how their account can earn interest income for them without them doing anything. Even though the interest from their bank account will probably be extremely small, emphasize how appealing it is that they earned that money without having to do anything at all. If you show them your excitement for this concept, they will be excited too. If you haven't opened or discussed the opening of their IRA or education fund, this may be their first opportunity to witness the power of passive income—the key to financial freedom and passing the PI≥E! As soon as you can, you'll want to get some of that money invested into their

Roth IRA. It is here that you will be able to demonstrate the true power of passive income. If they don't have much passive income themselves yet and you have an account statement you are willing to share with your child, you can show them how your account has grown (hopefully) over the last year or two and how you didn't have to work for it. Doing so serves as the demonstration phase from the five-step pilot training model as it pertains to passive income. Explain to them that the goal is to get your passive income to replace your active income. Once it does, you will have reached financial freedom and the whole world opens up to you.

Now would be a good time to review the beginning of Chapter 1 with your child to provide them some additional academics on passive income and remind them how we reach financial freedom by "passing the PI≥E." It won't be hard for them to recognize that PI≥E sounds a lot easier than sanding all day like Bret had to do to earn his active income.

## BASICS OF CREDIT CARDS, DEBIT CARDS, CHECKS, ETC.

In Chapter 4 when we first discussed teaching your child that money buys things, we recommended that you keep things simple by starting off purchasing food from the grocery store with cash in the form of bills or coins. This kept it simple for your child by showing them what was actually being exchanged and teaching them that money is a conduit for things they want or need. However, few people these days use cash for most of their purchases. By now, your child has probably noticed that you usually use something quite different than cash for your purchases. Even if you discussed the basics when they opened their first bank account, it's now time to teach them how things like credit cards, debit cards, ATMs, checks, and other assorted payment systems work.

Initiating the conversation about these money tools is easy. To do so we return to the pilot training model and use our tactic called demonstration. When your child is out with you buying something, show them what you are using for payment. Ask them, "Do you know what this is and how this works?" Explain that credit cards, debit cards, and ATMs are tools of convenience, so we don't have to carry around cash. They aren't magic money. Explain the similarities and differences between the different payment services and how they work with your bank account. Point out how other more modern payment services like Apple Pay, Square, and PayPal work in a similar fashion. Make sure to highlight the difference between credit cards versus checks, debit cards, ATMs, and other money transfer services. Point out which ones act like a debit card and are tied directly to the bank account and can only access funds that are already currently in the account.

Ensure that you call attention to the fact that credit cards, in contrast to debit cards, are basically a loan from the credit card company that you *do* have to pay back. As a result, make sure your child absorbs the fact that they shouldn't spend money they don't have. Further, help them realize that they should always pay credit cards off fully every month to avoid paying interest. You can remind them that when they put money in their bank account, they get to earn the interest. Conversely, if we don't pay our credit cards every month, we must pay interest to the credit card company, but at a much higher rate. As exciting as the interest is when it comes in, it's quite frightening how quickly it can go out if you hold a credit card balance. If they are ready for the math, it might be worth explaining the difference between gaining and paying interest with a fictional $100 account. Always use realistic interest amounts for the bank account versus the credit card to show the stark interest rate disparity. Here's a simple example:

**LORAL SAYS: I was recently speaking at a university and was approached by several college students after my talk, and the number one question was "What's the difference between a debit card and a credit card?" College-age kids should never reach this point in their life without understanding this basic information.**

The average interest rate on a savings account is currently approximately 1 percent. This won't provide much interest for our $100 account, but at least it won't lose it like the credit card will. Credit cards at the time of this writing are charging, on average, over 15 percent in interest. These interest rates are the annual rates, so they would assume 1 year of accrued interest.

| SAVING ACCOUNT AT 1% | CREDIT CARD AT 15% |
|---|---|
| $100 × 1% = $101 | $100 × 15% = $115 |

As you can see in the table, the credit card is growing interest against you 15 times faster than you can make it in the savings account. You could never keep up if you didn't pay off your credit cards. An even better lesson to teach your child is to never accrue bad debt like credit card debt in the first place. When your child is older you can eventually explain the exceptions to having a credit balance and when buying investments with credit might make sense. We'll discuss the general concept of credit later in this book. For now, keep it simple and emphasize the convenience factors and the dangers of things like credit cards. The idea is to give them an overview of the different payment options so they are familiar with them and can gain comfort in hearing them discussed before they use them.

## FINANCIAL DISCIPLINE

While we believe that people need to keep their spending under control, we do differ a bit on the importance of financial discipline. Perhaps some of this comes from Loral's earlier path to entrepreneurism. Recall the discussion in the first chapter where we showed the equation I > E where I represented income and E represented expenses. As an entrepreneur, Loral was able to create a surplus on income by making her business produce more income and keeping the expenses relatively stable. With this surplus income she could buy assets. Recall that Kyle, however, was tied to a demanding 12+-hour-a-day job (W-2 income) that left little opportunity to increase income. In fact, due to the 24-hour nature of the job, officers in the military must receive special permission to have another job or business. This permission is usually denied. Thus, to create the same surplus of income that allows one to buy assets at a rate necessary to become a millionaire, Kyle had to reduce his expenses significantly more than most people of a comparable income. He was only able to increase his income by acquiring assets that produced that income for him. Fortunately, his parents were excellent teachers of financial discipline and frugality and did a great job giving him the tools and mindset necessary to do so.

This is why we both believe so strongly in teaching financial discipline to our kids. Even though we are simultaneously teaching them how to improve their income, we know they may choose to chase a passion that doesn't provide large amounts of income. By having the skills to keep their expenses low, your child can still achieve the income surplus necessary to purchase assets and achieve great wealth.

So how does one teach a child to have financial discipline? The first step is reminding them that it is more important to *be* wealthy than to *look* wealthy. It doesn't matter what others think of your financial situation. An excellent book that talks about this concept is *The Millionaire Next Door* by Thomas Stanley and William Danko. In it the authors describe how many millionaires wouldn't appear so from the outside looking in. In fact, looking wealthy often only attracts solicitors, thieves, and litigators.

The next major way to help your children be financially disciplined is to set the example yourself, even if you have enough money that you don't have

**KYLE SAYS: Looking like you are rich is often a serious impediment to actually being rich. If you are doing it right, many of your friends and family probably won't even know you are wealthy. I'll take *being* rich over *looking* rich any day of the week.**

to. This sounds a lot like the demonstration phase of the pilot training model again, right? It doesn't mean you can never enjoy your money and buy nice things for yourself. It does mean that you should do so very thoughtfully and with great consideration for the value you are getting for your money. Why buy a new car for $30,000 when you can buy a slightly used one that looks and runs exactly the same for $20,000? Then you can use the remaining $10,000 as a down payment on an asset like a rental property that can provide a steady stream of income for life.

Financial discipline can also be displayed with smaller items like clothing and furniture. Savings in these things can really add up over time. Just make sure you don't spend 20 hours researching or shopping the best price just so you can save a mere $20. This is an easy trap to fall into for the hyper-frugal. Your time is worth *way* more than that.

The next way to promote financial discipline in your children is a tough one. In this day and age when the media and everyone around you equates showing that you are a good parent with providing your child everything he or she desires, remember this. You should shower your child with love, not gifts. Kyle recalls having the conversation with his son Bryce about one of his friends whose father had bought him a $50,000 truck for his sixteenth birthday. Kyle asked Bryce what he thought of that. Bryce said "Well, it is a really nice truck, but I guess it seems like a waste to spend that much on just a vehicle."

Kyle agreed but continued, "It's more than that, though. When your friend goes out on his own and has to make his own living and that truck gets old, what will he likely do? He'll almost certainly feel like he has to go out and buy an even nicer vehicle because it's really

> **LORAL SAYS:** Even though I don't stress the importance of expense reduction as much as Kyle, I'm still a firm believer that before you start spending on Lifestyle Cycle things, you must first contribute to your investments and get your Wealth Cycle running strong.

tough to take a step down in life, whether it be with a house or a vehicle. People psychologically need to feel like they are stepping up in the world. If your friend isn't making really good income when he buys his next vehicle, he won't be able to afford a truck like that, and he'll probably go into debt and take out a huge loan he can't afford, just to prove he's better off than he was when he was 16.

"Your friend's dad thought he was giving his son a wonderful gift. What he likely did instead was to doom him to a life of consumption addiction and consumer debt—constantly trying to make just enough income to keep his head above water and feed his ever-growing consumerism."

Bryce nodded and responded, "I might get a vehicle that nice someday, but not until I'm a millionaire." Kyle nodded quietly in agreement, but inside he was beaming. His lesson was hitting home. We'll talk more about car buying and the problem with spending too much on a vehicle in the Chapter 7 section titled "Buying a Car."

*The Millionaire Maker* describes this consumer debt trap as the Lifestyle Cycle. In the Lifestyle Cycle, wealth can never be built because money that comes in goes right out again to support perishable, onetime-use consumption. And in many Lifestyle Cycles, money is spent, thanks to credit cards, even before it's earned. Conversely, in the Wealth Cycle, money coming in supports assets—that is, money-making resources that will generate cash flow and create wealth. The difference between having wealth and not having wealth is the difference between living in a Lifestyle Cycle and living in a Wealth Cycle. As we mentioned in Chapter 2, a person earning $14,000 a year who understands the concept of a Wealth Cycle has a better chance of building and sustaining wealth than a person who makes $1 million a year and lives in a Lifestyle Cycle.

We're big fans of having money to buy yourself things. Achieving the wealth necessary to do that is part of what this book is all about. However, we also believe in using money primarily to buy yourself freedom and time so you can give those things to the loved ones in your life. In the end, they will appreciate those gifts from you much more than any expensive trapping of consumerism. If you absolutely must shower them with physical gifts, then at least make sure they realize that you are only able to do that because you first used your money in the Wealth Cycle before ever considering the Lifestyle Cycle.

## SUPPLY AND DEMAND

The law of supply and demand is one of the most basic tenets of capitalism. The law states that the price of goods is linked to both the availability (supply) of a given product and the desire (demand) that consumers have for that product. If a product is low in supply or high in demand, then the price of that product should rise. If the opposite factors are in play (high supply and/or low demand), it will lead to a drop in the price of that product. Note the graphic in Figure 5.5.

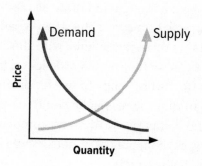

**Figure 5.5** Law of supply and demand

It's a simple concept, but the intricacies and implications of this simple relationship have filled libraries of books and been the subject of debate amongst countless economists. When your child is this young, it's probably easiest to describe the basics using an example business they are already involved in and can understand. Here's a story about a business Loral's son, Logan, started when he was only eight years old, and how he learned about supply and demand.

## Logan's Smoothie Store

Loral glanced to the back of the room as she had done so many times before. Logan was still sitting quietly at the back of her financial seminar. As a single mother, Loral often had to bring him to these seminars. "At least he's listening and being quiet," she thought. But she could tell he was getting restless. At the next break she walked to the back and gave him a high-five as recognition for being such a good kid. "I'm getting thirsty," she stated. "How about you?"

Logan nodded vigorously. "What I could really use," he exclaimed, "is one of those fruit smoothies you make for me!"

Loral agreed. "But if you are back here drinking a smoothie, then everybody else will be jealous and want one too." Logan's eyes lit up. He had a brilliant idea.

"What if I made smoothies for everybody and sold them?" Loral practically glowed with pride. "That's a genius plan!" she declared with another high-five.

The next day, Logan brought in Loral's blender. He then had one of Loral's employees walk him across the street to get fresh fruit, yogurt, and juice. Combining these ingredients with the ice they already provided for water, Logan was able to make delicious fresh smoothies that the seminar attendees were happy to pay for during the breaks. Loral explained to Logan that the reason he could make such a good profit was that he had no competition. With no competition, he controlled the supply. As long as the supply of smoothies was low, the price would stay high (demand being equal).

"But what if somebody else came in and also supplied smoothies?" she queried. "There would be plenty of smoothies for everybody, and you would probably have to lower your price to make sure people bought your smoothies instead of hers." Logan's furrowed brow made it clear he wasn't excited at the prospect of someone else moving in on his business.

Loral then asked Logan, "What would happen if you brought in extra fresh and juicy strawberries that were so delicious that everybody here wanted a smoothie, maybe even two smoothies, but you still only made a small amount of those smoothies for the entire room?"

Logan shook his head knowingly and responded, "If I did that, then I bet I could sell them for even more!"

Loral smiled and responded "Supply and demand. You just increased the demand, so . . ." But she wasn't able to finish. Logan had already absorbed the lesson and was sprinting off to get more strawberries.

## HOW YOU DO ANYTHING
## IS HOW YOU DO EVERYTHING

Consistently exhibiting attributes like hard work and attention to detail may not seem directly related to making money, but they do influence a person's success in money matters like having a job, starting a business, or even investing. It's easy to slack off on these traits when one doesn't think a task is important, or when nobody is watching. However, it's during these times that these traits are so important in order to have integrity within ourselves. Novelist Charles Marshall said, "Do the right thing, even when no one is watching. It's called integrity."

By doing things the right way even when no one is watching, we also create habit patterns that will carry through in all aspects of our lives. When your child does a chore or job for you, make sure they work hard (and smart) at it, and with attention to detail.

Kyle remembers passing on to his kids this lesson he learned from his father while sweeping out the garage. He wasn't allowed to be finished until every bit of dust had been swept up. Nor were his kids. Kyle's mother required a similar attention to detail when she would help edit his school papers. Why? Did it really matter? In the big picture it probably didn't matter that the garage was swept perfectly, but "any job worth doing is worth doing right" was always the answer.

Later in life, Kyle and many of his other fellow instructors passed a similar lesson on to their student pilots. Early in their training the aspiring fighter pilots would be chastised if they did not line up perfectly with the other jets at the end of the runway before taking off (even though it didn't seem necessary).

The reality is that doing even the little things with exactness and a fastidious nature creates inertia that drives people to hold higher standards for themselves in other areas of their life. In other words, how you do anything is how you do everything.

## Teamwork Is Fundamental

Even though fighter pilots in the movies are often glorified for their ability to take on the enemy by themselves, the reality is that they rarely ever do anything as individuals. They usually employ in groups (called flights) of several aircraft, or wingmen, to provide mutual support for each other. The term *wingman* has even entered popular culture as synonymous with someone who helps, protects, or guides. Even fighter pilots can't complete the mission alone. Building wealth is the same way. In Chapter 3 we explained that teamwork is one of the 12 building blocks of the Wealth Cycle. Millionaires don't become wealthy or stay that way by themselves. They do so with a team.

The wingmen of the financial world would include a cadre of field partners. These are people in the field who know the industry, the region, and the players in the arena you want to invest in. They provide the connections, legwork, and oversight, while you provide the cash, the credit, or the network of investors. Field partners include such people as realtors, business brokers, and regional financial planners. Additional people on your team might be other investors or business owners that you can

**KYLE SAYS: When a confused student would ask why it was so important that they line up perfectly, I would tell them, "In about four months you will be flying solo in formation in this jet with my aircraft a mere three feet away from you and occasionally upside-down or at 550 miles per hour. If you can't even line up on the ground with precision and attention to detail, how in the world can I depend on you to not kill me?"**

**LORAL SAYS: There is rarely such a thing as self-made millionaires. Instead, they are team-made millionaires.**

collaborate with, affiliate with, or mastermind with to help one another reach your financial goals. In the financial world, this team would be the professional advisors, lawyers, accountants, and even the house cleaners, gardeners, tutors, or childcare specialists, all of whom free up your time so you can focus on what you do best.

You cannot and should not try to be an expert in all the fields that asset generation requires. You just need to find the experts, get them on your team, and lead them to your goal. Contrary to popular opinion, you don't want to be the smartest or even richest person in the room. You want to be with people who have bigger brains and more experience. Motivational speaker Jim Rohn has said, "You are the average of the five people you spend the most time with." Wouldn't you want those people you spend time with to be the type of teammates who make you smarter and richer? Finding the best people for your wealth team is crucial to your success. Once you've voiced your vision and taken action to move toward it, others will be compelled by your leadership to join your pursuit. In the Wealth Cycle Process, it is your job to direct a team of professionals that helps you to develop and execute your strategy for building wealth and reaching your PI≥E.

**LORAL SAYS:** As a single mom, I had to become an expert in team building. I mastered the art of putting a team together. I believe in an integrated life. It all needs support.

Now that we've hopefully demonstrated the importance of teamwork, how do you show your child, and foster an environment for them that creates an appreciation of teamwork? Like always, it starts at home. Even at a very young age, your kids are part of a team. They are part of the family team. As team members they play a role in helping the family move toward its goals. Just as we discussed in the section "Never Pay Your Kid an Allowance" in Chapter 4, your child should have some chores that they do that are just a part of being in the family—part of the team. Let them know that just as families work together, they also play together and stick together. This should extend to siblings and extended family members as well. Set a good example by not trying to do everything yourself, but rather by bringing in the team members we described in the paragraph above.

When you have a transaction involving money, take advantage of the demonstration phase of the pilot training model and make sure to point out to your child the team that was involved. For example, if you buy a house, quiz them on who was involved. You might ask, "Who was included in the team to make that happen? Dad and Mom don't just buy a house by themselves. There was a broker, a lender, a title company, an inspector, and an appraiser, just to name a few." Talk to your child about the role each of these members play in the process, and how important they are. This is just a continuation of the theme we have discussed throughout this book, of constantly talking with your child about money.

Another way to help your child appreciate the importance of a team is to get them involved in team activities. These team activities could serve as the simulation phase of the pilot training model by letting kids learn the teamwork they will be required to take advantage of later in life. One of our favorite ways to accomplish this was to get our children involved in sports. Sports and other team-based activities help your child understand how to work with others and to socialize and develop the people skills that will be necessary to lead and be a part of teams later in life. Remind your child during these activities of the importance of collaboration. As a parent, remember to celebrate their team, not just individual accomplishments. It may seem like these activities are just for fun, but they are much more. They are simulation and practice for life. If your child's life is to include great wealth, it will be as a team-made millionaire.

## Leadership Is Vital

We described in the last section the importance of a team. Somebody has to guide and pilot that team. This leads us into the next topic we believe you should teach your child: leadership. Teaching your child leadership may seem unrelated to the subject of money. We assure you it's not. There is absolutely a correlation between one's leadership ability and one's wealth. As we described in Chapter 3, leadership is a key part of the Wealth Cycle. We must effectively lead our financial team to create the wealth we deserve. If we create a business, we must lead our employees to meet the objectives of that business. As adults we can lead our family to achieving its vision and financial future. Finally, personal leadership will drive us to continually improve ourselves and develop the money muscles we need to achieve our goals.

Wealthy people take a leadership role in their wealth plan: they literally lead their wealth team. Though you may, and should, choose to delegate the activities that support your wealth building, no one can drive it like you can. If you do not keep consistent and constant pressure on the aircraft throttles, the wealth engine will sputter to a stop and your flight will come to an abrupt end. No one cares as much as you do about your wealth, and your leadership is crucial to your success. You, and only you, must assume the leadership role to create the wealth you desire.

It can't be overstated how crucial leadership is to becoming a millionaire, achieving financial freedom, and "passing the PI≥E." But can leadership really be taught? We believe it can, especially if you start at a young age.

Legendary NFL coach and leader Vince Lombardi is known for saying, "Leaders are made, they are not born. They are made by hard effort, which is the price which all of us must pay to achieve any goal that is worthwhile." If you began teaching your child integrity and hard work, as described in the section "How You Do Anything is How You Do Everything," you are already on your way to teaching them leadership. Integrity is an important aspect of leadership. Unless they are forced by virtue of your position, people will only follow you if they

> **KYLE SAYS:** If it wasn't possible to teach leadership then there would be no reason for the military academies like West Point and the United States Air Force Academy I attended. One of the main purposes of these institutions is teaching leadership.

respect you. Integrity goes a long way toward that respect. Another aspect of a leader is that leaders are willing to step forward, even when no one else will. Former British Prime Minister Margaret Thatcher said, "Don't follow the crowd, let the crowd follow you."

This too can be taught. Lead your child by example, by letting them see you step up to meet the challenge in your profession, church, or community. Tell them stories about times you are proud of when you were willing to show initiative and take on a leadership role. Encourage them to do so, even if it's among their playmates or siblings. You might say things like, "Tristin, I know you don't want to apologize to your friend, but you need to be a leader and be the first to say you're sorry." Most important, when your young child does display moments of leadership, shower them with compliments. Tell them how proud you are of them when, for example, they don't hang their head and instead motivate and lead their entire baseball or softball team to keep battling despite long odds. As your child grows older, encourage them to take on leadership positions in their classroom, teams, or clubs. As Vince Lombardi said, leadership takes hard work. The more practice your child gets in leading and the more you encourage them to do so, the better the leader they will become. The better your child is as a leader, the more easily money will flow to them to make them wealthy. The following story is an example of a time when Bryce learned about leadership.

## Bryce's Apricot Epiphany

Bryce beamed with excitement. His young eyebrows rose to meet his blond locks and his eyes seemed to double in size. His seven-year-old mind raced nearly visibly with the possibilities of what he could do with his potential bounty. His father had just made an unusually lucrative proposal and promised him 5 cents per apricot pit that he picked up, and the yard was riddled with hundreds of them. To his mind it must have seemed like a field of gold nuggets. The contract had nary been set when he sprinted into action and began filling the bucket he had been provided. Only four handfuls into the endeavor, however, his fervor quickly turned to horror. His three-year-old brother, Bret, had just sauntered outside. Though Bret wasn't part of the agreement, sensing his brother's exhilaration, he had quickly grabbed his own bucket and was filling it with pits. Bryce recognized that his fortune was swiftly becoming half a fortune and pleaded angrily for his brother to stop. But it was too late. Bret was biologically compelled to follow his brother's lead.

As his father watched Bryce loom angrily over his younger brother, he knew he needed to act quickly to avoid bedlam between his children and to salvage the teachable moment. He called Bryce over and explained how, far from being a travesty, this incident was actually a lucky break. "Since my agreement for picking up pits was only with you, what if you were to hire your brother to help you pick up the apricot pits? You could pay him 2 cents per pit, and I would still pay you 5 cents per pit. Although you would make a little less, if you team up you can finish the job much more quickly, and while he is working you would be getting paid 3 cents for just being a good leader and teaching him. This way, you can both win!" Bryce's anger began to melt into a wide and approving smile as he contemplated the seven-year-old version of leadership and passive income. For better or worse, an entrepreneur was born.

As we mentioned in the first chapter, the money lessons you try to teach your children don't always work out the way you intend. Sometimes that can be for the best. Kyle thought he would take advantage of a yard full of apricot pits to teach Bryce about the value of hard work and how to earn money through what are today commonly referred to as "side hustles." Instead, the moment quickly pivoted to an entirely different learning point when Bryce's brother Bret decided to enter the picture. Kyle ended up teaching Bryce how to use teamwork, and more important, how to lead that team to complete a mission and make money. Bryce also learned a bit about the idea of passive income since he no longer had to be the one doing all the work. By taking advantage of the circumstances and rolling with the situation, Kyle was able to drive home entrepreneurial lessons about leadership and passive income even more powerfully than he originally intended. For years afterward, Kyle was able to refer to this successful example when he needed to remind Bryce about the power of teamwork, leadership, and passive income. As a result, Bryce remembers the lesson he learned then, even to this day.

## PLAY GAMES WITH YOUR KIDS THAT INVOLVE MONEY

Even though learning about money is a serious matter and we're going to ask you to teach your kids a lot in this book, remember to always keep it fun so that they become addicted to a lifetime of learning. This won't happen if your child feels like the learning is being shoved down their throat. One of the best ways to do this is to make the learning a game. After all, money is like a game; you just have to figure out the right way to win it. For example, you could have a stock-picking contest or a challenge to see who can save or make the most money or in the most creative ways. You can also play board games or computer games that teach people about money. We can think of several reasons why playing finance games is helpful. First, it helps kids to get comfortable with the terminology of money in a nonthreatening environment. When your child is having fun, they will retain information without even knowing it. Games also serve to reduce fear about money. One can take risks and try new things without the permanence associated with real life. In this respect, games can be considered like the simulator portion of the pilot training example where concepts are practiced in a safe and simulated environment before taking them on in the real airplane or real life.

Math can also be less intimidating when it's done involving money in a game. Your child may even forget they are doing math when they count up the money they won in "Free Parking." Many financial games also involve dealmaking and the art of negotiation. These skill sets are vital to success in real-life business. Finally, playing games is a great way to replicate the fun and competitive nature of money in real life. It can be incredibly gratifying to be successful with finances. Games can help cultivate the competitive edge necessary to realize this financial success.

**LORAL SAYS: I always suggest to my clients that they play two games in order: Monopoly and my game The Millionaire Maker.**

If you are already playing games involving money with your kids, that's a great start.

What better way to get started than by using games that have already been created? These games introduce your child to the basics of finance while recapturing the nostalgia many of us have associated with playing the games when we were kids.

Here are some of the money lessons you can learn from Monopoly:

- The value of money
- How to count money
- The basic concept of banking
- Being paid a salary
- Buying and selling properties
- Value of being a property owner
- Frustration of paying rent to owners
- Basics of a mortgage interest
- Negotiating and finding win-win deals
- Asking for the cash
- The importance of location with real estate
- Weighing risk versus reward for an investment
- Balance between having some cash and overextending yourself
- Getting started investing/purchasing properties early
- Overcoming bad luck and playing the long game

When you were playing as a child you may not have realized all the financial lessons you were being taught. Another excellent game is Loral's game, The Millionaire Maker. Like Monopoly, the purpose of this game is to increase your net worth. However, one of the key differences is the introduction to the concept of entrepreneurialism and building wealth through owning and growing businesses. Playing The Millionaire Maker teaches many valuable financial concepts including:

- Having regular cash flow
- Paying yourself first
- Owning and managing your own Cash Machines
- Having wealth accounts to allocate toward investments
- Buying real assets that generate income
- Reading and understanding a balance sheet
- Reading and understanding an income statement
- Building teams
- Allocating money resources appropriately
- Protecting your assets and businesses with entities and insurance
- Recognizing different asset classes other than just real estate
- Forecasting taxes, income, and expenses

Any of these lessons learned through real-life experiences would take a long time to absorb and could be incredibly costly. We all know that making mistakes can be one of the best learning tools. However, financial mistakes in real life can be devastating and take years to recover from. Games make financial learning fast and entertaining, while letting kids learn from their mistakes without jeopardizing their future. They serve as a great simulator for your child's Flight To Financial Freedom. Make money games a regular part of your family routine and your child will be better prepared for the game of life.

# CHAPTER 6

# AGES 9 TO 11

*Opportunity is missed by most people*
*because it is dressed in overalls and looks like work.*
—Thomas Edison, inventor of the light bulb

During the ages of 9 to 11 your child is getting more and more independent. Their growing independence will lead them to seek relationships outside the family, and they will begin to be more influenced by friends. This may make them more susceptible to peer pressure. It's imperative that you establish their values about money now so they don't fall victim to the pitfalls of addictive consumption brought on by peer pressure and the barrage of ads they'll be seeing on their phones, tablets, or computers they probably now possess. Also, don't forget to continue the discussions, activities, and exercises we introduced in the previous chapters. The good news is they're still willing to listen to you and their intellect is growing quickly. As a result, they can learn more and help around the house more, providing them ample opportunity to earn income and start learning how to use their money to work for them.

**Helpful reminder: Don't forget to continue teaching and doing all the things you introduced in the previous chapters and expanding on them as your child's understanding improves.**

# SPEND ONLY WHAT YOU HAVE OR MAKE MORE

The idea of only spending only what you have is similar to the discussion we had in the section "Financial Discipline" in the last chapter. However, at this age, we are focusing more on your child actually beginning to make and transact money, so it's important that we reiterate the points in that section. Furthermore, in this section we will go into further detail on how we recommend that you teach your child about spending as well as earning money, and the relationship they have to each other.

It's important to teach kids at a very early age that although money can be abundant in the long term, the amount of money we have at any given time is finite. They may still be too young to fully grasp the meaning of *finite*. It's important that children appreciate that their parents don't have an endless supply of money, so they can only spend what they have. If you as a parent have a consumer problem with credit card debt, you might need to take a hard look at yourself now to consider your awareness of this concept and the lesson you are teaching your kids.

We mentioned in the previous financial discipline section that Kyle is generally a bigger proponent of limiting your spending than Loral is, especially because he spent much of his life as a military member without a large salary. However, we agree on one thing. We both deviate from many financial advisors when it comes to the implications of the concept "Spend only what you have." It is true that you should only spend what you have, but that doesn't mean you can't work to make sure you *make* more. This is where the power of being an entrepreneur comes in. It's difficult for a salaried employee to simply turn on the money spigot and make more money. When Kyle was in the military, he had to do so primarily with investments, mostly stocks and real estate. Though these investments can increase your income, it can take several years before they grow enough to add significant cashflow.

Savvy business owners like Loral, however, can sometimes increase their income very quickly by opening additional revenue streams in their business or by creating additional businesses.

Loral's bestselling book *YES! Energy* is a great resource for encouraging people to create the income they desire. This concept isn't as incompatible with the idea of financial discipline as you might think. When you actually have to put in more hours of work to buy the things you want rather than just throwing it on a credit card, it's astonishing how much better you become at differentiating between the trivial things you want and those that really matter. The trivial tend to fall away. Recall in Chapter 2 we talked about the concept of keeping your income greater than your expenses. We used the equation:

**LORAL SAYS: My son, Logan, learned this very early as I advised him "money will always come and go, and you're in control and responsible for what comes and what goes. If you want more, make a bigger life." Some of the most damaging and limiting phrases you can teach your child are "We can't afford that" or "Do you think I'm made of money?" Instead, if there is something they really want, focus on saying "How can we create more income so that we can buy that?"**

$$\textbf{Income > Expenses}$$

or

$$\textbf{I > E}$$

Note that this equation could just as easily be flipped to say that we should keep our expenses less than our income, or E < I. Expenses and income might be concepts that are too advanced for kids this age, so it would probably be best to use terms like "spend" and "have." Therefore, if we replace the previous equation with these simpler terms, we will have the following:

$$\textbf{Spend < Have}$$

The difference between our approach and that of many financial educators is that rather than only lowering the left side of the equation (the Spend side) to match the right side (the Have side), we recommend also teaching your kids creative ways to grow and increase the right side (the Have side) to meet their desires on the left side (the Spend side). Even though you still need to teach your children about over-spending and financial discipline, you can simultaneously start them early with using positive language and vocabulary about money to help them think of money as an item of abundance, not scarcity. Loral has written several books on this concept alone. If you are looking for ways to implement this strategy, look no further than the following story where Loral silently reminds her daughter, Tristin, about this important concept. Consider using a similar tactic to help your child understand the relationship between what they spend and what they have.

### Tristin's Triumph

Tristin was famished. She had been hanging out in the back at her mom's financial event for an eternity—which in her 10-year-old time meant at least 30 minutes. She had spotted a snack machine and could feel herself beginning to salivate. Unfortunately, she had accidentally left her money at home. Because she had been earning income from small businesses for a few years already, she normally carried at least a little spending cash. "No worries," she thought. "I'll just ask my mom for some." She walked up to Loral, who was deep in conversation and had three clients hovered around her. After waiting for a pause, Tristin queried, "Mom, can I have some money for a snack?"

Loral's lips pursed, she looked at her daughter, and she dropped her chin with a look that silently pleaded, "If you don't have money, go earn some!" Loral then made an exaggerated, lateral sweeping motion with her arm as if to say, "There are 50 people in this room that you can get money from!" No words were necessary. Tristin dropped her head in admission. Her mom was right. She did know how to earn the money she needed for the snacks she so desperately desired.

Tristin reached into her backpack to make sure what she needed was still there. Fortunately, one of her businesses had been selling single-application teeth whitening paste. As her fingers reached through the pocket of her backpack, they clasped on the package of whitening paste she had intended to use for herself later that day. "Time to make some money!" she uttered under her breath as she strode confidently to the soon-to-be owner of whitening toothpaste. Mere moments later Tristin walked by her mother and, with a fling of her hair, flashed a cheesy grin as she waved her newly earned 10-dollar bill in the air and made a beeline to the snack machine. Loral let a proud smile briefly escape her lips as she continued uninterrupted with a sale of her own.

## START A TWENTY-FIRST-CENTURY LEMONADE STAND

Hopefully the last section helped motivate you toward enforcing the idea of money abundance in your child. Loral's daughter, Tristin, understood this concept at an early age. If you want more, you must earn more. If you haven't yet helped your child start a twenty-first-century lemonade stand, you need to do it now. A twenty-first-century lemonade stand is the modern-day version of a very simple business that allows your child to make income. It's like a side hustle for kids. In the section titled "Never Pay Your Kid an Allowance" in Chapter 4, we recommended creating income using Home Tasks and Home Pay. We're now going to recommend having your child create a Cash Machine, one of the 12 building blocks of the Wealth Cycle. We warned you that making your child a millionaire would require effort. It does, and not just from you.

As Thomas Edison said, don't let your child miss out on opportunity because it requires them to work. Edison also said, "Genius is 1 percent inspiration and 99 percent perspiration." Your child is old enough now to perspire a bit and do a variety of jobs that would enable them to earn a salary or start a small business. But don't worry. It doesn't have to be all sweat and no fun. When encouraging your child to be an entrepreneur, remember to emphasize the child's strengths. If they are good at drawing, consider having them sell their art. If they are good at writing, have them sell short stories or poems.

When Kyle was in junior high, he was good at writing and rhyming, so he would sell his friends personalized poems that they could gift to their girlfriends. Tristin is very artistic, so when Tristin was at Loral's events in the back of the room, she would sell paper wallets that she had created. The sky is the limit. The following is Loral's strategy for finding your child's Cash Machine.

Grab a piece of paper and your child and together brainstorm some of your child's strengths and things they like to do. Next, write down all the things your child already has experience with. These would generally be things they have done for your household as Home Tasks or possibly at school or in another organization they are a part of. For example, they may have already babysat a younger sibling, so they could also babysit other kids. Alternatively, they may be used to caring for your pet, so they could pet-sit for others. Write down their job experience on the same piece of paper where you wrote down their strengths. In a perfect world, your child's best Cash Machine would be ventures that are listed in both their strengths/likes and experience lists. If you can't find something that falls in both lists, we've found it is usually best to focus on their experience. In Loral's book *Put More Cash in Your Pocket* she calls these ventures the twenty-first-century lemonade stand. The point is to create cash using something they can already do. Later in life they can pursue what they enjoy and are naturally gifted at.

Our kids have done all of the following things to make money at this age:

- Mowing lawns
- Raking leaves
- Shoveling snow

- Car washing
- Sweeping garages
- Babysitting
- House-sitting
- Assisting elderly people
- Walking or sitting dogs
- Running lemonade stands
- Smoothie bars
- Helping paint investment properties
- Tutoring

Other common ideas would include:

- Gardening
- Computer/phone tech support
- Selling baked goods
- Pet grooming
- Delivering newspapers
- Reselling items on eBay or Facebook
- Making greeting cards
- Housecleaning
- Becoming a social media or YouTube star

In fact, if they have an interest in starting a YouTube channel, we believe you should encourage them to do it. It's our opinion that having YouTube and social media skills will be as important for young teens now as having computer skills was for teens of 20 or 30 years ago. An aptitude in these areas may very well turn into a future venture.

If your child uses the excuse that they can't think of anything they want to do, have them flex their internet skills and do a quick search for "business ideas for kids." If they need additional motivation, you can explain the numerous advantages of being an entrepreneur that are discussed in the section "Entrepreneur Mindset" in Chapter 2.

Even for their entrepreneurial ventures at this age, try to teach them about as many of the aspects of running a business as you can.

This Cash Machine isn't just for extra money. It acts as the simulation phase of the pilot training model for their entrepreneurial future. If they have a lemonade stand, make them create the signage to advertise for it. Make certain they understand that the costs of the lemonade supplies will come out of their revenue. Explain the difference between gross and net profit. Most of all, try to make it fun and profitable. Keeping it fun keeps them interested so they will do it longer and learn more entrepreneurial lessons.

Having income gives kids money. They need money so they can start learning how to earn, save, manage, and invest it. Having an income also allows kids to contribute to an IRA. By helping them start this IRA 15 or 20 years earlier than most people you are not only teaching them the valuable lesson of putting money aside for the future, but you are also giving them the opportunity for their investment returns to double at least two extra times. If you've been contributing on your child's behalf, this might be the time to have your child start contributing their own money to their IRA. Recall the section "Open a Roth IRA for Your Child" in Chapter 4 or "Investor Mindset: Compound Interest" in Chapter 2 if you are doubting the importance of having your child start investing while they are young.

The following is a story about how Kyle's son Bryce started his lawn mowing business.

### Bryce's Push-Mower Push

Bryce's mind was made up. He'd heard his dad's talks about businesses for years, and he finally had a great idea for one. He marched up to his dad with the undaunted resolve that only a 10-year-old can muster. "Dad, I want to start a lawn mowing business," he stated matter-of-factly. Kyle matched Bryce's serious tone and tried to conceal his excitement that his entrepreneurial lessons had been taken to heart.

Kyle's inner enthusiasm dampened when he realized that he wasn't really comfortable with Bryce using a normal lawnmower at only 10 years old. Kyle worked in the safety office at his base and had a friend who was missing two toes from a lawn mowing accident when he was a kid. Kyle didn't want to stymie Bryce's enthusiasm, but he just wasn't comfortable with the safety of Bryce's lawn mower plan. He was contemplating how he would break the bad news to Bryce when he suddenly thought about reel mowers, a type of mower that has no engine at all but is powered strictly by pushing it, which turns gears that spin the cutting blades. Though the blades are sharp, there is no danger of a runaway lawnmower cutting off toes or throwing projectiles across the yard. Push mowers are even known for keeping grass healthier by making a sharper cut. It was the perfect solution!

After talking with his wife, Tracy, Kyle pitched Bryce the plan. Bryce nodded his head slowly, gave an earnest look of resolve, and said, "Let's do it!" Kyle wanted Bryce to get the full experience of starting his own business. This meant Bryce had to pay the business startup expenses. Kyle had learned this valuable lesson from his own father. When Kyle was a child, he had a banner printing business and made a healthy profit (for a 12-year-old anyway), until his father wisely informed Kyle that he had to replace the printer ribbon on the family printer, effectively cutting Kyle's profit in half. For Bryce, this meant he had to pay the startup cost of the lawnmower. Kyle knew they had to find one that was easy to push since Bryce was only 10, and the difficulty in pushing reel mowers is one of their potential disadvantages. Together, they eventually found one that had great reviews online and even had one reviewer who said his 10-year-old kid could push it. Kyle and Bryce were sold. When the mower arrived, Kyle helped Bryce put it together. The grass hadn't come back from its winter dormancy, but Bryce was prepared to make his millions once the spring had fully sprung (Figure 6.1)!

The moment their yard's grass was ready to be cut, Bryce was out the door. Fifteen minutes later he was back in the door. "Dad, it's too hard to push," Bryce declared.

Kyle fed Bryce one of his favorite lines. "Son, you'll just have to cowboy up. We knew it would be hard to push, but just think, you won't

**FIGURE 6.1** Bryce with his new reel mower—
the Bermuda grass here is dormant, not dead

have to spend money on gas and it will make you stronger for football and wrestling."

Bryce begrudgingly trudged back outside. Twenty minutes later he was back again. "Dad, it's *really* hard to push," he pleaded, "can you please come make sure it's working right?" When Kyle ventured outside, he gave it a shot himself and could see what Bryce was talking about. Even for Kyle it was difficult. They lubricated the gears and sharpened the blades, which made it easy enough for Bryce to complete the yard, but it took forever. The next few times Bryce mowed a yard he was able to complete it, but it still took three or four times as long as it should.

After Bryce's sixth time mowing a lawn, even Kyle had troubles pushing it. Sharpening the blades and lubricating the gears was no longer helpful. It was becoming clear this wasn't going to work. Kyle tried not to reveal it, but he was perhaps even more frustrated than Bryce, especially since the reel mower had been his idea. He was afraid the experience would stymie Bryce's enthusiasm for entrepreneurship. After some thought, Kyle and Bryce sat down and discussed what lessons could be learned from the endeavor.

The first thing they learned was that reel mowers don't work very well in Oklahoma because of the thick, tough Bermuda grass that grows there. They realized that in their excitement to get started, they hadn't done enough research and due diligence before investing capital in the business. Bryce also learned about startup costs and that businesses don't always produce huge profits. After all the hours of labor he had put in, Bryce ended up with only a modest profit. You could say it was only a little better than a push on the push mower business (pun intended). Of course, the alternative was that he wouldn't have made any money at all, so fortunately Bryce wasn't too upset. It was also a great learning experience. In fact, when he was older, Bryce used the lessons he had learned and entered the lawn mowing business again with a traditional mower and grew the business to a highly profitable one with several employees mowing lawns throughout town.

Fortunately, the lessons Bryce learned didn't dampen his enthusiasm for different types of future entrepreneurial ventures either, as his other anecdote later in this book will demonstrate. Not every business works out as well as you hope. The world is full of people and businesses that failed many times before making it big. Thomas Edison purportedly failed over 10,000 times before successfully making the light bulb. Henry Ford founded two automotive companies that failed before turning Ford Motor Company into a multibillion-dollar company and one of the 10 largest automotive companies in the world. Media mogul Oprah Winfrey was once fired from a news reporter job at a Baltimore news station because they thought she was unfit for television news. Even Walt Disney was also reportedly once fired by a newspaper editor for not having good ideas or imagination. The important thing is that you learn from your mistakes and stay persistent.

# TAXES

Up until now, your child's entrepreneurial endeavors may not have produced enough income that they were required to pay taxes. Whether their business requires it now or not, it's time for your child to learn about taxes. The Merriam-Webster dictionary defines taxes as "a charge usually of money imposed by authority on persons or property for public purposes." For the purposes of this lesson, we are generally talking about taxes imposed by the government on the income we make.

To help your child appreciate the reason behind taxes it might be best to start by first asking them why they think taxes might be necessary. If they aren't sure, ask them how things like our public schools, roads, police forces, fire departments, trash services, and other publicly used facilities get paid for. Continue by asking them what other things taxes pay for. They get bonus points if they can recognize that things like our military, Medicare, and social security are paid by federal taxes as well. Since we can't all provide our own individual police, fire, and military services, it makes sense that we should each pay our own part.

Now ask your child if they think anybody should pay more than their fair share. They will most likely say that would not be fair. This is where you can describe the premise that we should all pay our taxes but it's important that we understand the rules behind taxes so that we don't pay more than our fair share. Use their business to explain how much taxes they would (or will) be required to pay. Explain the concept of graduated tax brackets and the fact that higher levels of income are taxed at higher rates, but only for those amounts that are above the lower tax bracket.

Another concept to discuss with your child regarding taxes is the fact that the government wants to encourage people to do certain activities that help the country, like buying real estate, running businesses, and even having kids. As a result, the government incentivizes these activities by giving tax deductions or credits for these activities. Thus, taking advantage of these tax breaks and making sure you pay only your fair share of taxes is not only not wrong, it's actually patriotic because it means you are doing the activities the government desires and has incentivized you to do. If your child doesn't have to pay taxes on their income yet, then just bringing up the concepts is probably sufficient for now. At a later age we'll discuss more details on taxes and specific strategies on how to pay the lowest fair share you can.

# ASSETS VERSUS LIABILITIES

In the financial world, an asset can be generally defined as something that is owned that provides economic value. For the purposes of teaching your children, the simplest way to explain the term "economic value" is that it means something gives you money. In other words, an asset is something you own that gives you money. Examples of this might be a savings account, stocks, or rental properties. Now let's talk about a liability. A liability is something that is owed that takes away economic value. Using the same definition for economic value as before leads us to the conclusion that a liability is something you owe that takes away money. Examples of this would be credit card debt, loans, and promissory notes. If you take the value of your assets minus the value of your liabilities, you will get your net worth.

### Assets – Liabilities = Net Worth

Unfortunately, many families have more liabilities than assets. The assets they do own are often depreciating assets that are going down in value each year (think cars, tools, electronics, toys, etc.). Though accountants may technically define these as assets because they have value, they don't give you money. These aren't the type of assets you should teach your child to accumulate. The assets we recommend for you either go up in value or provide cash flow. Therefore, we define real assets as those that give you money. The only

> The only way to grow your net worth and overall wealth is to grow your assets faster than your liabilities.

way to grow your net worth and overall wealth is to grow your assets faster than your liabilities.

Because your child won't have many assets, and hopefully has zero liabilities, the best way to teach them this concept is through examples. Quiz them about different things and ask them if they are an asset or a liability. Start with obvious things like credit card debt or an investment account, then work your way into more ambiguous items like your personal home or a personal car. Talk about ways these items have characteristics of both an asset and a liability. Though they are both something you own that has value, they do not provide cash flow. The car also generally depreciates in value. Even the personal home often takes away more economic value than it provides in appreciation, due to expensive home insurance, property taxes, and maintenance expenses. This doesn't mean we don't recommend owning a home. You have to live somewhere. It just means it is not the ideal asset to accumulate your wealth.

Assets other than a home can provide both appreciation and cash flow without the draining expenses. Loral, for example, didn't buy her first home until after she had already owned rental properties for several years. She believes in the concept "Live where you want and invest where it makes sense." Talking through different examples of assets and liabilities, including some you own and some you don't, will help your child recognize the differences between things they can spend their money on and the opportunity cost for those purchases. Understanding assets and liabilities is also foundational to comprehending the next concept, good debt versus bad debt.

## GOOD DEBT VERSUS BAD DEBT

Loral talks about the concept of good versus bad debt in her bestselling book *The Millionaire Maker*. She describes bad debt as consumer debt that purchases liabilities or depreciating assets. This usually takes the form of credit card debt used to support a lifestyle. Good debt, on the other hand, is used to buy assets that appreciate and make you money. In reality, the topic is more nuanced than this and you could always come up with exceptions to this general rule. For the sake of teaching your kids at this age, we recommend you keep it simple. Bad debt = consumer or liability debt. Good debt = appreciating asset debt. For example, debt on an investment property that is appreciating or providing you income would be considered good debt. Debt on credit cards that was used to buy toys and trinkets would be considered bad debt. The answer isn't always this straightforward.

What if Bryce had used debt to purchase his mower in the example titled "Bryce's Push-Mower Push" earlier in this chapter? Would this be good debt or bad debt? This is a bit more complicated example. The fact that Bryce had to sell the mower for less than he bought it for means the mower had depreciated. This might lead one to think it would have been bad debt. However, the mower actually helped provide income that was greater than the cost of the mower (though not by as much as anticipated). This means that using debt to pay for the mower would have actually been considered good debt. If your child has tried their hand at a business, ask them if using debt to purchase some of the tools or supplies needed for their business would have been considered good debt or bad debt. Their ability to answer and discuss their reasoning will let you know if the concept has been cemented in their brain.

Another way to reinforce the concept is to talk to your child about different examples of debt you have incurred over the years, and what category they fell into. As we've said before, this isn't the time to be proud and hide things from your children. Now is the time to help them learn from your bad or good examples and experiences. Nobody is perfect when it comes to money decisions. Airing your dirty laundry just might be the necessary catalyst to lead your child to not be afraid to seek your advice when they need financial guidance someday.

**LORAL SAYS: I tell clients, "The only reason you have bad debt is because you wanted a bigger life. Go make more money so you can have that life."**

Bad debt is the one of the greatest barriers to wealth. When you take on bad debt you lose precious dollars that could be used to invest and make more money. The same compound interest that works for us with our investments can work against us if we purchase bad debt. In the same way that paying yourself first equals paying your future self first, bad debt could be even more accurately described as stealing from your future self. Even worse, because of the high interest rates associated with most bad debt, it can grow very rapidly. We give an example of this high-interest debt in the section titled "Advanced Credit Cards—Friend or Foe?" in Chapter 8. People who have bad debt often get stuck in the vicious cycle of not being able to fully pay off that debt, which leads to even more debt.

Not only does bad debt steal from you, but it also ruins your reputation, or at least your credit reputation. We'll discuss credit more thoroughly in the Chapter 7 section "Credit and the Credit Score." For now, it's important to teach your child that the worse your reputation is, the higher the risk is to lenders and the more they will want to charge you for a loan. A ruined credit reputation means you may not qualify at all for a loan even on good debt. This may even prevent you from being able to buy a home. If you do qualify, you will likely have to pay a higher interest rate than someone who has a good credit reputation. This results in paying more money for your home. Nobody wants to pay more if they can help it. The good news is . . . you can help it. Keep a solid credit reputation.

Advise your child that avoiding bad debt is one of the best ways to be certain they keep a good financial reputation. It's hard not to fall victim to a culture that practically exalts immediate gratification, the urgency of consumption,

**Asset addiction can create a vigorous cycle of wealth even more powerful than the vicious cycle of debt if you'll embrace it.**

and the accumulation of bad debt. But fall victim we must not. Teach your kids to avoid the addiction of bad debt. Instead, teach them to get addicted to good debt, making more money, and buying assets. We call this asset addiction. Asset addiction can create a vigorous cycle of wealth even more powerful than the vicious cycle of debt if you'll embrace it.

## YOUR MONEY ISN'T THEIR MONEY . . . OR IS IT?

If you do have some wealth, this is the age when your kids may begin to recognize it. If you didn't make a decision on whether you will spend all your money or give much of it to your kids when we recommended it in the Chapter 4 section "Decide on a Legacy Plan," you really need to begin that conversation now. Reread that section again if you need to review some of the reasons you might choose one or the other. How you manage and teach your kids will change based on this decision. If you do have wealth but don't plan on giving it to your kids, make sure your kids realize that the wealth you have accumulated is yours and not theirs, and that you worked very hard for it. Here's how the conversation went for Kyle and his two boys:

"Boys, by now you have probably figured out that your mom and I have some wealth. It's true, but that wealth is ours. We may be able to help a bit with your college costs, but you are not wealthy. You are dirt poor. By now you've heard this phrase a thousand times, but I'll repeat it again to be sure it's clear. Give a man a fish and you feed him for a day. Teach a man to fish and you feed him for a lifetime. Boys, I'm not giving you our fish. I will, however, do everything I can to teach you everything I know about fishing. I'll spend all day every day if that's what it takes. I take great pride that I made my own wealth, and I want you to have that same pride. If you are willing to listen and put in the work, I will give you all the tools you need, and I have no doubt you will achieve your own wealth. Do you understand? Do you realize that your mother and I plan on spending our wealth, and you probably won't get anything other than the road map on how to get there yourself? Not leaving you money doesn't mean we don't love you. In fact, we're doing this because we love you. We want you to experience the pride we experienced from knowing we made our wealth ourselves."

What if you don't have wealth but your kids think you do because you live in the Lifestyle Cycle? It won't be easy, but it's time you let your kids be aware of that as well. Share your tough lessons so they aren't in the same boat when they are your age. The result for your child is basically the same as the parents who have wealth but don't plan on giving it to their children. The children need to understand that they will be expected to fend for themselves. The earlier you set this expectation, the better.

Thankfully, you are reading and (hopefully) teaching your child the concepts in this book so they will have a much better chance at creating wealth for themselves. If you can't or don't want to give them fish, at least teach them how to fish.

What about those of you who do have wealth and plan to pass it on to your children? When Loral decided to have Logan and become a single mom, she chose this path and wanted to prove that it was possible to create generational wealth. Generational wealth is wealth that lives beyond just your kids but on to their kids and their kids for several generations. If this is the plan you desire, you need to be setting up the financial instruments necessary to protect that wealth.

We introduced several of these instruments in Chapter 4. At the very least you should have a trust and life insurance. You should also have set up an IRA and education fund for your child. If you have a business, it should be protected with at least one incorporated entity like a corporation or limited liability company (LLC), and possibly several. If it's been a while since you reviewed the discussion in Chapter 4 on these topics, it's probably a good idea to do so now. Which entity and financial instruments you choose will be based on a multitude of factors that would include the amount of wealth you have or hope to have one day, your liability risk, your familial situation, your tax circumstances, and how much you want to leave to your heirs. You absolutely must leverage your team and get advice from a lawyer and accountant to help balance the intricacies of your personal situation. The larger your fortune, the more important it is that you seek the right professional help.

If you do plan on passing on a large portion of your wealth to your kids, you need to think about when you will explain to them how that transition will happen, and how much you want them to know. You should give them an idea of how much money they expect to inherit and your expectations for how it should be managed and passed along. You should let them in on the details of your trust and life insurance.

The advantage of telling your kids early about your legacy plan is that they can play a larger role in the planning and may have a better comprehension of the structure and responsibility that will be placed on them when they do eventually receive the money. This goes back to the concept of setting expectations for your child. The disadvantage is that you will be susceptible to potentially creating entitled and lazy kids. They may not be willing to make their own fortune if they know one is already headed their

**LORAL SAYS: If you don't tell your kids about your trust, you risk giving them "the surprise basket" after death, which will often lead to fights among your heirs. This never ends well.**

way. Hopefully this won't happen if you work hard to teach them the concepts discussed in this book, such as delayed gratification, financial discipline, teamwork, and giving back. Additionally, you can create conditions in your trust that will ensure responsible, financially disciplined, and contributing kids.

Deciding what you will do with your money and how you will tell your kids about it is one of the most important decisions you can make in your child's development, so we encourage you to put great consideration into the ramifications. You don't have to make the decision alone. We are building an expanding array of content at MakeYourKidsMillionaires.com where you can get in touch with a community of other parents who have already faced or are currently facing the decisions you have in front of you. As we've said several times already in this book, millionaires are made with a team.

# RISK VERSUS REWARD
# FOR INVESTMENTS

Though the concept of risk versus reward is somewhat straightforward, calculating it does require some math. In this section we'll be explaining this math so that parents can get a good sense for how expert investors consider risk and reward. If some of these concepts seem advanced for your child, we recommend starting with the basics. You might be surprised. Some kids will get this at this age. For others, you may have to stick with the basics for now and introduce more of the math later when they are ready. As they progress through this age group and perhaps into the next one, you will be able to add more and more facets from this section. Just remember to start integrating the ideas of risk and reward into your everyday conversations.

Believe it or not, by the end of this age group, your child has learned most of the math they need to calculate one of the basic principles of investing. The most important metric is quite simple to calculate. We are talking about return on investment, or ROI. ROI is a measure we can use to calculate the reward associated with an investment. We will be using this acronym throughout the rest of this book, so it's worth looking at how it is calculated:

$$\text{ROI} = (\text{Net Profit/Cost of Investment}) \times 100$$

ROI is usually reported as a percentage. For example, if an investment cost $100 to buy and we expected it to have a net profit of $10, the ROI could be computed as follows:

$$\text{ROI} = 10/100 \times 100 = 10\%$$

It just so happens that 10% ROI approximates the historical ROI of the stock market throughout its history. We will often use this as the baseline ROI we want to achieve. The beauty of ROI is that it doesn't just look at the return or reward only in terms of the money we will make (the numerator in the equation), but also in terms of the money we will have to invest or put at risk (the denominator). This distinction allows you to gauge the effects of using other people's money to leverage your returns. What if we used the example above, but you could lower your cost of investment by half while keeping the same net profit? Let's take a look.

$$ROI = 10/50 \times 100 = 20\%$$

As you can see, we were able to double our ROI by reducing our cost of investment. "But we're still only making $10," you might say. This is true, but we have avoided the opportunity cost of the other $50 (reference the "Basic Opportunity Cost" section in Chapter 4 if you need a refresher). We still have $50 from our original $100 to spend on other investments. If we wanted, we could put the other $50 into the same investment and we would yield $20 in returns. The other advantage of using ROI is that because it does consider the cost of the investment, it is a good metric for comparing different investment alternatives.

When speaking to your child about ROI, it might be good to give an example of how ROI could be used in an example business they can relate to. Loral has a client with a child whom we'll call Morgan. Morgan wanted to buy video equipment to make YouTube videos. Morgan wanted to spend $1,000 on the equipment but wasn't sure if it would be a good investment. Loral helped her evaluate the ROI on the equipment. They determined Morgan could make $50 per video. If she could sell 10 videos per month, Morgan would make a total of $500 per month. What would her monthly ROI be? Have your child actually run the math. To figure it, we would simply divide $500 by $1,000. In this example, Morgan would make an impressive 50 percent ROI per month. This translates to an amazing 600 percent ROI per year (50 × 12). Armed with this information, Morgan's parents were comfortable letting Morgan buy the video equipment. Of course, Morgan still has to do the work and we haven't accounted for her time, but simple ROI calculations like this are the sort of thing that you can bring into regular conversations with your child. The next time they have an entrepreneurial inspiration, at some point you should bring ROI into their decision-making.

ROI is one of the best metrics for comparing two investments, but it doesn't tell the whole story. If it did then nobody would ever invest in anything that had an ROI below the 10 percent average of the stock market. Yet they do. The reason, of course, is risk. Even though the stock market has returned an average of 10 percent per year, there is no guarantee it will do so in the future. Also, it has fluctuated significantly from its average in many years. Depending on your timeline, you could achieve much higher or much lower returns than 10 percent. This uncertainty of your returns is called risk.

One definition of risk would be that it is the chance that investment's actual gains will differ from the expected gains. Even if it does meet your expected gains in the long term, a risky investment may oscillate significantly along the way. This oscillation is similar to standard deviation and is sometimes called volatility. Since it's difficult to quantify the risk of an investment not meeting your expectations, we'll talk mostly about the type of risk that involves volatility and standard deviation. Depending on your child's progress in math, they may or may not have covered this subject yet. If not, you can put them ahead of their class by introducing the basics of it now. Don't worry. We won't be calculating it. We'll just talk about the concept. Have your child review Figure 6.2.

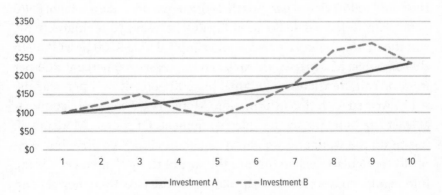

**Figure 6.2** Comparing Risk

Both of the investments shown had the exact same overall returns of 10 percent per year over the 10-year period. Thus, the ROI for both was 10 percent. If you owned Investment A it was a smooth, predictable climb from $100 to $236. But what if you owned Investment B? Your ride would have been a little more adventurous and unpredictable. Some years you made more than 10 percent returns, but others you lost money.

What if you sold in year 5? The value of your investment at that time had actually dropped to $90. If you needed the money then, you would be wishing you had invested in Investment A. You might even have given up on the investment and sold it that year due to its underperformance. Of course, in year 9 you would have been thinking you were pretty smart, as you were sporting much better returns than Investment A. The higher deviation or variance of Investment B from its long-term average returns means it has a much higher standard deviation. When evaluating stocks, investors use a similar evaluation called beta (β). Beta measures the volatility of an investment and how much it deviates from the overall market. Whether you use the term *volatility, standard deviation, beta,* or *risk,* the message is clear. Some investments are more unpredictable.

Which investment would you rather own? The answer you give says a lot about your risk tolerance. Some people don't mind risk and would be perfectly fine with Investment B. Others can't stand risk and would never even consider Investment B. It's important to understand your own risk tolerance and invest in a way that doesn't cause you to make poor long-term decisions. If you would have given up on Investment B when it was losing money in year 5, then you probably never should have invested in Investment B in the first place. This leads us to another factor when considering the risk of an investment—what is your time horizon? If our time horizon was short, we might have needed to sell in year 5 of Investment B when we actually lost money. The longer your time horizon, the more likely you will receive the actual ROI of the investment and the less concerned you are about risk from volatility.

If we knew with 100 percent certainty that the two investment returns would match Figure 6.2 and both investments would end up with the same returns, would there be any reason to invest in Investment B? The simple answer is no. The risk of Investment B was unnecessary if it had the same long-term ROI. This is why assessing risk relative to ROI is so important. Nearly every investment has risk, but we want to get the maximum returns for the minimum risk. The only reason to accept higher risk is if you expect it will bring you higher returns. The only reason to accept lower returns is if you expect it will bring you lower risk. This is the reason many people will put their money in much more conservative investments. They are willing to accept the lower returns to ensure they don't lose their money. Oftentimes ROI and risk are correlated. To properly evaluate an investment, we must consider what ROI we will get in the context of whether we are willing to accept the risk that will come with that ROI. The person who knows their own risk tolerance and time horizon and can best weigh the risk versus reward of an investment will win at the game of investing.

In the Chapter 5 section titled "Play Games with Your Kids That Involve Money," we discussed the numerous benefits of playing Monopoly. One of these is learning how to weigh risk versus reward for investments. When you are playing with your child, talk with them about the risk and reward for the decisions they make. For example, early in the game, some Monopoly players will buy properties until they are completely out of money—possibly even to the extent of having to mortgage the properties they do own in order to buy a new one. Since the game is all about getting properties and monopolies, buying as many properties as possible could have a high reward. However, it also carries the risk that you will land on somebody else's property before that reward pays off and you could end up broke and out of the game. If you and your child play Monopoly enough, you'll get a chance to see this tactic have both results—the thrill of victory and the agony of defeat. Other Monopoly players like to take a more conservative approach. They buy as many properties as they safely can, but they always reserve enough cash to be certain they can afford to land on other players' properties. The reward of this strategy may be lower, but it also carries much less risk of going broke early in the game.

While playing Monopoly or similar games, talk to your child about the balance of weighing this risk/reward ratio. From this discussion, it's easy to steer the talk to real-world risk/reward decisions. Explain some of the decisions your family has made to balance risk and reward, such as buying insurance, keeping an emergency fund, incorporating a business, or avoiding highly risky investments.

As your child gets older you will begin to see patterns in their willingness to take risks in the game. This can give you a glimpse into their risk tolerance. A person's risk tolerance is a huge factor in determining what investments are best for them. Investing should be fun and shouldn't keep us up at night. What one person might consider a conservative investment might be so volatile and risky that it drives another person crazy. The sooner you and your child can recognize your own risk tolerance, the quicker you will be able to find investments that fit that risk category. When you combine this risk balance with the ROI you need to meet your goals, you will be able to make informed decisions about where you should invest.

## A STOCK IS OWNERSHIP IN A BUSINESS

Stock ownership comes in two forms. There are public stocks and private stocks. Public stocks are generally associated with large companies that have offered their shares to the general public through the stock exchange via an IPO (initial public offering). Private stocks are similar but they often are associated with smaller companies and the shares are not offered via a stock exchange to the general public. Both revolve around fractional ownership of a business. In other words, when you own stock shares in a company, you own a fraction of the actual company. The percentage of your fractional ownership depends on how many shares you own versus the total shares that exist, often called the shares outstanding. Loral's experience is primarily with private stocks. Kyle's is mostly with public stocks. Private stocks are not for sale on the public market. Loral owned the private companies individually or along with some partners. Just like public stocks, the value of private stocks rests completely on the value of the underlying business. Since Loral was the owner of these businesses, her kids received a behind-the-scenes lesson on how to grow and improve the value of Loral's private stock.

When Logan was in this age range, Loral bought a laundromat. Logan traveled with her every week to count the coins with her and understand how the business operated and was important to the community. He was able to see firsthand which washing machines and dryers were more profitable than others. Effectively, he was assessing the ROI of each machine. When Tristin was in this age range, Loral bought a pizzeria. Again, several times a week, Tristin went with Loral to the pizzeria, helped make pizzas, took orders, and was on the front lines of witnessing how a food business works. She too was able to witness supply and demand and which menu items were profitable. All of these lessons were vital to teaching Loral's kids about businesses. If Loral had decided to put her businesses up for sale to the public, then her private stock would have transitioned to public stock.

Though Kyle has invested in some private stock, his experience is mostly with public stocks. The problem with the way many people trade public stocks is that they treat their stocks more like gambling bets than investments. They buy ticker symbols without even knowing what the underlying company does, much less comprehending the ins and outs of the business. This isn't the way you should invest in stocks. In the same way that Loral, Logan, and Tristin had to mind their laundromat and pizzeria businesses, owners of public stocks also need to keep track of their business. You should always remember that every stock ticker symbol is associated with an actual business with actual products and employees. Make sure your child is aware of this. To get them interested in thinking like a business, ask leading questions to get their business minds going. When they want to buy a toy that is popular among their friends, ask out loud, "I wonder who makes that toy? I wonder if investing in that company would be a good idea? If you could make that toy even better, how would you do it?" Then have them follow up by finding some answers. Talking to your kids about money can benefit you as well. Your conversations will help you learn from your kids what the interests of people their age are. Remember, they are the future adults of the world, and they are often the first ones to grasp onto concepts that will eventually be huge.

We're obviously not recommending you buy every stock your child likes and sell the stock of everything your child sours on. Any investment decision should involve plenty of due diligence and an evaluation of numerous factors, but the information you learn from your child may be one factor in your decisions. Children are usually much more connected to social media and can sometimes see trends changing quicker than adults. Sometimes these trends bring about long-term changes in the behavior of the masses, as was the case with YouTube, Twitter, and Instagram. Engaging your children in conversations about things they and their friends enjoy gives you a chance to be on the front end of what could be a tidal wave. It's then your job to figure out which trends are short-term and which trends and businesses have a model with long-term staying power.

One of the biggest advantages an individual investor can have versus the market in general is that investor's ability to evaluate the long-term prospects of the business he or she is investing in. If you've been following our guidance up until now, your child should be beginning to understand the basics of business. Explain to them how the actions of businesses affect the stock price. If Apple creates a great new phone that everybody likes, it will usually result in the Apple share price going up (at least in the long term). If it creates a new phone that nobody likes, then we can expect its stock price will often take a hit. Of course, Apple has many products and stock movement is never as simple as one factor, but the point remains that stock prices are inexorably linked to the success of the underlying business. Reiterate the concepts we discussed in the section "Basic Opportunity Cost" in Chapter 4.

Teach your kids that even though short-term stock movement can seem random (trust me, even long-term stock experts feel this way), in the long run, choosing businesses that execute well, put out great products, and have great futures will result in investment gains. Just remember to explain to your kids that the long term is measured in years, not days or weeks. This is a tough concept to grasp when a few years represents one-fifth of your life, but the sooner they can learn this investing lesson the better. Now that your child appreciates that stocks represent ownership in a business, it's time for them to get their feet wet with a stock simulator.

## START A STOCK SIMULATOR FOR YOUR CHILD

Think back to the theme we first discussed in Chapter 1 of this book regarding how teaching your kids about money should be like pilot training. With that theme in mind, the previous section provided some of the academics, or ground school, of stocks. The next step we will propose would be like letting your child start flying the simulator, except this time it is a stock simulator. A stock simulator is sometimes called a paper trading account, play account, or practice account. These accounts let you make trades without using real money so you can get practice trading stocks and testing your performance without the normal consequences of potentially losing money.

One of the few times that Kyle actually learned about investing in school (other than the compound interest lesson) was when his fifth-grade math class had a stock trading competition using paper trading accounts. Back then, a paper trading account consisted of just writing down on a piece of paper when you wanted to simulate buying that stock and how many shares you wanted to purchase. The process for finding out what you would have paid for the stock, unless you already had a stockbroker you could call, consisted of checking the newspaper the following morning to see what the closing price from the previous day had been. It's incredible how far stock trading has come. Now, paper trading accounts are much more advanced and no longer require any paper at all. A quick internet search for "paper trading account" will reveal dozens of options you could set up for your child to give them their first attempt at simulating the experience of buying stocks.

The simulated account lets you start with play money and buy whatever stocks you desire, including trying more complicated strategies like options if you want. After a set period your child could check their performance to see how they did. This is a great way for your child (or you) to begin feeling comfortable investing in the stock market. You could even set one up with the same amount of simulated money for every member of the family and set up a contest to get everyone's competitive juices flowing. This is yet another example of how playing games with your child can make learning about money interesting and exciting. Just remember, if you have real money to invest, you won't want to delay investing that money since stock market investing is generally about time *in* the market, not tim*ing* the market. We talked about this previously in the section "Open a Roth IRA for Your Child" in Chapter 4. After proving their acumen in the simulated account for a while, your child will have the confidence to eventually transition to actual money.

If your child is itching to put some real money into stocks, we recommend combining the tactic of a simulated account with the idea of selling your child a few shares from your own stock portfolio. In the pilot training model, this strategy would fall somewhere between a simulator and letting your child fly just a bit. Although it will be with real money, the amounts will be very small so they can't get hurt excessively by losing too much money.

Here's how Kyle accomplished this: After talking to his son Bryce about stocks and how the value could compound, Bryce wanted to buy some stocks. Of course, Kyle had already explained in detail that what Bryce would be buying was not just some certificate or ticker symbol but an actual part of a business. They discussed all the factors described in the previous section, "A Stock Is Ownership in a Business." After much deliberation on the merits of different businesses, Kyle and

Bryce finally decided on a few companies that Kyle already owned. Kyle decided to sell his son one share of Disney and one share of Activision Blizzard. Bryce was interested in Disney because they had been to Disney World and he was fully aware of the movies and other aspects of the brand. Bryce wanted to buy Activision Blizzard because, as we mentioned before, it was the maker of two of his favorite video games at the time—Guitar Hero and Skylanders. Since Kyle already owned both stocks through his discount brokerage, the transaction made sense.

You could still sell your child a share even if you don't own it if you are willing to give them the value of that stock when they are ready to sell it. In this case, Bryce bought these two stocks for a grand total of $55.80 that he had earned from doing chores. It doesn't have to be a formal transaction. Kyle simply wrote on a piece of paper "This paper entitles Bryce Boeckman to one share of DIS stock, purchased from his dad at the price of $45 on this date." They created a similar document for the ATVI stock. After both Kyle and Bryce signed both documents, Bryce stored them in his piggy bank so he would never lose them.

Bryce was excited to track his stocks' progress, and when the occasional dip happened it was the perfect opportunity to talk about the long-term nature of stocks and when a person should or should not sell them. The stocks Bryce bought are now, 11 years later, worth over four times what he paid for them. By the time you read this it might be even more. This won't always be the case, of course. Although it's unlikely if you choose carefully, it's possible your kid's stock could even lose value over a 10-year period. Even if so, this creates a great learning opportunity to talk about what went wrong with the company over that time.

A few years after Bryce's initial stock purchases, Kyle was describing to him his reasons for purchasing another batch of shares of Amazon. As a fan of the company himself, Bryce decided to purchase a share of Amazon from Kyle for its then-current price of $450. Only eight years later the stock is currently worth over seven times what he paid. The only downside for Kyle is that he now owns one less share for himself—a price he will happily pay for a positive and educational lesson that will inspire a lifetime of future investing for his son!

A few years later, Kyle's younger son, Bret, saw the success his brother was having and entered the investment game as well. Now he also owns shares of Activision Blizzard as well as Tencent Holdings Ltd. (majority owner of Epic Games, maker of his, until recently, favorite video game, Fortnite). If you don't know much about investing or stocks, make it a family affair to learn more. The more you understand, the more comfortable you will feel investing.

## THE VALUE OF REAL ESTATE INVESTING

Real estate investing can be a great way to grow your net worth. The fact that it's real and can be touched can also sometimes make it easier for children (and parents alike) to identify with. We have both made a large amount of our wealth through real estate. In fact, for almost all wealthy people, real estate plays a significant role in their accumulation of that wealth. In this section, we'll first discuss the advantages of real estate so that you, the parent, can appreciate its enormous benefits and so that hopefully you will get involved and buy some real estate so you can model the lessons for your child. Near the end of the section we'll talk about how to get your child thinking about real estate and interested as well.

The reason real estate plays such a significant role in the new worth of wealthy people lies primarily in two benefits of real estate: leverage and the tax code. First, let's discuss leverage. In investing terms, leverage is the use of debt to magnify the returns of an investment. Notably, although leverage can multiply your returns to the upside, it can do the same to the downside if things don't pan out. Since the purchase of real estate is such a large transaction for most, it often must be purchased with leverage. Most people don't have the funds to buy a home or condo outright. The power of leverage and debt allows these people to purchase and control much larger properties than they otherwise could. As a result, real estate investments provide one of the best ways to use other people's money to make yourself money. As we mentioned in Loral's story, she used this strategy to buy a significant amount of real estate in Oklahoma, which allowed her to become a millionaire in six months.

The next advantage of real estate involves the tax code. Governments give tax breaks to things they want to incentivize. Real estate is no different. Like other businesses, real estate investments let you deduct your rental expenses from the rental income you earn, thereby lowering your tax liability. Rental property expenses like repairs, maintenance, home office expenses, insurance, and even mortgage interest and property taxes can be deducted in the year you spend the money.

Perhaps the biggest tax advantage of real estate is the ability to depreciate your property. Real estate depreciation is a tax deduction based on the perceived decrease in the value of the real estate. Real estate depreciation assumes that the rental property is actually declining over time as a result of wear and tear. In the United States, for example, commercial real estate is depreciated using the price of the property, less the value of the land (since land cannot be depreciated), divided by the 27.5-year life of the property. Therefore, after 27.5 years a property would be fully depreciated. Even though most real estate investments appreciate over time, the government lets you depreciate these properties for tax purposes.

Let's look at a practical example of a $100,000 property. Since it depreciates over 27.5 years, each year it depreciates 3.636 percent. If the underlying land is worth $4,000, then this would leave the depreciable property at $96,000. Since $96,000 /27.5 is $3,490, you could subtract approximately $3,500 from the property's income for each year you own it, up to 27.5 years. This can often be the difference between a taxable income and a paper loss even though you had positive cash flow.

To recognize the full power of the leverage and tax advantages of real estate, let's look at an example. We have both invested in real estate investments like this. For the sake of math simplicity, let's use the same $100,000 price point we used before with that price including all the closing costs. In this example, the investment was a single-family home that Kyle and Tracy bought to rent out. We can't promise the assumptions in this example will work out in your area, but they are actual returns that Kyle received for a property at a very similar price point.

Since 1928 the annualized appreciation for housing nationwide has been 3.7 percent per year. Kyle's investment was in Oklahoma. After doing considerable research and talking to several real estate agents, he learned that appreciation in his area was closer to 3 percent. If he had purchased the house outright with cash his return on investment (ROI) would be $3,000 or 3 percent.

$$\$3,000/\$100,000 = 3\% \text{ ROI}$$

Instead Kyle chose to take advantage of leverage. The bank required that he make a minimum down payment of $20,000, or 20 percent of the purchase price. Since appreciation applies to the entire house and not just the $20,000 he paid, his ROI is significantly higher using leverage.

$$\$3,000/\$20,000 = 15 \text{ percent ROI}$$

Investment returns of 15 percent beat the historical stock market return and would constitute a nice investment, but Kyle did his research and made sure he bought a property that was cash flow positive as well. In this case, the property generally makes Kyle approximately $3,500 in cash flow even after all expenses. When this $3,500 is added to the $3,000 in appreciation, it results in an overall return of $6,500. Let's look at the updated ROI:

$$\$6,500/\$20,000 = 32.5\% \text{ ROI}$$

Now we're talking. This alone would be an excellent ROI, but we still haven't considered depreciation. Recall that earlier we found that the $100,000 property would depreciate each year by approximately $3,500. On paper, this completely wipes out the $3,500 in cash flow and makes it appear that this property only broke even for tax purposes, even though we still get to keep the $3,500. We are receiving that $3,500 completely free of tax. If that income had been added to our wage/business income then we would be taxed at our marginal tax rate. Let's use a 25 percent tax rate for simple math.

$$\$3{,}500 \times .25 = \$875$$

Granted, we don't receive this money in any measurable way, but that $875 is money we saved versus a comparable income. If we add this $875 to the previous $6,500 we get $7,375.

$$\$7{,}375/\$20{,}000 = 36.87\% \text{ ROI}$$

If this was the entire ROI Kyle would be very happy, but we've not yet addressed another form of value—principle paydown. When Kyle is paying off the mortgage, a portion of the payment goes toward mortgage interest that we have already expensed. The other portion goes to principle, or equity, in paying off the home. Although Kyle can't access this principle or the appreciation on a yearly basis, when he sells or refinances the property it still adds to the value of his investment. Given a 30-year mortgage at 4 percent, Kyle's monthly payment for the loan would be $381.93. Of this, $115 each month would be principle, with this amount going up each month. Therefore, each year Kyle's tenants would be paying approximately $1,500 off of the mortgage. If we add this $1,500 to the previous $7,375 we get $8,875.

$$\$8{,}875/\$20{,}000 = 44.37\% \text{ ROI}$$

Now do you see why Kyle describes real estate as the surest way to get rich slowly but surely? We can't promise you'll be able to match these returns, but the example shows how real estate offers several built-in advantages that make it an excellent potential investment.

Homes are just one example of how you can invest in real estate. Recently, Loral and her team have begun investing in RV parks. Each individual spot in the RV park could have a similar ROI calculation to the one above. The exciting thing about RVs is that you can often get excellent cash flow because you can squeeze as many spots on the land as possible. Adding a few extra spots can quickly increase both your ROI and cash flow. For example, the difference between 40 spots and

50 spots that are profiting by $500 a night is $5,000 per month. Many families can live on the cash flow of that alone.

Now that we've watered your eyes with the benefits of real estate, let's talk about some of the downsides. Kyle and Tracy spent dozens of hours searching out the best market and property to invest in. Then he and his family spent dozens more making renovations to the property after he bought it. Finally, he and mostly Tracy spent even more time managing the property themselves. What's the point? Real estate requires work and time. You may be able to find a team to help you with these tasks, but it takes time and experience to find that team. Once you do find a good team, you still have to manage them to keep them on track. Hiring that team also bites into your profits. Kyle's cash flow wouldn't have been the same if he had to hire people to do all those things. That being said, spending that time himself to improve the cash flow of his investment is one of the ways W-2 wage earners can increase their income to keep their I > E. It might even lead to a business as it did for Kyle and Tracy.

Real estate also isn't without risk of loss. Properties don't always appreciate, and you sometimes must deal with vacancy or terrible tenants. Economic downturns, neighborhood deterioration, demographic shifts, and even natural disasters are just a few of the other potential risks. Finally, when you own a real estate property you always risk liability and potential litigation. That's why it's vital to have umbrella insurance and own your real estate in an entity like a limited liability company that allows you to protect your personal assets from litigation associated with your real estate investments. We discussed this concept in the section "Start a Business and Get Incorporated" in Chapter 4. In the end, real estate can be a great way to get started, and it can become a valuable part of your portfolio. Just make certain you do your homework.

Whether you own real estate or not, you can start discussions with your child about real estate by asking questions when you drive around town. Loral would ask her kids, "Who owns that building?" This is a great way to instigate conversations with your child. The best way to teach your kids about real estate is to have commonsense conversations about it.

If you as the parent are already involved in real estate, it's a great idea to take your child with you when you investigate a new property and view the properties you already own. Show them the things you look for when inspecting and evaluating a property. As your child gets older, you can run them through a numbers example for your property like the one above or start crunching numbers of real estate properties in your area to see how the returns look. Talk to them about your experiences as a renter, homeowner, and landlord, if applicable. If you already own properties, have them join you in making the repairs. By the time our kids were teenagers they could already lay tile, paint, do basic carpentry, and even do some plumbing. Even if your children don't aspire to do these things themselves when they buy their first rental property, the experience will help them when they hire other people to do the work.

## HAVE YOUR CHILD CREATE A CAR ACCOUNT

In Chapter 5 you set up a bank account for your child. Part of the reason for doing this was so your child could begin saving for some longer-term purchases. Especially if you live in rural America, one of the purchases that is almost essential to getting around is a vehicle—whether it be a car, truck, or even motorcycle. Whether you plan on letting them borrow the family car for a while or not, eventually they will want their own "wheels." At this age, don't make the mistake of buying their car (or yours) with a loan. This is the definition of bad debt. A car is a depreciating item that does not bring in cash flow—in fact, the more expensive it is, the more it produces negative cash flow via loan interest and more expensive insurance rates. We don't advise using debt for these types of items. Getting a loan is probably just going to trigger you to get more car than you need, causing you to lose even more money through negative cash flow. Instead, earn and save more money so you can afford to pay in cash and buy a vehicle you can afford without having to go into debt.

Now that you've decided your child's car will be purchased outright, it is time to designate an account, or portion of an account, for your child to begin saving. You might be tempted to save the money in a safe place at home, but we always recommend using interest-bearing bank accounts whenever possible. This is safer and more reflective of how your child will handle money as an adult, and eventually a millionaire. The "Car Account" could be a traditional savings account, a money market fund, or even short-term bonds or certificates of deposit. Since you know approximately when the money will be spent it doesn't need to be as "liquid" (immediately accessible) in the short term as other spending accounts might need to be. Ideally, your child would set up a different account than their regular checking or savings account to ensure that they don't mistakenly spend some of the money that is supposed to be set aside for the car. Does this make their banking more complicated? Yes, it does. They might as well get used to it. The wealthy usually have multiple bank accounts. It's not complication for complication's sake. These separate accounts are necessary to safeguard against mixing money between different business entities, an accounting error known as "comingling." The sooner your child gets used to being able to manage multiple accounts, the better.

Who should pay for your child's car? We believe your child should, at the very least, pay a significant portion of the costs for their car. Kyle makes his kids pay for the entire car. Since he warned them of this early in their life, this provided greater incentive for them to start earning money at an early age. Loral used a different technique for her kids. She agreed to match the amount they put away into their car account between the ages of 10 and 16 but only up to a total of $10,000, ensuring the vehicle would not cost over $20,000. It was up to them how much they spent up to that amount. This way she was able to help her child afford something a bit more expensive but still incentivize them to make money and work hard enough to get something they wanted.

Another technique might be to pay a set amount like $5,000 to get them a basic car but require them to pay for the rest if they wanted to get something nicer. Now is the time to put thought into what your plan will be, and to communicate that plan to your child. You need to set the expectation for them so they can set a goal and know how much money they will need to earn. At this age they may not yet comprehend the importance of a car and why they should begin saving for it. Explain to your child how important that car will be toward freeing up your time and stopping the parent taxi service that has been hauling them around from event to event for years. Better yet, approach it from their perspective and describe the freedom it will provide them.

Even if you can afford to pay for your child's entire car, we think you should resist the urge to do so. Here are some reasons. First, recall the example where we compared teaching your kids about finance to teaching people how to fly. We slowly let them take the controls and try to fly for themselves. Fully implementing this approach requires your child not only making money, but also saving and spending that money. While they are still under your roof, they need to learn the lessons of saving and making large purchases with their own money. Telling them up front when they are young that they will have to buy their own car will also incentivize them to work and save more than if they thought a car would be gifted to them. It will also allow them to flex their goal-setting muscles and feel the pride and success of reaching their goals. As always, we are trying to foster an attitude of independence and hard work, not one of taking handouts.

This also leads to another reason your child should pay for at least some of their own car. They will take better care of it. When your child has spent hours and hours of their own time earning the money for their car, they will be much more likely to be more careful with it. This means they will be more likely to follow the required maintenance necessary to maintain its value. More important, they may be safer drivers because they won't want to wreck it. Safety alone is probably reason enough to make your child buy their own car.

Speaking of safety, some of you may be thinking that safety and reliability are the very reasons you want to buy your child a car. You don't want your child driving something likely to break down or get in an accident. We agree wholeheartedly, but the safety and reliability you seek can probably be obtained for less than $5,000. It may not be the prettiest car ever, but there are plenty of cars under $5,000 that can safely and reliably get your child wherever he or she needs to go. The extra money your child saves by investing versus spending it could make them a millionaire on its own.

If your child started earning income at an early age and faithfully saved their money, there is no reason they shouldn't have more than $5,000 available to spend. They may want something flashy, but what they need is something functional. If you realize later that they made an honest effort to earn money but couldn't afford what you consider a reliable car, only then should you ponder supplementing their funds more than you had previously agreed. If you do consider paying for more of your child's car than originally agreed, just be sure they had a good reason for not earning enough and that you don't let them get away with avoiding work. This isn't the time to get soft. Your child needs to understand that life has consequences. If they end up having to drive around a clunker because they didn't put in the work, they will learn a valuable lesson for later in life. You might want to peek ahead into the section "Buying a Car" in the next chapter to get a better idea on our thoughts on the car-buying process and how much your child should plan to spend on a car. For now, these three steps are the most important:

1. Decide your plan for who will pay for your child's car—a loan is not a plan.
2. Have your child create a Car Account.
3. Motivate your child to get started working and saving for their car.

## THE IMPORTANCE OF GIVING BACK

The primary purpose of this book is to help teach you how to make your child financially free by making them wealthy. However, wealth alone won't bring them fulfillment. Fulfillment comes from giving back. We've talked about the freedom that can come from having enough wealth to not have to worry about working and to be able to do what you want to do with your life. Another benefit of wealth is that it allows you to give to others on a greater scale. The more money you have—the more you can give. The more freedom you have of your time—the more of your time you can give. Winston Churchill may have said it best when he said, "We make a living by what we get, but we make a life by what we give." We couldn't agree more. If you teach your children to be rich in money but not rich in life you are robbing them of true fulfillment. It's important to teach them in their childhood about the importance of giving back.

Giving back comes in many forms. If you don't have much money yet, that's OK. Give of your time. Teach your child to do so. Have them get involved in volunteer activities. Show them how great it feels to help others before they get tainted by a consumption-based society that espouses the value of the latest and greatest gadget over the greatest gift—helping others. Children can often get involved in volunteer activities through their church or school.

One volunteer activity we liked for our children at this age was spending time at nursing homes. The residents loved spending time with children and were happy to play games or read books with them. It was truly a mutually beneficial arrangement. The children were able to benefit from the wisdom of the elderly residents, and the visits helped alleviate the loneliness of the residents while giving them a sense of community and purpose. One shouldn't volunteer only for the benefits for oneself, but it's a bonus when it's a symbiotic relationship.

At a later age, Kyle's children also volunteered through charities like Habitat for Humanity. This charity brings families, volunteers, and resources together to build simple, decent, and affordable housing in low-income areas. We especially like Habitat for Humanity because not only does your child get to give of their time, they can also learn and practice a home construction/repair skill that may prove useful later in their life. For example, Bryce was able to use and practice his skill at laying tile floors that he first learned while helping Kyle and his wife, Tracy, renovate one of their investment properties. He ended up spending several hours at Habitat for Humanity laying the tile floor for the home they were building for the community. Later in life he'll be able to use that practice to help him renovate his own investment properties.

Loral and her family often give back during Christmas by adopting a needy family. She and her kids would help decorate their house, give gifts, and provide donations of food, coats, and hats. What Loral and her children decided to do each year would usually be decided in large part on what her kids wanted to do. Loral also played a large part in helping during the creation of Lifeschool, a program that has helped thousands of young teens get outdoors to learn life skills, financial literacy, team building, and leadership. As a child, Logan helped fundraise for the organization and even sat as an honorary board member. Loral's family has always been involved in the charity work of her business. Getting them involved in the decision-making helps build the habit of giving.

It's also important for your child to see you set an example of giving not just your money but also your time. For example, we have both donated time toward our children's teams and organizations as well as for outside causes. Among other things, Kyle has given free financial education at his local base and to other Air Force members. Loral has created Serve Out Loud, a program aimed at providing discounted education in financial literacy to United States veterans. More recently, she has given free financial advice at universities when asked. When we show our children that we care about giving back it sets an example that can create a cycle of charity for others to follow as well. In our opinion, the world could use a little more selflessness.

## THE VALUE OF CHALLENGING
## THEIR COMFORT ZONE

As Timothy Ferriss noted in his book *The 4-Hour Work Week,* "A person's success in life can usually be measured by the number of uncomfortable conversations he or she is willing to have." This is quite true. In fact, we've found an even greater correlation between success and uncomfortable actions. So many people stay in their comfortable cocoons and never have the uncomfortable conversations or take the uncomfortable actions necessary to bring them success. These new and unpleasant actions, once accomplished, help us to grow and expand our skill set and experiences.

Recall in Chapter 2 when we discussed money muscles and the way our body's muscles work. When pushed to their limits through uncomfortable exercise, our body's muscle fibers undergo trauma and break down. Our body repairs these fibers by fusing them, which increases their mass and size. The next time you work out, the muscle is stronger. Similarly, after undergoing uncomfortable situations, our minds grow stronger and better able to handle future situations. Circumstances that were once uncomfortable are no longer so. When we are no longer uncomfortable, we can be confident. Confidence breeds success. The more you can encourage your children to take on unpleasant challenges, the more their confidence will grow. The following is a story in which Kyle's son Bret, as well as his cousin Nick, challenged their comfort zone.

> **So many people stay in their comfortable cocoons and never have the uncomfortable conversations or take the uncomfortable actions necessary to bring them success.**

### Bret's Leaf Business Leaves Him a Profit

Kyle's nine-year-old son Bret and his classmate and cousin Nick approached Kyle with a walk of determination and a grin. Kyle was a bit worried what these two might be up to since the most recent time they had approached him like this was to report that they had added dish soap to the front fountain and turned it into a mountain of bubbles. This time their intentions were much more productive. Bret and Nick had decided they wanted to make some money and were going to rake leaves to do so. Kyle concealed a sigh of relief that it wasn't something more disturbing and congratulated them on their wonderful idea. They said they wanted him to pay them to rake the leaves but wanted to start with the neighbors' houses first since they knew the neighbors would pay better than he would. Clever boys.

Wanting them to succeed and knowing their leaf-raking experience was minimal, Kyle knew he had to give them a hand. He convinced them to rake a small portion of his yard first so he could teach them the basics of raking techniques and how best to get the leaves in the bags. "How are you going to find your customers?" he queried.

"Um, you can call them, I guess," answered his son.

"Not a chance," Kyle replied. "The most important part of this business is that you learn to find your own customers." Kyle lived in a great neighborhood and he knew most of the neighbors, so he pointed out several houses they should try first. He explained that they would have to knock on the doors themselves and try to get the customers' business.

At first Bret was apprehensive, but the peer pressure of not wanting to seem weak in front of his cousin helped Kyle persuade him. Kyle and the boys went over a basic script for what they should say and figured out some fair pricing options. After a few practice runs, Kyle was impressed at how adeptly they made their sales pitch. He gave them a clap on the back and sent them off to make their millions. To his surprise they found two customers that afternoon and spent over four hours raking leaves with three trips back to the house for extra leaf bags. One of the two elderly gentlemen they had raked leaves for had even given them a $5 bonus for their efforts.

Bret and Nick were visibly exhausted and bedraggled when they came home. They hadn't realized raking leaves was so hard. They could barely walk, but their sunburnt faces lit up when they announced to Kyle they had made $30 each in profit. "Well, not exactly all profit," he reminded them. "You made $30 in revenue, but you used practically my entire box of leaf bags. That means your business had expenses. You have to subtract that out to get your profit." Their brows furrowed. "How much do those bags cost?" asked Nick.

Seeing their extreme fatigue, Kyle didn't have the heart to discourage them and charge them too much. "I'll tell you what," he bargained. "Do you have any one-dollar bills?" They did. "I'll just charge you one dollar for all those bags you used, and you two can split your profits however you want." They agreed and sauntered off to figure out how they would spend their new wealth.

Kyle tried to remind them that they still had him as a customer for their leaf-raking business, but they muttered something about the backbreaking labor and fact that they were already rich with the $29.50 they had each earned. He tried reminding them of how he'd walked to school uphill both ways in the snow, but it was to no avail. At least they learned some valuable lessons. The first was the value of hard physical work and how tiring it could be. The second lesson was the difference between revenue and profit—the same lesson Kyle had learned from his father in his first entrepreneurial endeavor.

The final lesson Bret and Nick learned was the most important, and the one Kyle was the proudest of them for. They were willing to put themselves in the uncomfortable situation of knocking on doors and asking for their customers' business. Today when kids would rather text than talk, even asking them to interact with people face-to-face and eye-to-eye is challenging. Getting them to do that alone is valuable.

Loral taught Logan a similar lesson on dealing with uncomfortable situations when she made him go on a job interview and get a job. He had been an entrepreneur so long that Loral felt he needed to experience what it was like to be an employee and be subjected to a boss and time schedules. Although Loral only made him do it for 60 days, he was able to learn the respect and responsibility of having a job, even though the experience made him highly uncomfortable. Embrace every opportunity to encourage and celebrate your child's attempts to face their fears and meet their discomfort head-on. Confidence and success will be their reward.

# CHAPTER 7

# AGES 12 TO 15

*Do not save what is left after spending, but
spend what is left after saving.*
—Warren Buffett, legendary billionaire investor

Psychologists have found that much of a child's overall belief systems are cemented by the time they are 14 or 15. Teaching the financial concepts in this chapter while your children are still under this age is pivotal because we must be certain they have the right belief systems about money. Recall Chapter 2 on the "Millionaire Mindset" and review it if necessary. If you haven't already, commit to talking to your children regularly about the differences between the negative and limiting mindset about money and the positive mindset of financial abundance.

One thing to consider is setting aside a time for regular, weekly talks about money. You still have a few years to hone your child's money skills, but you need to get their mindset right very soon. Very soon they will be driving and have more independence, so your time with them will start to diminish. You have a few more years to highly influence them. This age category is also the time period when your child is finally able to start taking the controls a bit on their Flight To Financial Freedom. It's important that

> **Helpful reminder: Don't forget to continue teaching and doing all the things you introduced in the previous chapters and expanding on them as your child's understanding improves.**

you give them that opportunity, but keep a close eye on them so you can course-correct when necessary.

## SET UP A CHECKING ACCOUNT AND DEBIT CARD FOR YOUR CHILD

In the Chapter 5 section "Set Up a Bank Account in Their Name (and Yours)" we advised you to set up a savings account or money market account for your child. The main purpose of that account was to get them started in banking and teach them about interest. Now that your child is starting to make income and potentially run a small business, they need a way to conveniently pay expenses with that business.

If you haven't already, it's now time for you to open a checking account for them—one that they'll have access to. As before, you will have to be the custodian for the account and your name will be on the account along with theirs. The main disadvantage of a checking account is that they usually don't pay interest. If they do, the amount is even smaller than a savings account. This is why we want your child to keep their savings accounts for the use of their wealth account and long-term savings. The checking account's advantage is that it allows easier withdrawals of funds. This is pivotal if your child has a business or needs to pay expenses out of the account. It's also necessary to exe-cute the more technological ways of paying yourself first that we will discuss in the upcoming section "Advanced Pay Yourself First."

The other reason we want you to open a checking account for your child is so they can begin using checks and get a debit card. In Chapter 5 you taught your child the basic academics of the debit card and checks in the section "Basics of Credit Cards, Debit Cards, Checks, Etc." Now you are going to help them use these things under your supervision (step 4 of the pilot training model). Since you are the cus-todian to the checking account and have access to it, you can watch over the account and make certain your child doesn't abuse the use of their debit card. It's even a good idea to show your child how to balance their checkbook and supervise them and confirm it's right. Just like in the pilot training model, when you see any dangerous behavior, you can "take over the controls." For example, if your child overdrafts their account by writing a check when there are insufficient funds, they will receive an NSF (not sufficient funds) fee, often ranging from $10 to $35.

Fixing the poor money behavior of your child may even require them taking a step back and getting an additional demonstration or refreshed academics on the proper use of checks or a debit card. The point is that getting a checking account for them early allows you to provide that supervision and guidance. As a result, they aren't left trying to learn how to use a debit card and checking account when they are on their own and susceptible to crashing their own personal finances. Understanding how to manage their expenses and income through their checking account will be discussed in the next section and several more in this chapter.

> **LORAL SAYS: My rule for over-drafts was that my children would get one strike, and if it happened again, they had to pay for any future mistakes themselves.**

## FORECASTING

With a checking account set up, your child now has the main financial account they need to manage the expenses and income for their business, employment income, or even just their Home Pay. The key thing you need to teach them now is how to use that account properly and to make intelligent and informed decisions about their income and spending like a business does. In earlier sections like

> **LORAL SAYS: Forecasting is very similar to the idea that many of you have been introduced to called budgeting. The problem with budgeting is that, like a diet, it is very limiting and unappealing. As a result, just like a diet, hardly anybody sticks to a budget and it seldom works.**

"Pay Yourself First" in Chapter 4 we helped you teach your child the basics of how to save their money. Now that they hopefully have a little more money, they need to learn how to responsibly spend it.

This age is the perfect time to teach them about the Wealth Cycle building block of Forecasting.

In the Wealth Cycle Process, we do not think only about what you can't do, which is what budgeting forces you to do, but instead challenge you to deliberately and purposefully plan how you will both earn and spend your money. Recall in Chapter 2 when we discussed the ridiculously simple formula for wealth, which was keeping:

**Income > Expenses**

or

**I > E**

If you'll remember, we explained that we recommend working on both sides of the equation. The problem with budgeting is that it only addresses the E or expenses side of the equation. Forecasting is more comprehensive than just budgeting because it addresses both sides, the income and the expenses. If you want to eat, drink, and be merry, that's fine, but then you need to "learn to earn" more income to keep up with your expenses. This means you need to plan, or forecast, for what your earnings as well as your expenses will be. That's the way businesses and millionaires manage their money.

In addition to projecting your income and expenses, forecasting also evaluates what your future assets and liabilities will be. We'll talk more about how to track and assess income, expenses, assets, and liabilities in this chapter in the upcoming sections "The Balance Sheet" and "The Income Statement." The earlier you can get your children to start thinking and planning like a business, the better. Just like businesses, individuals should be mindful of what money comes in, as well as what they spend their money on. Kids need to be taught, as well as shown, that frivolous purchases won't help them achieve their long-term goals. If you don't control your expenses, your expenses will control you. In the next several sections we will talk about several topics related to forecasting, as well as give your child the tools they need to do their own forecasting.

## ADVANCED PAY YOURSELF FIRST

By this age most children are old enough to fully understand the concept of delayed gratification. A good way to enforce this concept is to teach them about paying themselves first. As discussed before, this means setting money aside toward your savings goals before you spend any money. Paying yourself first is just one aspect of forecasting. The quote at the beginning of this chapter by Warren Buffett deserves repeating: "Do not save what is left after spending, but spend what is left after saving."

**KYLE SAYS: When talking about the concept of paying yourself first, I like to break people's financial behavior into three categories. Where would your current spending habits fall on the following chart?**

| | |
|---|---|
| Predictably Poor | Income – Expenses = Play money |
| Methodically Middle-Class | Income – Expenses = Savings |
| Reliably Rich | Income – Investments = Expenses |

If you are like the Predictably Poor, any money that makes it to your bank account after expenses gets spent as play money, otherwise known as Lifestyle Cycle spending. This is assuming you don't spend the money even before the expenses are paid and create bad debt for yourself. The Methodically Middle-Class are better because they at least save the money they have left over after expenses. The problem with this strategy is the "savings" or "emergency accounts" often don't get invested, or they justify lifestyle purchases as necessary expenses and don't end up with any savings at all. Many people simply don't have the discipline to put these savings to work buying assets instead of liabilities masquerading as legitimate expenses.

The way to ensure you are in the Reliably Rich category is to move the money into your wealth account and investments before you have a chance to spend it. Expenses are only paid for with what remains. This results in your expenses staying small and limited to only what are truly necessary expenses, not those you justify as such because you think you have extra money. In the last "Pay Yourself First" section in Chapter 4 we focused on helping your child to pay themselves first by using a jar system. If you missed or forgot that chapter, it might be worth reviewing the content. Now that your child is older and hopefully is familiar with the mechanics of paying themselves first, we will move to more advanced ways of doing so.

The best way to guarantee that you and your teenage child will pay yourselves first is through "automatic investment plans." Automatic investment plans are programs that automatically contribute funds toward an investment. Don't be worried. Despite their official-sounding name, they are incredibly easy to set up. Automatic investment plans can usually be established in less than five minutes by simply going to your brokerage or investment account and setting up automatic deposits that will be transferred electronically at whatever frequency and amount you desire.

Nearly every investment account has this as an option. The only information you need is usually the bank name, account number, and routing number for the bank you are pulling the deposits from. We recommend aligning this with right after your income arrives in your bank account, if possible, to make certain the money is sent to your investment account before you have a chance to spend it. This acts in the same way that placing the money in your wealth account jar did, except it's automatic. If you haven't already set this up for yourself, we highly recommend you do so now so you can provide a good demonstration for your child. After you're done, set one up for your child. We promise it will be time well spent—setting up an automatic investment plan is debatably the five minutes with the "most bang for your buck" toward your child's financial future.

If you set up an automatic investment plan for your child, then even if they aren't great at delaying gratification, they will still contribute at least the monthly amount you set up. They just need to take care that they contribute their weekly Home Pay or other income into their bank account soon enough to have funds available in their account to transfer for the automatic investment. Depending on what type of investment account they are using, they may still need to go to

> **Setting up an automatic investment plan is debatably the five minutes with the "most bang for your buck" toward your child's financial future.**

the investment account and allocate those funds on a monthly basis into whichever investment they prefer. However, at least you have kept their money from sitting in their bank account where it might entice your child to spend it on something frivolous. Another advantage of the automatic investment plan is that it provides dollar-cost averaging.

Dollar-cost averaging is a strategy where investors divide up their overall investment into multiple smaller and equal-sized purchases at regular intervals. The advantage of doing this is that it can reduce some of the risk of mistiming the market, particularly if the investment has high volatility, or beta ($\beta$), as we discussed in Chapter 6 in the section "Risk Versus Reward for Investments." People often like to dollar-cost average when buying stocks. Since you invest the same amount of money every time, if the stock price is high, you would buy fewer shares. However, if the stock price went down, you would be able to purchase more shares with the same amount of money. Therefore, you would avoid putting all your money into an investment when it is at its peak. Of course, the downside is that if the stock keeps going up you will buy fewer and fewer shares. Despite this downside, especially for people who have a low risk tolerance, dollar-cost averaging can be a smart strategy, especially when it's done with an automatic investment plan.

Recent innovations have created other ways to automatically pay yourself first. Check out our website MakeYourKidsMillionaires.com for a few of our recommendations.

Whether you choose to use the jar system, manual transfers, or an automatic investment plan, the fact remains that you need to find a way to pay yourself first. We prefer the automatic investment plan because it is the easiest and most, well . . . automatic. Automatic is good when we all, including your children, have so many things competing for our time. Automatic is also good when you aren't great at delaying gratification and you need to save your future self from your present self. Finally, automatic is good if you suffer from indecisiveness and can never decide how much and when to contribute to your investments. There's no "analysis paralysis" when it's done automatically for you. So do your child (and yourself) a favor and set up an automatic investment plan to pay your future self first. The financial reward you receive may be your future freedom.

## THE BALANCE SHEET

In order to figure out where we are going financially, we must first know where we are starting from. In Loral's books this is one of the 12 building blocks of the Wealth Cycle, which she calls your Financial Baseline. Your financial baseline is an overview of your current financial situation in the form of two tools—the balance sheet and the income statement. These are the tools that businesses use to figure out where they stand financially. In fact, they are two of the main financial statements that all publicly traded companies must report to the Securities and Exchange Commission (SEC) every quarter.

As financially savvy individuals, we should track the same things. The balance sheet and income statement are important tools for building the foundation for your child's financial plan. These financial instruments bring action to many of the concepts we discuss in this book. In this section and the next one we'll provide an example of both tools so you can help your child read and produce their own. Feel free to use our example balance sheet and income statement at the end of this book or go to our website MakeYourKidsMillionaires.com for an electronic version that you can alter to suit your needs. First, some background discussion is required to explain why these tools are so important.

Management theorist Peter Drucker stated in his 1954 classic book *The Practice of Management* that "what gets measured, gets managed." His point was that when organizations tracked and measured something, it caused them to manage it. The only obvious reason to manage a goal is to meet it.

The added attention you place on your goals when you measure them will help you make the decisions (like reading this book) that will help you reach those goals.

In the book and film *The Secret*, Loral and others also describe how the mere process of continuously thinking about your financial goals can help them come to fruition. Whether you believe in the metaphysical attraction of thoughts or just the practical belief that "What gets measured, gets met," having a financial baseline will help

> **KYLE SAYS: I tell students, "What gets measured, gets met." When you measure your progress toward your financial goals, you will naturally pay more attention to them.**

you know where you are starting from so you can track how to reach your goals. Creating a balance sheet provides you that baseline. We will discuss the balance sheet now and the income statement in the next section.

A balance sheet is a financial statement that lists your assets and liabilities and allows you to measure your net worth. This tool shows the financial baseline for where we are currently so we can figure out how to get to our goals. Thus, the balance sheet is the starting line or takeoff airport for our financial flight. The finish line, or landing destination, is the goals we discussed in the Chapter 5 sections "Your Child's Money Goals" and "Family Financial Goal Setting." Recall the story about Loral's son, Logan, and his smoothie store in the Chapter 5 section "Supply and Demand." Although these numbers are fictional for simplification purchases and don't depict Logan's actual numbers from that time period (to protect his privacy), it's a good representation of how a balance sheet might look for a child this age (Figure 7.1).

| Logan Langemeier | Balance Sheet |
|---|---|
| **Assets** | |
| Wealth Account | 1,000 |
| Car Account | 1,000 |
| Charity Account | 75 |
| Other cash | 63 |
| **Total Assets** | **$2,138** |
| **Liabilities** | |
| Short-term loan from Mom | 20 |
| **Total Liabilities** | **$20** |
| **Net Worth** | |
| **Total Net Worth** | **$2,118** |

**Figure 7.1** Logan's Balance Sheet

In this balance sheet we can see that Logan had accumulated $1,000 so far in both his wealth account and car account. He started saving in both of these when he was 10 and created his car account. He had also put away $75 in a charity account. Finally, he had $63 in other cash that he was using for spending money. Together, he had $2,138 in assets. Thankfully, as a child, he had very little debt. He had borrowed $20 from Loral a few days prior to pay for supplies for his smoothies. His total liabilities were $20. When we subtract his assets from his liabilities, we find that Logan had a net worth of $2,118. More important, he had a financial baseline from which to start his financial flight. In the next section we'll show how Logan can use the income statement to plan the flight from his baseline to his goals.

# THE INCOME STATEMENT

In the last section we talked about the importance of two financial tools, the balance sheet and the income statement. We explained how important it was to track our progress toward our goals since "What gets measured, gets met." We further described how the balance sheet was the takeoff airport, or financial baseline, on the financial flight to your goals. Now we will describe the income statement, which helps formulate the flight path you will take on your "Flight To Financial Freedom."

The income statement, sometimes called a profit and loss statement, shows revenue and expenses for a company or your personal finances. This tool brings to life the forecasting and *pay yourself first* concepts we talked about earlier in this chapter. It also serves as a tool to do another of the Wealth Cycle building blocks called the Gap Analysis.

We figured out where we were starting from with our balance sheet in the last section. We figured out where we want to go in the goals sections in Chapter 5. Now, we just need to figure out a gap analysis so we can chart the flight path between the two. The best way to do this is just to figure out the math of how to get there. Once you know the math you merely have to create forecasted income statements to get you there. Let's go over an example.

In the previous section "The Balance Sheet" we discussed the story of Loral's son, Logan, and his smoothie store, which was described in the

**LORAL SAYS: Recall from the Chapter 3 section "Wealth Cycle Actions" that the gap analysis is a financial model that will create a map from where you are—your financial baseline—to where you want to go—your goals.**

Chapter 5 section "Supply and Demand." We showed a balance sheet for Logan that served as his financial baseline and talked about the gap between his starting financial situation and the goal he had of buying a car and investing for future financial freedom. Review that balance sheet again (Figure 7.1) if it's been a while since you looked at it. Now we will talk about how that gap analysis can be put into action by forecasting his income statement.

In the scenario we described, Logan was age 12 with $1,000 toward his wealth account and $1,000 already toward his car since he had started at age 10. Although his real numbers were different, for the sake of this fictional example, let's say his goal was to accumulate $7,000 for both accounts before he reached age 16. How could he get there? Logan knew he would be able to earn more as he got older and could start a business that had more cash flow if necessary. He also knew that even though he had a good start, there was no time to waste. Since he needed to save $6,000 more for each account over four years, he came up with the following forecast for wealth account/car account deposits for each year:

Age 12:  $600
Age 13:  $1,000
Age 14:  $1,800
Age 15:  $2,600
——————————
Total:   $6,000

Logan knew it was ambitious, but he really wanted a nice car and he particularly wanted to get his wealth account started early while he had plenty of time to let it compound. He also knew he was a hard worker and that he could meet his goals if he forecast the income he needed each month, paid himself first, and did whatever it took to meet his numbers. Since Logan was older and had been running the smoothie business for several years, he found that he could forecast what his revenue would be for the following month fairly accurately. He also knew what his expenses would be for the most part. By planning these out on a projected income statement he was using pen and paper to put into action the concept of forecasting that was described earlier in this chapter. Since Logan needed to put $600 into both his wealth account and car account this year, he knew he needed to forecast $50 per month into each account ($600/12 months = $50). Figure 7.2 is an example income statement for Logan's projected month.

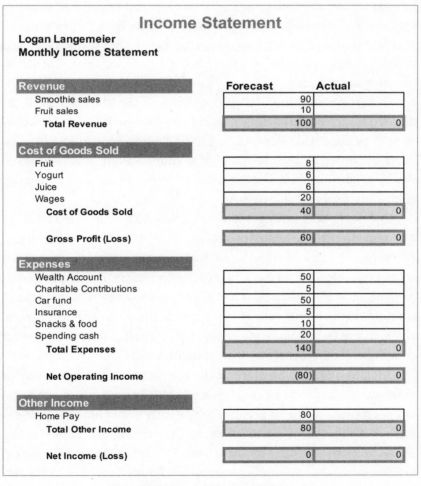

| Income Statement | | |
|---|---|---|
| **Logan Langemeier**<br>**Monthly Income Statement** | | |
| **Revenue** | **Forecast** | **Actual** |
| Smoothie sales | 90 | |
| Fruit sales | 10 | |
| **Total Revenue** | 100 | 0 |
| **Cost of Goods Sold** | | |
| Fruit | 8 | |
| Yogurt | 6 | |
| Juice | 6 | |
| Wages | 20 | |
| **Cost of Goods Sold** | 40 | 0 |
| **Gross Profit (Loss)** | 60 | 0 |
| **Expenses** | | |
| Wealth Account | 50 | |
| Charitable Contributions | 5 | |
| Car fund | 50 | |
| Insurance | 5 | |
| Snacks & food | 10 | |
| Spending cash | 20 | |
| **Total Expenses** | 140 | 0 |
| **Net Operating Income** | (80) | 0 |
| **Other Income** | | |
| Home Pay | 80 | |
| **Total Other Income** | 80 | 0 |
| **Net Income (Loss)** | 0 | 0 |

**Figure 7.2** Logan's Income Statement

Remember, this is just a forecast for now—not the actual results. Note that Logan projected he would sell $90 in smoothies over the course of the month as well as $10 in fruit on the side, for a total revenue of $100. Loral made sure he accounted for and paid for his own cost of goods to make the smoothies. As he grew older, Loral also had him reimburse her for the time he used her employees to help him get supplies from the store. Between the cost of goods and the wages he had to reimburse Loral's employees, Logan forecast his overall cost of goods sold was $40. This left his forecast gross profit at $60. For the purpose of this income statement, Logan was forecasting not just his business revenue and expenses but also his whole life's revenue and expenses— the business of Logan.

Observe under the expenses column of the statement that he decided to pay himself first by counting $50 toward his wealth account as an expense, rather than waiting to find out what was left over, just like we discussed in the sections "Pay Yourself First" and "Advanced Pay Yourself First." He also set aside an expense of $5 for charitable contributions, as we also discussed.

The next expense Logan projected was $50 for his car fund. We discussed this in the Chapter 6 section "Have Your Child Create a Car Account." The insurance expense was another addition Loral added when Logan was a little older, to represent a concept similar to disability insurance. If Logan paid it and ended up unavoidably unable to sell smoothies that month, she would pay him his projected gross profit. The idea was to introduce the concept of insurance so he could better comprehend different types of insurance later.

All told, after adding a forecast for snacks and spending cash to his expenses, Logan had total expenses of $140. This gave him a forecast net operating income of negative $80, which would have been pretty bad except that he also had a forecast for making $80 in Home Pay, as we described in the section "Never Pay Your Kid an Allowance" in Chapter 4. This resulted in a projected net income of $0. This may sound bad, but remember he paid his wealth account, charity, and car account first and counted these as expenses. He also accounted for all his expenses, so having a projected net income of $0 is fine given how he chose to do his accounting. Of course, he could have accounted for things differently and paid his life-related expenses with the net income, but this way Logan made sure he paid himself first.

Note the process Logan went through, which is exactly the process successful businesses go through. He figured out his financial baseline via a balance sheet. He decided what his goals were. He then planned the flight to get from one to the other by doing a gap analysis. As part of that gap analysis, he figured out the income, or cash flow, he needed and the amount he would need to "pay himself first" toward each account for each year. He then took those yearly totals and broke them down to monthly forecast totals. If his business operated more regularly, he could have even broken the monthly totals into weekly and daily income goals to ensure he had something to shoot for on a daily basis. The only thing left was to actually execute his plan and see how he did. All the forecasting in the world doesn't mean much if you don't stick to the plan.

In order to see how you are doing, you must track the money to verify that you are conforming to your forecasting. Tracking the money includes following along with all the income coming in and the expenses going out. Some of the most tedious but necessary tasks required to track the money are balancing your checkbook and checking your bank and credit card records. Doing so accomplishes a few things. First, it allows you to check up on your forecast to see if you are complying with what you planned to spend for that month. It will also alert you to potential upcoming shortfalls in your account or maybe even excess money that needs to be redirected into your wealth account.

Finally, it makes sure there haven't been any bank errors or unauthorized purchases or withdrawals from your account. Electronic fraud is prevalent these days, and there are hundreds of ways for criminals to accomplish it. One of the best ways you can prevent electronic fraud is to keep an eye on your accounts to ensure thieves can't steal from you without your knowledge.

Take care to explain all the above-listed reasons to your child for why they should care about accomplishing these tasks. If you don't talk to them about these reasons, you can be sure they won't do it. We've learned that, for kids, if something isn't fun, there'd better be a really good explanation for why they should do it, or they will do everything they can to avoid it. If you don't explain the "why" while they are young you can be sure they won't continue it as adults once they are no longer under your watchful eye.

Once your child grasps the importance of tracking their money, you'll probably need to walk them through the steps with your own accounts. This would be where your expert demonstration (phase 3 of the pilot training teaching model) will provide your child with the basic skills and tactics that underlie the strategy you've been teaching them. Even though many people don't use checks very often anymore, if you haven't already, it's probably still a good idea to start by showing your child how you can keep track of your bank account by balancing your checkbook. Sometimes having something physical in front of them helps things make sense. Having a checkbook that automatically makes a carbon copy of each check inside your checkbook also helps to ensure you don't lose track of checks. Next, show your child how you go through your bank statement, whether it be paper or electronic, to confirm that all the deposits and withdrawals make sense and align with your expenses and income. Finally, do the same thing with your credit card statement, paper or online, to show how you double-check all those purchases. If you do come up with a discrepancy in your bank statement or credit card statement, show them how to fix it. If the fix requires a phone call, let them listen to the phone call you have with your bank or credit card company so they will have an idea of what the conversation should sound like. We've found that kids these days spend so much time texting that they are sometimes intimidated by talking on the phone with adults, especially those in positions of authority. Giving them an expert demonstration of phone etiquette will go a long way toward easing their apprehension.

Now that you've confirmed all your account transactions and balances are what they should be, there is one last step. This step might be the most important. Show your child how you compare your income and expenses to those you anticipated in your monthly forecast, as represented by the income statement. Did you spend more or less? Was your revenue more or less? Was there a good reason if not? Do you need to adjust your forecast for future months? If not, what will you do to get back on track? These are all questions you need to be asking yourself, as well as teaching your child to ask themselves about their finances. This post-action review is extremely important to validate that you are staying on track with your goals. If you can't take a close objective look at your performance to see how you can get better, how can you hope to improve?

Now that your child has seen your demonstration, have them follow along by doing the same thing with their checking account. Help them do a thorough review of their checkbook, bank account, and credit card statements. Then teach your child to do a thorough debrief to see how they did relative to their forecast and adjust accordingly. Eventually, especially if they own a business, they can use software that will automatically track some of these things. In the meantime, it's helpful for them to see where the numbers come from and learn to do it from scratch.

Now let's go back to Logan and his smoothie business. After tracking the money through his bank accounts to figure out his revenue and expenses, he

**KYLE SAYS: In the Air Force flying world, such a review would be called a debrief. When I was a fighter pilot, we would sometimes spend more time in the debrief than the actual flight. In fact, in my opinion, this is one of the biggest factors that makes the United States Air Force the best in the world. When I would fly with international pilots from some countries, I found that they had no interest in spending time debriefing the flight. They didn't realize what the US pilots knew. Most of the learning takes place in the debrief.**

was able to assemble the true numbers for his business. Figure 7.3 is the income statement showing his actual performance for the month he forecast. Let's see how he did.

## Income Statement

**Logan Langemeier**
**Monthly Income Statement**

| | Forecast | Actual |
|---|---|---|
| **Revenue** | | |
| Smoothie sales | 90 | 116 |
| Fruit sales | 10 | 15 |
| **Total Revenue** | 100 | 131 |
| **Cost of Goods Sold** | | |
| Fruit | 8 | 11 |
| Yogurt | 6 | 7 |
| Juice | 6 | 8 |
| Wages | 20 | 20 |
| **Cost of Goods Sold** | 40 | 46 |
| **Gross Profit (Loss)** | 60 | 85 |
| **Expenses** | | |
| Wealth Account | 50 | 50 |
| Charitable Contributions | 5 | 5 |
| Car fund | 50 | 50 |
| Insurance | 5 | 5 |
| Snacks & food | 10 | 7 |
| Spending cash | 20 | 13 |
| **Total Expenses** | 140 | 130 |
| **Net Operating Income** | (80) | (45) |
| **Other Income** | | |
| Home Pay | 80 | 90 |
| **Total Other Income** | 80 | 90 |
| **Net Income (Loss)** | 0 | 45 |

**Figure 7.3** Logan's Income Statement: Forecast Versus Actual Performance

It looks like Logan had a good month. As can be seen under the revenue section, his smoothie and fruit sales were higher than expected, giving him an actual total revenue of $131. Due to having to make more smoothies, his cost of goods sold went up, but not as much as his total revenue. As a result, his profit was $25 over his forecast and resulted in $85 in gross profit. As for expenses, Logan kept to his forecast by paying himself first for his wealth account, charitable contributions, and car fund. He also skipped a few snacks and miscellaneous expenses to keep an additional $10 in expenses for a total expenses of $130 and a net operating income of $45.

Since Logan was tracking his business so closely, he became even more motivated by its success and decided to do some extra Home Tasks around the house so he could earn $10 extra in Home Pay for a total other income of $90. All told, he was able to earn a net income of $45. Since he had already accounted for his expenses, he was free to use that $45 however he wanted. He could invest it in more inventory or advertising to improve his business, or he could contribute more to one of his accounts. If he wanted, he could even have spent a little bit to celebrate how hard he worked. In the end, Logan decided to split the extra $45 between his wealth account and car account so he would be closer to his goals.

Let's talk about some of the "debrief" items Logan should look at. Fortunately, he beat his expectations on revenue and income. If the business of Logan were a company this would be called "beating on the top and bottom lines." Just as it is displayed in the income statement, the "top line" represents revenue and the "bottom line" represents income. Now when your child is listening on TV to a company's quarterly earnings call, they'll know what this statement means! If Logan had a "miss" on the top or bottom lines he would need to take a hard look at his business and figure out why. If he missed on the top line, then he would need to figure out how he could improve his sales. Maybe he needed more marketing or different pricing. If he "hit" his top line targets but missed on the bottom line, that would mean his expenses were higher than he anticipated. Could he get the ingredients cheaper elsewhere or by buying in bulk? Could he lower the wages he had to pay Loral's assistants?

Given all that he learned, the next question would be how he should adjust for the next month. Should he raise his revenue forecast, or was this just a one-time situation? How could he try to drive his revenue numbers even higher or his costs lower? Does he need to adjust his goals higher to account for the extra contributions? These are just a few of the questions Logan could ask himself in order to do a thorough debrief of his monthly performance.

Hopefully it's clear from this exercise the multitude of lessons your child can learn from creating an income statement. If it didn't work, then Fortune 500 companies and all publicly traded businesses wouldn't do it. The combination of the balance sheet and the income statement provides the perfect tools to take you from your financial baseline, through your gap analysis and forecasting, and to your goals. With some hard work and these tools at their disposal, your child can fly from takeoff to landing on their Flight To Financial Freedom.

## REAL-WORLD COST OF LIVING

As your child begins to grow wealth and accumulate some money at this age, it's not uncommon for them to think they don't have to work so hard anymore. After all, they should have enough cash to buy some snacks and the occasional electronic gadget. What else could they possibly need? Why are these adults always so stressed out about money? This game is easy. If you start to sense these attitudes from your teenager, it's time to snap them back to reality. They probably have no idea how expensive life can really be.

Different parents have different beliefs about what they will buy for their kids. Some parents pay not only for their kid's needs but also everything they want. Loral's rule is her kids share the price for extras that go beyond their needs. Kyle covers all their needs but often makes them pay for things they don't need unless it is a gift for their birthday or the holidays. The choice is yours. Pick a path and make a plan. The key is that you are consistent and set the expectation early.

Now is the time to break the news to your child and show them some of the real costs of living. Show them your bills and how you go about paying them, even if they are on automatic payment (which they probably should be). Show them the electric and water bills. Show them the insurance and medical bills. Show it all to them. There's no reason to be secretive at this point. Your child needs to know what it really costs to live independently or support a family. It might even be worth showing them a sample income statement for your expenses to compare it to theirs. Not only will this teach them how to handle these bills when they are on their own, it might even help them appreciate your efforts at saving by helping them realize the cost of things.

For the full heartbreaker, show your child their own cell phone bill. How many months' worth of cell phone bills could they pay if they had to pay it themselves? This might also be a good time to talk about the pay differences between different jobs or professions. Even if they want to eventually be an entrepreneur, they may have to work at a job for a while. The sooner they learn that all jobs have limits to the level of income they can earn, the quicker they will be open to learning how to run their own businesses as Cash Machines so they can generate larger cash flows.

> **KYLE SAYS:** I remember my son's amazement the first time he saw the electric bill and how expensive it was just to run the household. The next time he was reminded to turn off his lights before leaving his room, he had a greater appreciation for why that was important and was much more willing to pay attention to it.

Talking with teenagers about what it means to be an adult usually generates a list of fun "adulting" things they will get to do once they come of age, such as driving a car, eating out at restaurants, or attending a sporting event or movie. Talk about the costs of these activities and how quickly they can add up. It might also be a good idea to talk about the future cost of these activities as well as the opportunity cost of what they are giving up in future investment profits by instead spending the money on entertainment. We don't want to depress them into not wanting to grow up, but it's a good idea to temper their expectations of how much extra income they will have.

It's better to slowly ease them into the realities of being an adult than to wait until they are on their own and let them get slapped in the face by the harsh realities of bills they didn't expect and hadn't even thought about. It might even make them a little more sympathetic of your perspective when they don't get to spend and party like teenage rock stars.

## CREDIT AND THE CREDIT SCORE

This may seem early to begin teaching this, but you need to start bringing up the principles. The idea of credit in financial matters started long before the credit card or modern-day credit score. It started as a contractual promise. Nobody knows for sure, but the first use of credit probably occurred thousands of years ago when a shop owner decided they would allow a customer to purchase bread for their family that day with the promise that they would pay later. The shop owner had to trust that the customer would keep his word. Such a transaction wouldn't have been without risk for the shop owner. There was always the chance that the customer wouldn't pay. The more trustworthy the customer, the less the risk. Over the years, shop owners learned to keep lists of who they could trust and who they couldn't. Sometimes they would share these lists amongst other shop owners so each shop could better gauge the risk they were taking on with each customer. Eventually, these lists became formalized as credit scores. A person's credit score is a number that indicates to lenders that person's creditworthiness, or likelihood of repaying a debt.

Today when people talk about credit scores they are usually talking about a FICO score. Fair Isaac Corporation (FICO) developed a proprietary algorithm that scores borrowers numerically based on their creditworthiness. Explain to your child that this is not unlike the grades they receive in school. Much like school grades, the FICO score judges their performance, only this time it's their credit performance and not their math or language skills being graded. The other difference is that instead of being on a scale of 0 to 100 like school, the FICO score is on a scale of 300 to 850. There are three credit reporting agencies that report information that goes into your FICO: Equifax, Experian, and TransUnion. According to Experian's website www.experian.com, your FICO score can be categorized as shown in Figure 7.4.

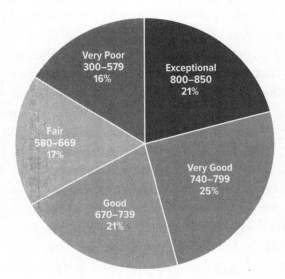

**Figure 7.4** FICO Scores

The lower your score, the riskier you are to lenders. As we discussed last chapter in the section "Risk Versus Reward for Investments," people want a higher reward if they must take on higher risk. As mentioned in the "Good Debt Versus Bad Debt" section in Chapter 6, this means the creditors will charge you a higher interest rate for loans if you have a low FICO score. Therefore, even when you purchase good debt, you will be punished by having to pay more interest than those with a higher credit score. Worse yet, if your credit score is very low, you may not even qualify for a loan at all. This means you may not be able to purchase a home. Your credit score may also influence your ability to obtain and the price for obtaining a car, cell phone, home utilities, apartment or rental home, insurance, investments, or even a job. That's right! Your credit score can keep you from getting a job as well. Additionally, because negative information generally stays on your credit report for seven years, it can take a very long time to atone for financial mistakes you have made in your life.

This is why it's so important that you emphasize to your child the importance of keeping a good credit score and credit reputation. Explain the concept of credit score, and how difficult it is to fix once it's been damaged, to your children. You've probably taught them how important your family's reputation is and what it means for people to respect and trust you. Your credit reputation, as reflected by your credit score, is almost as important and perhaps more influential on your financial life. Advise your child that avoiding bad debt is one of the best ways to ensure that you keep a good financial reputation.

For young people, sometimes the problem isn't that they have a bad credit score, it's that they have no credit score at all. If you don't have a credit score at all you are an unknown risk to credit lenders. Remember, your credit score tells lenders not just your creditworthiness but effectively your trustworthiness and risk scope. Without a credit score, it's not that they assume you are untrustworthy and not creditworthy, it's just that they have no proof that you *are* creditworthy. This too can prevent you from getting a loan or taking advantage of credit when you need it.

Now that your child recognizes the importance of both having a credit score and having a good credit score, how do they accomplish it? How do you make certain you are considered trustworthy to lenders and a low risk? The answer lies in knowing the rules of the game. We discussed how the FICO score is like a grading scale in school. If your child were trying to get a good grade in school, they would first want to be told how the grading scale would be applied. Realizing which percentages of their grade were attributed to tests, homework, quizzes, and attendance would be incredibly useful. The good news is we know at least the basic grading standards for the FICO score.

As you can see from the FICO Grading Standards chart (Figure 7.5), the most important factor is payment history, making up 35 percent of the score. This just means paying your bills on time. If we revisit

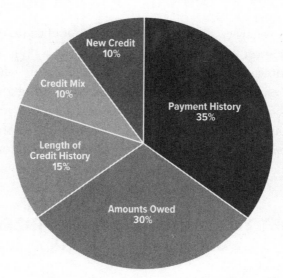

**Figure 7.5** FICO Grading Standards

the school analogy, over a third of your grade is just for turning in your homework on time. The next largest part of your grade is amounts owed at 30 percent. This just refers to the amount of credit available to you that you use. The lower percentage that you use, the higher your score. For example, if you have a credit limit of $1,000 but only regularly use $50 of that available credit, this will provide you a greater percentage of the available 30 percent of your score than if you regularly maxed out that $1,000 worth of credit. This is another good reason you should persuade your children to not max out their credit cards.

The third largest factor in determining your FICO score makes up 15 percent of the score. It is the length of your credit history. If you have a 50-year history of paying your bills on time, this will be given more credit than if you have only been doing so for a year. This is why it's so important for your child to start their credit history right away. The next factor in determining your credit score, tied for fourth at 10 percent, is credit mix. The person who has multiple types of loan accounts, such as credit cards, student loans, and car loans, is considered to have a more balanced profile that proves they are trustworthy with various types of debt. The final factor, which influences 10 percent of your credit score, is new credit. Applying for a new credit card or loan may temporarily lower your score.

Now that we know how the credit teacher grades us, what can your child do to ensure they get the right start on creating an outstanding credit score? In the next section we'll discuss a way you can start your child off right and put them on the fast track to exceptional credit and the type of credit score that will open up opportunities and save them money.

## GET YOUR CHILD AN AUTHORIZED USER CREDIT CARD

We discussed in the last section the importance of establishing a good credit score. We also mentioned how 15 percent of your credit score is associated with the length of your credit history. It stands to reason that the sooner you can help your child establish a credit score, the better off they will be. Fortunately for you, there is a way to do so without giving up oversight of your child's behavior. As we discussed in the Chapter 1 discussion of the pilot training model for teaching your child, we don't want to kick our children out of the nest and just hope they can fly. The best way to teach them to fly financially is to provide supervision, or oversight, of their financial habits. This is especially important for the use of credit cards. Adding your child as an "authorized user" on your credit card provides the first step on their credit journey and the most oversight possible. It also allows you to conduct the supervision of step 4 of the pilot training model. Equally as important, for most credit card companies, it also serves as the first opportunity to establish credit for your child. The only exception to using this strategy is if you try adding your child as an authorized user on a business account that has really high utilization and spending.

An authorized user is someone to whom you give permission to use your credit card via a card with their name on it. Although they get to have their name on the credit card, you are still the primary cardholder in charge of the account and are ultimately responsible for all their charges. You are also still the one getting the statements so you can and should closely monitor their spending. Before you add your child to your card, call your card issuer to confirm that their activity will be reported to the credit bureaus (most major credit card companies do). Otherwise, it will have no benefit to helping them establish a credit history. As long as the company does report it, your child will begin to create their own credit score. The minimum age for an authorized user varies by credit card company, but for some there is actually no limit. Usually there is no cost in adding an authorized user, but for cards with an annual fee there may be, so be sure to ask your credit card company if extra fees apply.

A parent has a few options for how to handle the child's card as an authorized user. If you don't think your child is ready for the responsibility of credit yet, you can simply get the card and add them as an authorized user but never give them the card. This way you can begin establishing their credit history without worrying about them running up your credit card balance. This technique has practically no risk, and even if you don't want to encourage your child to use a credit card, it is the very least you should do for your child.

If you've been reading this far, you've probably learned that we don't believe in doing the least you can for your child. We believe in doing the most. We also don't believe in shielding children from risk, especially risks as important and potentially lucrative as credit. Instead, as you probably know by now, we believe in using the pilot training model to teach them the academics of risks, then slowly expose them to those risks through simulation, demonstration, and supervision before they finally are ready to go solo. An authorized user card is a great way to take them through this process.

If we use the pilot training model for teaching our kids about credit, the first step would be teaching them about how a credit card works, as well as the benefits and dangers of credit cards. We discussed these academics in the last two sections as well as several other sections throughout this book including "Basics of Credit Cards, Debit

Card, Checks, Etc." in Chapter 5 and "Good Debt Versus Bad Debt" in Chapter 6. Review these sections with your child now if you think they need a refresher. We'll discuss advanced credit card academics even more in the next chapter in the section "Advanced Credit Cards— Friend or Foe?"

The next step after academics is simulation. As you may recall from Chapter 1, the simulation phase allows the student to learn with part-task training to keep them from getting overwhelmed and in a safe environment where their mistakes aren't fatal. To meet this criteria, we recommend that you start by only giving your child use of their authorized user card when they are with you and you have approved them to make a purchase. Although this obviously uses real money, it does meet the intent of the simulation phase in that it's a relatively safe environment and your strict oversight means they can't make any decisions that are financially fatal. As your child begins to recognize how to use the card better you can open up their freedom a bit, but for now, we recommend keeping a close eye on their account and setting up rules for what they are allowed to purchase. In the next chapter, when your child is a bit older, we will expand that freedom even more.

At the same time you are setting up an authorized user card for your child for simulation, you should also be providing an expert demonstration. This can be accomplished by showing your child how you use credit in a safe and effective manner and by talking to them about your credit card purchases and showing them your statements. In addition to showing them your statement, reinforce that the credit card is associated with their credit card statement, while the debit card is linked to their bank statement. This may seem obvious ,but you have to demonstrate the basics to your child or they may not understand these things. This would also include demonstrating how to pay off the entire balance each month to avoid paying interest.

It may also include telling your children about examples when you made decisions to avoid the pitfalls of credit cards. Instead of just saying you can't afford something, provide a more educational answer like "Honey, I really like that dress for you, but we need to make more money this month before we can buy it because I don't have the money in the bank to pay for it yet, and even though my credit card would allow me to buy it, we must always pay off our credit card every month." If you've struggled with credit card debt let them know how frustrating it was trying to claw out of that debt. These are the types of horror stories that are truly instructional for your child. Most important, do your best to lead by example. Regardless of what you did in the past, resolve in the future to show your child it is possible to never carry a credit card balance that results in paying interest.

The subject of credit cards is a somewhat controversial one in the financial teaching realm. We can almost feel the tension that this prospect creates for some of you. Don't worry. Of course, credit card abuse can and does happen. However, we've found that abuse generally only happens to people who weren't taught about money as kids. If you teach them the principles from this book, your children will understand enough to avoid hurting themselves. Also, by having them added as an authorized user to a credit card you already use while they are still under your roof, you can monitor that card and guarantee that they use it correctly. We'll talk much more about this subject in the next chapter in the section "Advanced Credit Cards—Friend or Foe?" Feel free to read ahead if you still need convincing to get your child started on their credit card journey.

## THE HIGH COST OF BORROWING

What if your child wanted to buy a $1,000 computer to improve their gaming? What if they "really, really, really" want the computer but don't have the funds yet? Should you pay the difference yourself? Should you make him wait? What if there was another choice? Have you ever learned a lesson the hard way? What if you gave your child a loan? The idea is counter to much of what we are teaching in this book, so take it on at your own risk. The intent of this loan would be to teach them how loans and borrowing work. In this way, the loan would serve as the simulation phase of the five-step pilot training model. The secret intent would be to teach them a relatively inexpensive lesson about the high costs of consumer borrowing, without the concern of ruining their credit or having collection agencies beating down their door.

If you do decide to give your child a loan, it is crucial that you have them draw up a formal promissory note to record the date, amount, and repayment schedule. Just like all simulators, the more accurately you can make the process replicate reality, in this case a bank loan, the better the learning experience will be. This absolutely must be accomplished before you give them any money and before they buy the item. If they are borrowing for bad debt (see the "Good Debt Versus Bad Debt" section in Chapter 6), we also highly recommend that you charge a large interest rate, just like they would receive from a credit card company. Remember, the intent is not to give them a good deal. The intent is to give them a realistic experience of what can happen when they have consumer debt. Continuing with the previous example, let's assume your child has $500 to buy a $1,000 computer but is short the other $500. You could give them a loan for the $500 at 15 percent annual interest. This may sound high, but it's actually the average US credit card interest rate at the time of this writing. If the payments were split up over a year, then the total amount your child would have to pay back would be $575. If this were paid the simple way, in 12 equal monthly installments, then each payment would be $47.92.

$$\$500 \times .15 = \$75$$

$$\$500 + \$75 = \$575$$

$$\$575/12 = \$47.92$$

When they see that they will end up having to pay an extra $75 by the end of the loan, they may back out altogether. This wouldn't be a terrible result and would get the point across. If they do take on the loan, they will learn about being responsible for making payments and will experience firsthand what they will have to earn or give up in order to buy the item immediately. The more painful the lesson is for your child, the more vividly it will be remembered. It's also worth pointing out that if this were a credit card transaction and they only paid the minimum balance on the card, the 15 percent interest would continue not just for the first year but continually until the balance was paid off. This could cost them $75 or even more every year! Hopefully, after this experience, your child would more clearly comprehend what they were getting themselves into when taking out a loan or when taking on credit card debt. This may prove to be a valuable lesson that will later keep them out of that debt. Learning the lesson now to *not* take on bad debt and borrow for the purchase of consumer or luxury items that quickly go out of fashion or functionality can save your child large amounts of money over time. The lesson Loral would teach here would be that instead of taking on debt, you should have collaborated with your child to make the money for the computer together.

## BEGIN RELINQUISHING CONTROL OF THEIR STOCK INVESTMENTS

Recall the pilot training model for teaching your kids. Much like pilot ground school, we recommended you start talking to your child about stocks at an early age. In Chapter 6 we recommended that you discuss the fact that buying a stock is actually buying a small part of a business. We then encouraged you to have your child try out a stock simulator. Next, they had their first opportunity to touch the flight controls when we encouraged you to sell a few shares to your child so they could learn firsthand the value of investing in stocks. If you need a refresher on those topics, reread the sections "A Stock Is Ownership in a Business" and "Start a Stock Simulator for Your Child" in Chapter 6. Now that your child is older and capable of grasping more complicated matters, it's time to begin relinquishing more and more of the flight controls to their investments. It's the perfect time to begin letting them help make some choices on what stocks or other investments are owned in their IRA and college fund you faithfully set up for them when they were a baby. We're not suggesting you fully hand over the controls. Just let them fly for small segments of the flight until they prove they are proficient.

The first step toward letting your child take a more active role in their own investments is to discuss your own investments. If you've been following along in this book and talking with your child about money and investing for years, they can probably now grasp most adult concepts related to money. It is pivotal that you begin talking to them like an adult. Explain to them why you make the investment decisions you make. Not only will this help your child, but discussing it and having to explain it will ensure you understand your own methodology. We always absorb things better when forced to teach them. Sometimes explaining something to our child can even make us realize a flaw in our original thinking. If you can't clearly teach why you made an investment decision, then maybe you should have given that decision some extra consideration. When your child hears your reasoning behind an investment, it will help them learn not just what to do but how they should do it. For example, you might say, "I bought shares of Disney today. One of the reasons I did so is because I was thinking about how powerful their brand is and because I was so impressed with the operations at Disney World when we were there." You may be shocked at the conversations this might create. We've often been amazed at how much our kids have retained and the intelligent questions they ask when we instigate a conversation in this way. As your child gets older, they may even be a good springboard to bounce investment ideas off.

Before, when we recommended your kids buy a few shares of stock from you, the monetary amounts were small, and the idea was to get your kids interested in the idea of stocks. Now that they are beginning to take the controls of larger amounts of money, it's important that we advise them to be serious and deliberate in how they invest that money. This leads us to the next step in slowly relinquishing control of your child's investments—due diligence. The next section will discuss how to accomplish due diligence to make sure your child is aware of some of the things they need to investigate before purchasing an investment.

# DUE DILIGENCE

Due diligence is a difficult concept. Many adults don't know how to properly perform due diligence. In this section, we'll attempt to teach first you, the parent, some of the considerations we go through when we're considering an investment. We don't recommend that you bombard your child with all these concepts at once. Slowly integrate the following concepts into discussions throughout their daily lives and conversations.

The first step in conducting due diligence on any investment is not whether the investment you are considering is a good one; it's whether the investment is a good one *for you*. In order to figure this out, you need to understand yourself. The first step in this process is understanding your own money psychology. As we mentioned in the section "Risk Versus Reward for Investments" in Chapter 6, one of the most important things to know about yourself is your risk tolerance. Investing shouldn't make you afraid, stressed out, or keep you up at night. If it does, the risk profile of your investments is probably too high for your risk tolerance. This isn't to say you should keep your money under your mattress. Hopefully this book is teaching you how important it is to keep your money invested and working for you. You just need to find your balance. That balance may not be the same for you as it is for your child. That's OK. Your job is to be the wise one and help your child recognize their own risk tolerance. As we mentioned before, you can figure this out through games like Monopoly or through other life situations you witness your child experiencing. Although it's not a perfect correlation, even non-money-related situations can tell you a lot about your child's risk tolerance. When considering an investment, have your child weigh the reward of the investment versus the risk, and ensure the child is comfortable with

> **LORAL SAYS: I talk more about the concept of due diligence in my book *The Millionaire Maker's Guide to Wealth Cycle Investing.***

that risk. Just as we talked about before, if a greater reward is possible, one might be willing to take on more risk, but it still needs to be risk they are comfortable with. Therefore, the big questions would be the following:

- What is my risk tolerance?
- What is the investment's potential reward?
- What is the investment risk, and is it within my tolerance?

The next factors you need to know about yourself are related to your current financial situation. In her books, Loral calls these factors your Money Rules. Here's a list of a few of the factors:

- Time horizon—short-term versus long-term?
- Liquidity needed or not?
- Active versus passive?
- Tax-advantaged or not?
- Cash flow versus appreciation?

For example, how quickly will you need the money? Children generally have a very long time horizon for when they need the money, but they might need some money available to buy a car or pay for college. It wouldn't make sense to put their money in an investment that couldn't be pulled out for five years if they need it in two. Also, investments with a high volatility, as we also described in the section "Risk Versus Reward for Investments," are better suited for long-term time horizons because, even though they may have good overall returns, they may lose money in the short term.

A similar question would be how much liquidity is needed for the investment. In other words, do the investment funds need to be accessible while they are invested or not? Could they be pulled out in an emergency? An additional question you should ask yourself would be how much time and activity you would like to dedicate to the investment. Are you looking for an active, passive, or "pactive" investment? Recall the discussion in the Chapter 5 section "Active Income Versus

Passive Income." Kids are often quite busy with school and activities, so they probably can't invest in something that is quite active.

Another question to ask would be, is the investment best served in a tax-advantaged account or not? Different investments serve different tax strategies, so you need to consider if your child plans on making the investment with their IRA or a non-tax-advantaged account.

Finally, are you looking for cash flow or appreciation? Cash flow will help provide you money now but may raise your taxes. If you need money to live off of, then you'll need an investment that provides cash flow. Appreciation won't necessarily give you money immediately but may have a better overall return, and it may save you money in taxes. Your child doesn't need immediate cash flow from their investment, so they can probably choose an option that provides the best ROI. All these factors play a large role in determining what kind of investment is best for you or your child.

Due diligence is an ongoing discussion. The type of investment that is best for you may not be best for someone else. The type of investment that is best for you now might not be best for you in five years. In this section, we only discussed what type of investments are best for you. If you are interested in learning more about due diligence and how to do due diligence on specific investments, go to our website MakeYourKidsMillionaires.com for more resources.

## BUYING A CAR

The day is quickly approaching. Whether you dread it because you can't protect them, or you are looking forward to not being a taxi, soon your child will be driving. If you want to quit your second job as your child's personal Uber driver, this means they will need a vehicle. Your child will probably remember their first car forever. What will their memories be of that car? If your first reaction to this question was to go out and buy them a brand-new Ferrari, then you haven't been listening along the way. As we see it, there are two main questions you need to address when considering a vehicle for your child:

1. Who will pay for it?
2. How much should be paid for it?

We addressed the first question extensively in the Chapter 6 section "Have Your Child Create a Car Account." If you haven't read it or are having second thoughts about buying your child's car for them, please read it now. If you followed our advice before, your child began setting aside a significant amount of their income earned toward a car account. The reason they needed those savings was to help pay for their own car, or at least a significant portion of the costs. The only question remaining then is, how much should your child pay for their car? The answer will be determined in large part by how much they saved. This is by design. Isn't this how it works in the real world? If your child sat on the couch all day and ate bonbons, then they shouldn't get a very nice car. If they worked their rear off making money so they could afford a nicer car, it's OK to let them have a nicer car—with a few caveats.

## Four Reasons Not to Let Your Child Buy an Expensive Car

There are four main reasons we think you should avoid letting your child purchase an expensive car, even if they can afford it:

1. Insurance will be more expensive.
2. Depreciation will be larger.
3. You may be tempted to get a car loan.
4. The "regression rejection effect."

We'll discuss each of these in turn.

### Insurance Will Be More Expensive

It's no secret that insurance rates are much higher for 16-year-old drivers than adults. In many cases the insurance for a 16-year-old will be five times more expensive. Since insurance rates go up relative to the cost of the car, each incremental increase in car value creates a huge increase in insurance rates. Also, if they buy a very inexpensive car, it may not even make sense to purchase comprehensive or collision insurance, especially if they have saved up extra for repairs.

### Depreciation Will Be Larger

Although there are some rare exceptions, more expensive cars usually depreciate more than less expensive cars. In large part this is because more expensive cars are often newer. Newer cars depreciate very quickly in the first several years. In many cases a new car will lose 25 percent of its value in the first year. After three years new cars have usually lost 40 percent or more of their value, despite the fact that with normal mileage usage that three-year-old car has probably used less than 15 percent of its serviceable life span. Although supply constraints starting in 2020 reduced the depreciation on new vehicles, the previous depreciation trends had existed for many years across almost all models of vehicles and will almost certainly continue when the supply issues clear up.

Let's look at an example of typical car depreciation. Although this example is hypothetical to avoid becoming dated, we have actual examples using NADA price guide data on our website MakeYourKidsMillionaires.com. After three years, the 40 percent depreciation on a new car that was purchased for $30,000 would be $12,000. In other words, even on a relatively inexpensive new car you or your child would have lost $12,000 in value in a mere three years. But what if you had instead purchased a car that was already three years old? You could have saved the loss of that $12,000. Of course, the three-year-old car still depreciates in that time frame, but it depreciates much less per year since the percentage depreciation on cars is reduced as they get older and that percentage is coming off a smaller car value. By the time they are three years old, many cars only depreciate about $1,000 per year. Thus, if you instead purchased a three-year-old car you would only lose about $3,000 to depreciation in those same three years. A loss of $12,000 versus a loss of $3,000 is a difference of $9,000. If one accounts for the cheaper insurance we mentioned above, the cost savings for buying the three-year-old car is probably closer to $10,000. What if your child invested that $10,000 they saved?

Using the 10X Tactic from Chapter 3, we know that we can calculate the approximate value of that invested $10,000 (given 10 percent returns) after 25 years by simply adding a zero to the end. Thus, the $10,000 in savings from buying a three-year-old car instead of a new car would grow to approximately

**The $10,000 in savings from buying a three-year old car instead of a new car would grow to approximately $100,000 if invested for 25 years and $1 million if invested for 50 years. One decision like this could make you or your child a millionaire!**

$100,000 if invested for 25 years and $1 million if invested for 50 years. One decision like this could make you or your child a millionaire! Just think how much money your child could have if they did this every time they bought a car. Since car companies often only change their models every four or five years, it is quite possible to buy a three- or four-year-old vehicle that looks exactly the same as a new car. Only true car aficionados could tell the difference.

If you really want to ramp up your child's potential savings and future investments, you could purchase a car approximately eight years old. This would lower the price point significantly, greatly decrease the depreciation (often down to $500 per year) and insurance, and probably save over $20,000, resulting in double the future value. Even an eight-year-old car is still a depreciating asset, but at least it's not depreciating as much as the newer versions. Older models would suffer from even less depreciation. The lower your price point, the less depreciation you will have to endure. A pre-owned vehicle may not be new, but it's still new to your child. We believe an inexpensive car is a small sacrifice relative to its huge impact toward helping them become a millionaire.

### You May Be Tempted to Get a Car Loan

The most sensible way to buy a car is nearly always to pay in cash. A car loan is the definition of bad debt because, as we just described, it is on a depreciating asset. If you let your child buy a car with debt, not only will their net worth be drained by depreciation of the car and the insurance for the car, but it would be further depleted by the interest they would have to pay on the loan. Because of the depreciation, people often end up owing more on the loan than their car is worth. Please don't put your child in this predicament. If they don't have enough to buy an expensive car with cash, then they certainly don't have enough to buy it with debt.

### The "Regression Rejection Effect"

Letting your child purchase an expensive car for their first vehicle, even if it is paid for in cash, may set them up for a lifetime of Lifestyle Cycle debt. Here's why. Psychologically, it is difficult for people to be willing to go backward and take a step down in life. We always want to feel like we are progressing, getting better things, and stepping up in the world. Some might call it "leveling up." We talked about this concept earlier in the "Financial Discipline" section in Chapter 5.

If you buy your 16-year-old child a $50,000 Porsche, what will happen five years later in life when they tire of their "old" Porsche? They'll feel like they need to "step up" to a $60,000 vehicle. Do you know many 21-year-olds who can afford a $60,000 vehicle? They would probably have to take out a large car loan of bad debt. Even if they could afford a car this expensive or make the payments, what would that do to their saving rate? In the years they should be investing and taking advantage of the compounding effects of time—the main advantage young people have— they'll instead be trying to pay off a car loan on a depreciating vehicle. Unless

**KYLE SAYS: People will go to extraordinary lengths to not regress in life, including rejecting the prospect of doing so, even when it makes logical sense. This effect is so pervasive that I've even created a name for it. I call it the "regression rejection effect." The "regression rejection effect" can make normally prudent and thrifty people go into consumer debt even when they know better. They just can't help themselves.**

they happen to be a Mark Zuckerberg, you are practically dooming them to a life of battling the Lifestyle Cycle and burgeoning debt. If you haven't figured it out yet—almost all kids think they will be the next Mark Zuckerberg. Most won't. The "regression rejection effect" is real. Don't set your child up for it by letting them get a first vehicle that is too expensive.

### Our Recommendations

Overwhelmed yet? In summary, here are our recommendations:

1. When your child is young, decide what portion of their vehicle they will have to buy themselves. They should pay a significant amount.
2. Communicate your decision to your child by the age of 10 so they will have several years to earn the money for the car they want.
3. When they reach age 16, follow through and only let them spend what they have earned or what was otherwise agreed upon when they were age 10.
4. Don't let your child (or yourself) use a loan to purchase a car, or any other depreciating asset. If they can't afford the car they want, then they need to learn the lesson that they should have worked harder to make more money.

# INSURANCE

We've discussed insurance a few times already in this book. We addressed it when we talked about the disability insurance Logan paid his mother in case he couldn't work for a specific time period. The main purpose of this would be to introduce the concept of insurance to your child at an early age so they can begin understanding how it can provide protection from risk. We also discussed insurance in the previous section "Buying a Car." Whether you want to pay your child's car insurance or let them pay it themselves is up to you. Some people believe making them pay it themselves will make them less likely to get in accidents. You could consider a hybrid plan in which you paid for their insurance, but they would pay the difference if your insurance rates went up due to something they did like an accident or traffic ticket. Either way, it's important that they recognize that their actions have a monetary effect on what gets paid for insurance. It's a good way to enforce the concept that actions have consequences. Think back to the discussions on credit when we described how your credit rating follows you for a long time. Remind them that their driving record does the same thing.

Another factor to discuss with your child regarding car insurance would be how much they should get. Explain the different types of car insurance like liability, comprehensive, and collision. You should also probably discuss the terms associated with insurance like deductible, premium, claim, appraisal, and adjuster. These are common terms that most adults know but your kids probably don't. Show them your insurance bill to help them understand what each version costs, and how you would file an insurance claim if you needed to. This would also be a good time to explain why liability insurance is required and what they should do if they get in an accident. As we mentioned in the last section, if they buy a very inexpensive car, they may not even need to purchase comprehensive or collision insurance, especially if they have saved up extra for repairs. This would be a form of self-insuring. After all, Geico doesn't make all those hilarious commercials because it is losing money. Explain that they could reduce the cost of the insurance and keep a liquid fund available for repairs, allowing them to forgo all but the legally required insurance. In general, if your risk is lower than your perceived risk in the eye of the insurance company, then it might be more economical in the long run to self-insure. You just need to ensure that you have funds to fix your car so that your car damage doesn't cause you income damage when you can no longer drive to work or your business.

So far, we've talked mostly about car insurance since that is probably the only insurance that is of immediate concern to your child at this age. However, while you are talking about car insurance with your child, it's probably worth mentioning and briefly discussing some of the other types of insurance they may eventually choose to purchase. These would include homeowner's insurance, renter's insurance, flood insurance, health insurance, disability insurance (which we touched on before), life insurance, long-term care insurance, valuable personal property insurance, and umbrella insurance.

Warranties are another topic related to insurance that could also be discussed at this time, including car warranties, home warranties, and merchandise warranties. Although we aren't generally a big fan of warranties, we have used home warranties to successfully reduce unexpected expenses on investment properties at times.

Identity protection is another item related to insurance that you should probably have yourself and should also discuss with your child. As the world gets more digital and we conduct an increasing amount of our business and transactions online, our exposure to identity theft goes up considerably.

You don't need to go into great depth on any of these topics at this point in their life, but it is worth talking about how they work and why they might be useful. It's also worth talking about situations when you might want to self-insure and what the risks of that could be. Like many things, choosing which insurance to get, how much of it to get, and what deductible you want often comes down to your risk tolerance and how much emergency funds you have set aside to pay for any uninsured losses. Talking through these factors with your child will help them make informed decisions about what insurance they will need in the future.

# CHAPTER 8

# AGES 16 AND 17

*Your economic security does not lie in your job; it lies in your own power to produce—to think, to learn, to create, to adapt. That's true financial independence. It's not having wealth; it's having the power to produce wealth. It's intrinsic.*
—Stephen R. Covey

Can you believe your child is driving now? With the newfound independence of being able to get around town on their own comes even more independence and pulling away from their parents. You may have to be more creative in finding engaging ways to get your child to keep learning about money and entrepreneurship. We have some ideas to help. Hands-on is the lesson of this age group. Recall the pilot training model from earlier in the book comparing your child's journey to financial freedom to flight school. By now, your child has mostly completed their academics part of training. It's time for them to take the controls of their own financial flight and show off the money savvy you've been teaching them for so many years. You are still there to supervise and keep an eye on them, but you need to give them some real-world experience. Don't let them shy away. Engage them and get them to say YES! These are your final years to impact their development. Their solo flight is only a few years away. We know. That's a scary thought.

**Helpful reminder: Don't forget to continue teaching and doing all the things you introduced in the previous chapters and expanding on them as your child's understanding improves.**

# STARTING A REAL BUSINESS

Whether your child's earlier entrepreneurial endeavors panned out or not, now is the time to help them grow wings and fly. They are now nearly adults, as intimidating as it may seem. They are capable of adult dreams and ideas. Some of the billion-dollar ideas and businesses began in the brains of teenagers. If you've cultivated their business spirit, their mind is probably constantly spinning with potential business ideas, but they aren't always willing to share them with their parents. If they are like some kids this age, they barely want to talk to their parents at all. What better way to create some shared time together than helping them start a real business—a real Cash Machine?

You may be able to get their mind working or get them to open up about their own ideas by saying things like, "I've been thinking it would be cool to start a business, but I can't decide exactly what it would be. Do you have any ideas?" Perhaps you might even be able to lead them to the idea by talking about what they love doing or have been told they were good at. Remember, the best Cash Machines involve businesses using skill sets your child already possesses. This is just a starter business to help them learn how to earn. To begin feeding their Wealth Cycle, the Cash Machine needs to generate revenue immediately.

## Cash Machine Action Plan

- Discover the skills you already have.
- Generate a business idea based on those skills.
- Model the idea after a similar business.
- Test the sales potential through revenue modeling.
- Design a Cash Machine plan.
- Build a team.
- Develop the marketing and sales strategies.

The story that follows describes how Kyle helped inspire his son to start a real business at age 16. At the end of the story, we'll analyze how Bryce followed the Cash Machine Action Plan.

### "Cyborspace": The Virtual Reality Business That Was Real

One day Kyle's 16-year-old son Bryce came home super excited. He had just been at his best friend's house, who had recently received a new virtual reality (VR) headset and gaming system for Christmas. Bryce raved about how amazing it was and how much better it was than traditional gaming. He said he wanted to spend $400 of the money he had earned the year before mowing lawns to buy the headset. Kyle reminded him that most of the money he had earned would be needed for him to eventually upgrade the old truck he had bought with his own money earlier that year. Bryce was undeterred. He went on to explain how he and his friend Peyton had already discussed ideas to use the VR headset he intended to buy for a business.

> **LORAL SAYS:** In my book *The Millionaire Maker's Guide to Creating a Cash Machine for Life*, I talk about the best way I've found to start a business. It's called the Cash Machine Action Plan.

Now he had Kyle's attention. Kyle had always tried to foster Bryce's entrepreneurial mindset, but now Bryce was old enough that simple ideas weren't enough. Kyle wanted details. They chatted for several minutes about possible ways Bryce could create a business, but it was clear this business idea was still in its infant stages. Kyle told him he would consider letting him buy the headset but only if he could prove he could monetize it by making the money back with his business.

Peyton brought the VR system to their house the next day, and Kyle too was impressed with how immersive the VR gaming experience could be. He could see how people would pay to play it, but it still wasn't a business yet. Bryce and Peyton and Kyle talked for over an hour about the possible ways they could make it a business. Kyle let the two teens do most of the talking, but he asked questions to help them clarify their ideas for how the business would work. In the end, they decided they would do a business where they would provide in-home virtual reality gaming for parties. The party host would purchase their services for a set period of time, and they would bring their computer and virtual reality gaming gear. They would also provide instruction and assistance throughout the event.

As the details began to crystalize, Kyle could see the teens' excitement growing with every passing moment. However, Kyle had witnessed the difference between business exuberance and actual work, so he told them he wanted to see a business plan. Bryce had heard of a business plan but admitted he had no idea what it entailed. Kyle explained the details of a business plan and told them they could search for a template online. If they could provide him with that, he promised to help with their business. However, the purchase of a VR headset for Bryce would have to wait on "proof of concept." "What's that?" they queried. "Let's deal with the business plan first," Kyle advised. It took a few days, but the teens did produce a business plan. The first draft was a little less detailed than Kyle desired, but by the second draft he was happy with what they had provided and convinced their plan could work.

Over the next several months Bryce and Peyton labored through all the steps toward setting up a real business. They began marketing when they purchased a website domain, created their own website, set up a Facebook page and Instagram account, purchased a banner, and made fliers. They also started accounting when they opened a bank account, set up an online payment system, and created invoices and receipts. Then they started their sales process when they practiced their sales script, ops-tested the system, performed dry runs, and had their first client. They even set up a tent at the local "First Friday" event downtown and sold gaming time by the minute to passers-by as they generated enthusiasm and marketed their business. Their customers loved it. This was the proof of concept Kyle was looking for.

When Bryce mentioned that he could purchase a used headset from another friend at a discount, Kyle was finally convinced that he could monetize the idea and gave him his blessing. As their business began to take off and they started bringing in revenue, Kyle and Bryce continued talking about things like marketing, accounting, sales, logistics, customer relations, and all the other aspects of a business. Bryce and Peyton often surprised Kyle with their ingenuity, and they even used targeted Facebook marketing to reach their focused audience. The whole experience was extremely educational for them, and the business was thriving right up until the Covid-19 pandemic made a direct assault on their business model. Despite this setback, they were still profitable and looked forward to starting the business back up in the future. More important, by opening a Cash Machine they learned important lessons about being entrepreneurs. They also learned how to turn their passions into a business and that, if they want something, they have to put in the work to get it.

Even though Bryce wasn't aware of the Cash Machine Action Plan at the time, he unknowingly followed many of its steps. For more details and specifics, read Loral's book *The Millionaire Maker's Guide to Building a Cash Machine*.

### Cash Machine Action Plan

**Discover the skills you already have.** Bryce and his friend Peyton had strong computer and gaming skills, so starting a business around these two concepts made a lot of sense. Peyton also had experience making websites.

**Generate a business idea based on those skills.** Even before Kyle became involved, Bryce and Peyton had already formed the beginning of a business idea centered around their skills.

**Model the idea after a similar business.** One of the reasons Bryce and Peyton settled on the idea of the party catering business model was because there were two similar business models already in town. One had a trailer with non-VR video games inside that could be brought to parties. A different local business brought a projector and large screen to parties so they could have outdoor movie nights. Bryce knew the owner of this business, and it was very profitable.

**Test the sales potential through revenue modeling.** During the First Friday event, Bryce and Peyton were able to test the sales potential of the product. They spent much of the time asking customers for feedback on pricing models and their interest levels for various pricing options. They also tested different pricing plans and discount options to find the best combination. Then they estimated how much revenue they thought the business could bring in on a monthly and weekly basis.

**Design a Cash Machine plan.** Kyle insisted on a business plan to be certain Bryce and Peyton were serious. The business plan outlined all the details for the business and how it would generate revenue and handle expenses.

**Build a team.** Bryce and Peyton were a team from the beginning. They had complementary skill sets to help run the business. They also hired another employee to help run the events when neither of them could attend. Kyle and his wife Tracy provided guidance and mentorship.

**Develop the marketing and sales strategies.** Bryce and Peyton had taken some online marketing classes already, so they knew most of the marketing basics. Their strategy for directing ads at specific age groups and demographics with targeted Facebook advertising was impressive. They also used the First Friday event to good effect, along with encouraging customers to tell their friends. Because they recognized that most people couldn't really comprehend the immersive experience of virtual reality until they tried it, they offered event discounts to anybody who tried the event at their booth during First Friday events.

Sometimes your child's entrepreneurial inspiration originates in their imagination like Bryce and Peyton's. Sometimes it's right in front of them, happens organically, and doesn't require huge amounts of planning. In the following story, the situation required Logan to act quickly.

## Logan's Limo Service

Loral's son, Logan, was 16 and had just bought his first 4x4 truck. He and his mother had just returned home from a day of skiing at Heavenly ski resort in Lake Tahoe, Nevada, where they lived. They lived in an area where many people would off-trail ski and end at the bottom of a hill near their house far away from the lifts. The off-trail skiers would have to hike back to the lift, which for some could take hours. Ridesharing services were just beginning to become more prevalent back then, and Logan recognized an opportunity similar to the one that eventually made these services so successful and widespread. Logan asked Loral if she thought he could get paid to pick the skiers up and take them to the lift. Loral said "I bet you could get $20 per person for doing that. Go get in your truck and try it!" Together they came up with a quick script of what to say. Though Logan was a little uncomfortable at first having to talk to strangers, Loral said "If I have to do it, I get half the money." Out the door he went alone.

To Logan's surprise, on his first trip he picked up four people and made $80. He quickly came back for another load. The skiers kept coming, and he kept driving them. Next thing he knew he had made a handsome profit. With practice he learned several lessons. For example, he needed to get the money up front. He also needed to ensure he had change. This became a regular weekend business. Logan even expanded his business later to include driving his friends around town to wherever they needed to go. Since he drove a 4x4 truck rather than an actual limo, he could take people up the snowy mountains where other ride services couldn't go. Over the course of the next few years, he made several thousand dollars from this pop-up business that was right in front of him all along.

What businesses can you plan for, and what businesses are right in front of you? Though Logan's business was more like a twenty-first-century lemonade stand than a cash machine, it still made him a lot of money. It's important that you have the conversation with your child to figure out which model works for your child's situation and that you are in a constant conversation about making money.

# PAYING TAXES ON THEIR BUSINESS

Hopefully by now your child has a thriving, profitable business. Whether your child goes on to be an entrepreneur or not, it's important they understand basic bookkeeping, including how to pay their taxes. If your child is like ours was at this age, they love making money but hate keeping up with the books. Come to think of it, this is still one of our least favorite parts of owning a business. Unfortunately, it's also one of the most important parts.

We've already covered in this book many of the topics that will help your child's accounting and taxes. In Chapter 7, we covered "Forecasting," "The Balance Sheet," and "The Income Statement." If these processes are accomplished and kept up to date, the bookkeeping during tax time comes much easier. One of the big reasons so many small businesses go out of business is because they don't know how to track the money flow in their own organization. If you don't realize which activities or clients are providing most of your income, how can you find more of those clients or activities? How can you improve or get rid of those that aren't providing you income? How can you track which expenses are helping or hindering your bottom line?

Here's where the basic accounting fundamentals we taught earlier like keeping an income statement will come in handy. As businesses get more complex, they often turn to accounting software to help manage their profits and losses. This software isn't free and does have a learning curve. Your child may prefer to use basic spreadsheet software like Microsoft Excel or Google Sheets. These can be obtained much cheaper (or possibly free), and your child probably already has some experience with them at this age. If not, it's a great time to learn. It's easy to either download a template or start your own. The key is that the spreadsheet or program keeps track of all the money flow within the company. At a minimum, the earnings entries should include the date, amount, who paid, what was sold, and whether the payment cleared. Expenses should include the date, amount, who it was paid to, what was purchased, and perhaps a comments section for why it was purchased. We like to create separate columns on our expense sheet to account for the different expense categories like rent, utilities, office supplies, advertising, website and software, internet and telephone, vehicle expenses, licenses and permits, dues and membership fees, insurance, bank fees, legal and professional fees, training and education, equipment, business meals, charity, and home office costs. Most of these coincide with categories you report as deductions on your taxes that will save you money, so sorting them as you go makes it easier at tax time. Obviously, your child's business will not have all these categories of expenses and may have a few other categories.

Your child should keep business receipts and invoices as a "burden of proof" to the IRS if they are ever audited. Will your 16-year-old's business be audited? We hope not, and it's unlikely. Still, it's a good idea to get them in the habit of keeping good records for their future businesses. The main reason to keep good records is so they can deduct all the expenses they can legally take. As we said in the "Taxes" section in Chapter 6, there is nothing wrong with making sure you don't pay more than your fair share of taxes. Deductions and expenses were created so business owners would take them. Have your child take a close look at the expense categories we listed in the previous paragraph and think about whether any of them could be applied to their business. One of the best benefits of being a business owner is having the ability to pay your expenses before you are taxed instead of with after-tax money like employees. Tax professionals can be worth their weight in gold when it comes to finding allowable expenses and should be consulted often. We've found that having a tax professional on your wealth team can often save you more money than their fees. Your child's business may not rival Amazon yet, but that doesn't mean they can't look for legal ways to lower their taxes.

Now that your child has mastered bookkeeping, it's time for them to use all the information they've been tracking to file their taxes. If your child is just an employee, they could probably file an IRS Form 1040EZ. If they have a business but it is a sole proprietorship, they will file an IRS Form 1040 and may have to fill out a Schedule C and

Schedule SE. At the most basic level, your child needs to understand what portion of their business profit they will get to keep. Walk them through filing their taxes and how to get their refund, if any. If your child doesn't need to file taxes, walk them through yours so they can get a feel for it. If you are clueless about taxes as well and rely on an accountant, then have them sit in while you talk to your accountant about your taxes. Have your child write down some questions they may have. Make note of the actual effective rate of tax for your taxes or theirs. Remind them that the tax brackets are graduated. If their income is small, their effective tax rate should be very low or possibly even zero. If they will owe taxes and it isn't already pulled out, it's a good idea to set aside a portion of their monthly income to make sure they can pay the taxes when they are due.

Now would be a good time to revisit the concept of the Roth IRA and other tax-advantaged accounts discussed in Chapter 2 in the section "Investor Mindset: Tax-Advantaged Accounts" and how these accounts can help them avoid paying more taxes later when they are likely in a higher tax bracket. Speaking to your child about taxes isn't always fun. If your child does find it fun, then congratulations! You might be raising your own future family accountant! Either way, showing your child that the business of tracking their money and paying their fair share of taxes isn't as scary as they may have thought will demystify the intimidating part of owning a business. It might even make them more likely to pursue their dream and start a business.

## REVEAL YOUR FINANCIAL LEGACY PLAN

If you have followed the guidance in this book, your child at this age has a considerable amount of knowledge about money. In fact, they probably know more than most adults. Several years have now passed since the Chapter 6 section "Your Money Isn't Their Money . . . or Is It?" when we advised you to begin discussing your personal financial situation with your child and discuss with them whether your money was also theirs or not. This is a continuation of your legacy conversation. This conversation will be more detailed than the previous one.

Your child is only a few years from potentially being out on their own. They can handle it now.

Wouldn't you share your knowledge about your experiences with life and love with them? Money should be no different. If you made some great choices with your investments and have a healthy nest egg, now is the time to reveal it and have a conversation about it. Don't you want them to know so they can make similar decisions? The temptation is to be worried that revealing your full financial situation may cause them to be spoiled. If you've been teaching them the concepts in this book all along, that should be very unlikely. Trust your parenting. This is especially true if you revealed to them after reading the section "Your Money Isn't Their Money . . . or Is It?" that your money indeed is not theirs. If you aren't giving them any money, they have no reason to be spoiled.

**LORAL SAYS: Remember, it's important to "Live out loud." This means talking about money with your child and sharing your financial successes as well as failures with your teenager.**

If you do plan on giving your children a portion of your wealth, it is important that they understand how that wealth transfer will occur. Now is the time to explain any IRAs, trusts, entities, life insurance, or special education funds you may have set up. The availability of college funds may change their plans and potential choices, so they need to be aware of these accounts now. Explain when they will take possession of these accounts and what their responsibilities will be. Though the full transfer may not occur until their thirties as with Loral's estate plan, they still need to know what to expect.

Remember, the goal is to slowly transition them into these responsibilities, so giving them a surprise windfall when they turn 18 or older won't help them be responsible managers of that wealth. You need to be sure they are ready and groom them for generational wealth. They need to appreciate your motivation for why you are guiding them in order to comprehend how to take over these entities and accounts. Revealing the details of these accounts and entities should get them excited to learn.

Of course, not everybody has been fortunate enough to build wealth. If you made some mistaken decisions and are in a lot of bad debt, it's OK to tell your children about it so they can learn from your mistakes. In fact, it's your duty. It's important to share the lessons of your choices. Knowing them will help them avoid these choices for themselves. Remember the famous quote from George Santayana, who stated, "Those who cannot remember the past are condemned to repeat it." Don't condemn your children over a history they haven't even been taught. Explain to them the lessons you learned and how you are making better decisions now and in the future. They probably already realize more about your financial situation than you think. Children are very perceptive. Whether they admit it or not they are constantly listening to us. Ignoring conversations about your choices while pretending you did everything right will only make them mistrust you and not listen to your guidance.

## COLLEGE PREP AND STUDENT LOANS

Earlier in this book, in the Chapter 4 section "Set Up a Tax-Advantaged Education Account," we began introducing the topic of college preparation. It's a good time to go back to that section and review. By now, this should have been part of your plans and conversations for years. This section will discuss whether your child is going to college or not and how they are going to pay for it.

The first thing you and your child need to consider is whether they want to go to college at this time. Though we've been encouraging you to make your kids entrepreneurs, we still think college is a great experience and a good idea. That being said, some kids will not be interested in college and will want to do something else like start a business, get a job in an industry they are interested in, or even join the military. There is no singular path that is right for every child. Though you may have had a plan for them when they were born, the reality is that they will soon be an adult and will ultimately have the final say in what they do with their life. Now is the time to have the conversation with your child about what *they* want to do.

If college is the choice for your child, let's look at how it will be funded. Scholarships are always an option. It's not too late to motivate your child to do what it takes to get as many scholarships as possible. As mentioned before, there are numerous scholarships that don't even get used, so start getting smart on how to find them. Don't forget to look at local scholarships. If you did set up an education account when we recommended it before, then you are already set. If you didn't, you have some alternative planning to do and your options are more limited. For you, student debt might be a solution.

Student loans are a hot topic these days. In the spectrum of good debt versus bad debt, we believe that student loans fall closer to good debt than they do to bad debt. However, there are a few caveats. In theory, student debt should be an investment in the student's future. In theory, student loans allow the student to attend college when they otherwise couldn't. If this allows them to eventually have a higher paying job or be a better entrepreneur, then that student debt can be considered an investment. The fact that student loans usually have very low rates is also in their favor. In fact, the rates are so low that it might be a better investment to take on the student debt than to pay for the tuition outright. In Logan's situation, that's what they did. They took the zero percent loans and kept the money invested with an average investment return of 15 percent. When the student loan interest rate kicks into a higher multiple, they will then pay it off with the money from the investments, including the returns from those investments.

Although student loans could be considered an investment, not all investments are good investments. For a school loan to be a good investment it must have a positive return. Returns from attending college can come in many different forms, including social, intellectual, spiritual, and emotional growth. Colleges can also have a monetary return in their ability to improve the graduate's capacity to make more money as either an entrepreneur or employee. Of course, every person's situation is different and there are a hundred other factors we haven't considered. Just a few of these would include the degree one gets, the earning years lost while attending college, and the business acumen one has before attending college. If you teach your kids the concepts in this book, they will be much more prepared to have a higher income whether they attend college or not.

Even if you decide that college may have a positive return for your child, it's not obvious whether the return is equal for different priced schools. For example, although attending one college may be a good financial investment, that doesn't mean a less expensive college might not have a better return. If an expensive college were twice as expensive (assuming twice the student debt) as another one, it would have to result in twice the income difference to maintain the same returns. This isn't to say that all less expensive schools have a better return. The results completely depend on your assumptions regarding how much extra your child would earn in the expensive school versus the less expensive school.

The college decision can be life-defining. The sooner you start having serious conversations with your child about this topic, the better informed they will be.

## ADVANCED CREDIT CARDS—
## FRIEND OR FOE?

In the last section on credit cards in Chapter 6, we encourage you to "Get Your Child an Authorized User Credit Card." At that point we wanted you to use a credit card you already had so that you could provide a simulation experience for your child and demonstrate how to appropriately use a credit card without ever paying interest. Now we are going to move to the next phase of the pilot training model—supervision. Though you supervised your child before, they will now be given more freedom to "fly the jet" by allowing them to have their own credit card.

Though children aren't allowed to open a credit card by themselves until they are 18, that doesn't prevent you from opening an additional card for yourself that will effectively be used only by your child. You merely need to open the new card and again add your child as an authorized user. The difference from before is that you will expect your child to handle all the aspects of this new card, including paying it off and managing their expenditures. Of course, you are still ultimately responsible to the credit card company for ensuring the card gets paid and your name is still on the card, but this credit card will be treated like your child's card alone. You will still need to supervise their use of this card. After all, your credit score is still on the line. But the goal is to let them handle the entire process. After all, in a few short years when they turn 18, they will be besieged by credit card companies trying to get them started with or without your consent. Wouldn't you feel more comfortable knowing you had a few years of supervising their good credit card habits before their first solo flight?

Despite our best efforts to persuade you, some of you may still feel that credit cards are a bad idea. After all, credit cards get a bad reputation. Many financial gurus dismiss them as inherently evil. We believe this characterization to be misguided. These gurus believe that you don't have the discipline to use credit cards as they were intended— as a tool to help you use your money. This is like saying that all knives (including steak knives and paring knives) are bad because some people get cut by them. Everybody has the power to be disciplined enough to use credit cards to their benefit and to not be cut. If you teach the principles in this book, your child will not be the lowest common denominator, for whom the only way forward is to cut up their credit cards.

In Chapter 6 we talked about "Good Debt Versus Bad Debt." Though we previously spoke about the dangers of credit card debt, the reality is that credit card debt can be good debt or bad debt depending on how you use it. In the previous debt section, we focused primarily on what you buy with your debt. We made the case that if you are buying assets, that debt could be considered good. Conversely, if you are buying liabilities, that debt would be considered bad. This same concept could apply to credit cards. Credit cards are obviously a bad idea if they make you more likely to purchase more liabilities and feed the Lifestyle Cycle by getting further and further into bad debt. This type of behavior can make you enter a credit card debt spiral and end up on the wrong side of the compound interest equation.

Let's look at an example of how compound interest can work against you. Note how it contrasts with the compound interest example where compound interest is working for you. Much like a savings account's interest, interest calculation on a credit card is usually compounded daily. Although this would make the interest accrue more quickly, we'll just use the annual percentage rate (APR) to make the math simpler. It is worth noting, however, that for larger interest rates like those associated with credit cards, the fact that the interest is compounded daily can have a much larger effect than for small interest rates like those of a savings account.

For this example, let's assume your child accrued $1,000 in credit card debt. His credit card interest rate is 15 percent. At this rate, if your child didn't make any payments on his credit card at all, his debt would double in less than five years. Fortunately, credit card companies generally require a minimum payment. If you don't pay at least the minimum payment each month you will destroy your credit rating and eventually have debt collectors knocking at your door or garnishing your wages. For this example, we'll assume your child's credit card company requires a minimum payment of 2 percent of the balance, not uncommon in the credit card world. If your child paid only the minimum balance, how long would it take to pay off the debt? How much would they pay in interest?

*Time to pay off debt: 118 months*

*Total interest paid: $851.01*

That's right. It would take nearly 10 years to pay off that $1,000 debt! Even though they would pay off more than the monthly accrued interest each month, they wouldn't pay off much principal, so the interest would just keep accruing on most of the $1,000 balance.

The example above demonstrates why you absolutely *must* teach your child not to carry a balance on their credit card. There may be some extremely rare cases where it might make sense, but these are so unlikely they aren't even worth discussing with your child. Credit cards aren't evil, but unpaid credit card balances can be. To the uneducated or undisciplined person who carries a balance and lets the interest work against them, credit cards can indeed be a dangerous foe. But what if credit cards are used with discipline and don't lead to rampant consumerism and spending in the Lifestyle Cycle? What if they were only used to purchase things you really needed or even wealth-generating assets? Could credit cards be your child's friend? What if they were paid off fully every month so that you didn't have to pay any interest at all? Believe it or not, to the disciplined individual, credit cards can be a good thing.

Let's discuss a few ways credit cards can be your friend. First, credit cards are very convenient. Not having to haul around a wallet or purse full of cash makes life simpler and potentially even safer. Most cards also have built-in fraud insurance to protect your purchases. If you know your card is stolen you can call your credit card company to put a hold on the card. You can't do that with cash.

Next, if you pay your bill in full every month, credit cards can be considered a 30-day interest-free loan from the company that provides them. In some cases, you may even have an introductory period up to one year with zero percent interest. This would be a one-year interest-free loan. This allows you to use other people's money, at least in the short term, to pay your expenses or possibly even buy assets. Additionally, most credit cards have rewards programs that give you points when you use them. These points have real value that often ranges from 1 to 2.5 percent of every purchase. Though it doesn't seem like much, these points can add up, especially if you use them for business expenses. When these points get added up over the course of a year, they can often fund airline trips or other perks, or even be redeemed for cash.

We've both funded much of our travel through credit card points we've accrued. The credit cards give you these points to incentivize you to use their card in part because they know full well that many people will not pay their balance in full and the interest payments they receive from these misguided people will more than fund the points they reward. Finally, regardless of whether you like it or not, digital currency is the future. In the past, debit cards and credit cards were the ways that digital currency was transacted. In the future, digital currencies like cryptocurrency will likely play a huge role in how your kids live their life.

What if you and your child chose to beat the credit cards at their own game and never carry a balance that required you to pay interest? You would be getting these credit card companies to pay you (in points) to let them give you a 30-day (or longer) loan. It really is that easy. Teach your children to be disciplined. Don't let them be the lowest common denominator that fills the credit card company's coffers. The final and perhaps biggest advantage and most important reason to establish an authorized user credit card for your child is to begin developing their credit. We discussed this at length in the section "Get Your Child an Authorized User Credit Card" in Chapter 7. By building a good credit history early on, your child will be able to use that credit to help them buy a house or even an investment property. Without a seasoned credit history, their credit score will be affected, and they will either have higher interest rates or may not be able to take advantage of these profitable investments at all. This circumstance would put a huge roadblock on their ability to use other people's money to make them money. Once your child turns 18, they can open their own credit card and build their positive credit reputation even more.

Many people prefer the use of debit cards to credit cards. Debit cards are not a loan like a credit card, and they only provide access to funds that are in your account. You can't spend what isn't in the account, so you can't amass debt like you can with a credit card. If your child is the type of person who doesn't have the discipline to pay off his or her credit card balance every month, we would agree that your child should stick to a debit card. If your child is particularly poor at delaying gratification or is especially impulsive in making purchases, these might be other reasons to stick with a debit card. Debit cards have the same advantage of convenience and preventing you from having to carry around a wallet or purse full of cash. However, they do not have any of the other advantages associated with credit cards. These advantages can be quite substantial depending on the situation. We prefer educating and coaching people with the empowering belief that they can use credit cards intelligently and with discipline rather than assuming they are incapable of doing so.

In the end, as with all things, it will be up to you to decide how you want to teach your child and whether you want to encourage credit cards or not. However, we encourage you to think of it in the following way. By this age (16 to 18), would you hesitate to give your child a steak knife to help cut their food? Of course not. You taught your child the dangers of knives when they were much younger, demonstrated how to use them, and supervised your child the first several times they used one. By now your kids are smart enough to avoid the dangers of knives in order to make cutting their food much easier and more convenient. Don't make your kids saw away at that financial steak with a spoon. Give them the best tools for the job and trust that you have given them the knowledge and training to succeed.

## ADVANCED FORECASTING: FINANCE TRACKING PROGRAMS

In the second section of Chapter 7 we introduced you to the concept of Forecasting. We explained how important it is to plan for both your expenses and income and to pay yourself first. In the following sections we went on to describe some of the tools like balance sheets and income statements that can help you forecast. The means for filling these out was either by hand or by using a digital spreadsheet tool like Microsoft Excel or Google Sheets. These tools are still important, but there are easier ways to compile the data in your balance sheet and income statement than hand-typing or cutting and pasting the data directly from your checkbook or bank accounts. Now that they are older and have some money to play with, it's time to let your child get in the actual aircraft and start trying out the controls themselves. Just keep a close eye on their forecasting so you can step in and take the controls to correct their flight path if necessary. Finance tracking programs are the modern way to manage your balance sheets and income statements and, thus, conduct the forecasting that is necessary to stay on track for your goals.

If you haven't already set up a finance tracking program for yourself, we highly recommend that you do so right away. Not only does it simplify forecasting and potentially bill-paying, it also keeps your goals in the forefront of your mind. With these programs in place, it only takes a few minutes to check up on your progress toward reaching PI$\geq$E.

By this age, your child is likely very familiar with "apps" and computer programs and spends a good deal of their time on their "screens" anyway, so why not take advantage of that? The internet has a multitude of programs and apps available that can help your child keep track of their income and expenses. Some programs you can get them started on include Quicken, Personal Capital, EveryDollar, Mint, Goodbudget, or YNAB. Many of these programs are free. Most have a desktop as well as a mobile version so you can manage your finances at home or on the go, although the functionality may be limited for the mobile version. New applications in this field are constantly appearing, so we recommend doing some browsing to see which one is currently top-rated. These apps allow you to sync your bank and investment accounts directly to the app. The advantages of this are many. First, it can automatically keep track of all your balances in one place with one easy logon. Because it's done automatically, this can prevent transcription errors. It also allows you to quickly and daily review your assets, liabilities, income, and expenses. Many of these programs can produce numerous reports with the touch of a button, like the balance sheet and income statement, or even accounts payable and receivable reports or cash flow statements.

Another advantage of finance tracking programs is that they can usually automatically categorize the expenses they import from your bank. This functionality assists forecasting when you have decided to give yourself spending limits for specific expense categories. Some finance tracking programs even allow you to use automatic bill-paying functions and produce invoices. Finally, depending on the program, they may allow you to import your data into some tax software. In addition to tracking income and expenses, you can also track your progress toward your wealth goals. They often have charts and simulations that allow you to project where your net worth will be in the future given your current income, spending, and investment activity. Although we haven't tried all of the finance tracking programs listed above, we have tried the first two and can attest to how helpful they can be with forecasting as well as keeping track of your investments and accounts. Eventually your child may progress to even more advanced options like QuickBooks to handle their accounting. QuickBooks is generally considered the preferred system for accountants and small to even fairly large businesses, so unless your business grows extremely large, it can probably accommodate your growing needs for many years. The important thing is that you use something to make it simple enough to quickly and easily measure your progress relative to your goals. Remember what we said in the original Forecasting section: "What gets measured, gets met."

Depending on how many accounts you have and how much you plan to do with it, setting up a financial tracking program can take anywhere from 15 minutes to several hours. You may have to set it up on your computer, but the information you input should eventually sync to a mobile app you can download. Inevitably there will be some issues with one or more of your accounts not syncing correctly with your financial institution. When this happens, you may be tempted to give up. Don't. The time you save in the long run will be well worth the pain required to get the program up and running. Be sure to set up the bill-pay and other functions that may be useful to you. Once you have a good grasp of your chosen program, have your child set up their own separate finance tracking account with the same program you use. Thanks to your experience and their likely much shorter list of accounts, the process of setting them up shouldn't be too daunting or frustrating.

> **KYLE SAYS: Though the saying "more money, more problems" isn't necessarily true, the saying "more money, more money tracking" usually is true. Since your child is going to be a millionaire someday, they need to be able to track and forecast their money like a millionaire.**

It may seem redundant to set up a financial tracking program for your child when they probably only have a few accounts to monitor. The point, as it has been throughout this book, is to lay the foundation for them so that when their finances get more complicated and they have more accounts, they will already have the framework in place. Knowing they can easily add a new account to their tracking program may also ensure they aren't afraid to open new accounts when it is appropriate, such as when avoiding comingling of personal and business accounts is necessary. Another reason to have your child open their own finance tracking software is to set up the habit pattern of checking their accounts and being mindful of tracking the money.

## HAVE THEM START A FINANCE OR ENTREPRENEUR CLUB

One of the best ways for adults and kids alike to keep learning about money is to surround themselves with other people who like to learn about money. As parents, we advise that you join programs like the Make Your Kids Millionaires Facebook page, Integrated Wealth

Systems, or other programs that allow you to connect with like-minded people to grow your financial acumen. Children can do the same thing at school by starting or joining a finance or entrepreneur club.

Starting a finance or entrepreneur club is a great way for your teen to transition to learning not only under your careful tutelage but outside of the home as well. This will help foster the "lifetime of learning" concept that is so important with money. It could also be a great opportunity for them to flex their social skills. The process of getting your child to approach the faculty to start a club entails important learning points as well. They will have to formulate an argument and likely a position paper or presentation explaining to school leadership why they think the club is important for the school. They will also have to put themselves in the uncomfortable and incredibly educational position of convincing (selling) an adult other than their parents. As founder, they stand a good chance at being named president of the club. Not only does this help them develop their leadership, but "president and founder of the high school Finance/Entrepreneur Club" also sounds pretty good on a scholarship application. Who couldn't use a little extra scholarship money?

After the vast knowledge you've acquired as a parent reading this book and nurturing your child's money mastery, you could even be the club's first guest speaker. Enlisting business leaders from the community to serve as guest speakers will not only enlighten the teens in the club but could provide future internship or business connections for them (or even you). The teachings and references in this book alone (plus future references to accompany this book) could fill an entire year's curriculum. Finally, starting a high school club is another step toward our dream goal of educating the youth in this world on money and creating financial independence for our next generation.

# CHAPTER 9

# AGES 18 AND BEYOND

*Formal education will make you a living;*
*self-education will make you a fortune.*

—Jim Rohn, financial author and motivational speaker

Y ou did it! Your child is technically an adult now and you can wipe your hands clean of ever having to teach them again, right? Not so fast. They might not be a child anymore, but they will forever be your child. Even if you have cut the metaphorical financial umbilical cord and are no longer supporting them with money, they still need your guidance. No matter how well you have taught them up until now, they are likely still about to receive a few financial slaps in the face. Rent is how much? My cell phone plan costs me what? My car insurance costs me five times what it would if I were 30? Even if you warned them about these things, the staunch reality of having to pay these expenses themselves will be frustrating.

Transitioning from having most of their income be discretionary to having little or no discretionary income can be overwhelming for some. Depending on how financially independent they have been forced to become, you might even find that you have magically begun to get a little smarter in your child's eyes. Mark Twain famously said, "When I was a boy of fourteen, my father was so ignorant I could hardly stand to have the old man around. But when I got to be twenty-one, I was astonished at how much he had learned in seven years." Take advantage of your newly recognized wisdom and make sure you are there to provide guidance to them going forward. Just like when they were a baby learning to walk, they will take some tumbles as they toddle along through the financial pitfalls of adulthood. You can't always prevent those falls anymore. Your job now is to be sure they

**Helpful reminder: Don't forget to continue teaching and doing all the things you introduced in the previous chapters and expanding on them as your child's understanding improves.**

are OK afterward and to help them learn the lessons they need to take from those stumbles. The following sections can help you provide them the guidance they need as they fly their own path to financial freedom.

## TIME FOR SOME ADULT GOALS

Up until now, many of your child's goals have probably centered on short-term aspirations like buying a new car or perhaps paying for college. It's time for them to consider making some longer-term goals about what they want out of life. Don't let them get stressed out by this exercise to the extent they don't do it. They can always change their goals if they need to. The point is to figure out a destination so they can start planning the route to get there. Review the previous section titled "Your Child's Money Goals." Their new goal should have all the characteristics of previously discussed goals like being SMAA or SMART and meeting the Underlying Why. The difference is that this goal should be long-term—around 20 years is probably best. Perhaps reaching PI≥E is attainable in this time frame. If your

**KYLE SAYS: I vaguely recall having one of my teachers during high school ask the class to write down their long-term goals. Much like your child probably, I was skeptical about the exercise of writing down my goals. Despite this, I completed the assignment. Only recently did I realize the significance of that assignment.**

child follows the teachings from this book it is quite probable that they can be a millionaire by then and financially free.

When Kyle's teacher asked him to write down his goals he wrote down the following:

1. Be a certified scuba diver
2. Become a pilot
3. Be a millionaire by age 40

At the time Kyle wrote down these goals he didn't have any experience in any of the three categories. He wanted to achieve these goals, but he had never actually written them down until that day. In fact, until a few years ago, Kyle didn't even remember writing down these goals. He was rummaging through some of his old high school books when a notecard fell out. The notecard was simply titled "Goals" and had the three goals from above written on it. Only then did he remember the exercise of writing down the goals that he had done so many years before. How was high-schooler Kyle's success on the three goals he wrote down so many years ago?

1. **Be a certified scuba diver.** Not only did he become a certified scuba diver, but he became an advanced open water diver who has enjoyed scuba diving in seven different countries.
2. **Become a pilot.** Kyle went on to be a fighter pilot and instructor pilot in the Air Force with over 2,500 hours.
3. **Be a millionaire by age 40.** Kyle achieved this goal three years early by becoming a millionaire at age 37.

The point of this example is not to gloat. Others have probably accomplished much more ambitious goals with less. The point is that even though Kyle didn't remember writing these goals down, the mere process of writing them down seemed to help them come to fruition. This is the magic of writing down your goals. Putting pen to paper engages several senses. We must first think about what we want to write. We then have to convert that thought into language. Next, we move the pencil (or fingers if typing) to create the text and engage our tactile senses. We then read that text to ensure it is correct. If we follow the guidance listed in the previous chapter on goal setting, we will then display that goal in a place where we will see it daily. All of these actions reinforce and ingrain that goal into our mindset and bring it into the world. In fact, we recommend taking it a step further and considering the goal to be an actual written contract—a contract with your future self. This can help make the goal even more tangible. If Kyle was able to achieve his goals simply by writing them down, how much more likely will it be that your child can achieve their goals when they add the additional steps of reinforcement?

Why do we keep beating the drum of having your child set, write, and review their goals? It's not just our experiences. Hundreds and maybe even thousands of books have been written about it. Tens of thousands of hours of research have been accomplished by scholars for a hundred years. Its efficacy has been known and passed down for centuries. It simply just works. Thoughts lead to actions. If we constantly have our goals in our thoughts, then it will lead to actions, which lead to achievement of those goals. It's that simple. See our website MakeYourKidsMillionaires.com for more resources on goal setting. Encourage your child to follow our recommendations about goals and let them thank you later.

## THE VALUE OF FINDING A MENTOR OR COACH

We all hope to be a mentor for our children. If we do things right, we will be the most important mentor in their lives. The mere fact that you are reading this book means that you at least are trying your best to provide the mentorship your child needs. However, we cannot be everything to our kids, no matter how much we would like to be. Even if you knew everything there was to know about financial matters, occasionally they just won't listen to you. Sometimes our kids have heard (and apparently ignored) a teaching point we were making, only to come back the next week and profess that they learned the exact same point in some social media video. Sometimes it's just easier for them to learn the lessons from sources other than their parents. Sometimes these sources can fill in the gaps of teaching subjects we might not have a strong background in or may have simply failed to discuss.

Finally, hearing differing viewpoints teaches them critical thinking and lets them form and develop their own beliefs and values. This is great as long as those sources are trustworthy. With social media these days there is no dearth of so-called experts in practically any topic under the sun. Financial matters are no different. Some of these experts have good information and some do not. When we peruse social media, we are sometimes appalled by some of the incorrect information out there. Some of these experts have no credibility whatsoever, other than their ability to be entertaining and amass viewers, likes, and subscriptions. Since your children are probably digesting a lot of their content online, make sure you know what they are swallowing.

We are obviously biased, but you can't go wrong referencing our website MakeYourKidsMillionaires.com, Loral's website Integratedwealthsystems.com, or Kyle's content on Flight To Financial Freedom. Loral became a financial coach and mentor in 1996 and has been doing it as a career, mentoring hundreds of thousands of clients from six continents. For other sources, we suggest checking out the content to be sure it is credible before recommending it to your child. Since Loral has been in this industry for so long, she knows who is credible and real and who is not. Connect with us on our website if you want to discuss options.

So far, we've talked about virtual mentors, but the best mentors of all are not virtual at all. We've both been highly influenced by mentors. Kyle had a mentor who taught him about real estate and helped him escape analysis paralysis and make the leap into his first investment property. Loral had her first mentor at age 17 and employed the services of several mentors, including some of the biggest in the self-help industry. She was mentored by industry powerhouses such as Bob Proctor, Jay Conrad Levinson, Michael Gerber, and John Gray, and has become a powerhouse in her own right. Kyle has used her mentorship on coaching and business matters. In fact, many of the most successful people in all walks of life have had a coach or mentor to help them achieve their success. Encourage your child to seek out and find a coach or mentor to help them on their path to financial literacy.

Hopefully you can appreciate the value of a mentor to help guide your child along their Flight To Financial Freedom. But how do you find a coach or mentor? The same people who provide content online often have coaching programs. Loral offers several coaching programs on her website and even offers high-level mentorship through her program. Kyle has mentored several people on finances and offers courses as well. Finding a mentor isn't always easy. In the case of high-profile mentors, it may cost tens of thousands of dollars. Other times, the mentorship might be offered free of charge. Mentors are usually most willing to offer their guidance to students they believe they can truly help. Mentors can be found as near as your local town or neighborhood or as far away as distant countries. They can be bosses or teachers or relatives. With today's technology and global reach there is no limit to where they can be found. Sometimes they can be found by joining investment or business organizations or clubs.

Seek out the person who already has or knows what you want. If there is somebody in your community who is successful at what your child wants to do, have your child seek them out and ask if they can have a few minutes of their time. Logan, for example, went straight to the dean of the business school at his college and asked if he could be mentored and guided by him on his decisions. Make sure your child is respectful of mentors' time and help. It often helps to offer something in return for the mentorship, even if it isn't monetary. The key is finding something you have to offer that the mentor needs. Sometimes this is simply the opportunity to pass on their knowledge. Other times the mentor may be looking for an assistant or even a successor. Perhaps the best thing your child has to offer is their time and enthusiasm.

Following is an example of a scenario where a young man we'll call Edgar was hoping to learn from a real estate investor named

Mr. Mooney in his local town. Mr. Mooney had dozens of rental properties and was widely respected as a prominent investor. Edgar contacted Mr. Mooney and asked if he could meet with him the following week to discuss a proposal where Edgar would help Mr. Mooney find more investment properties at no charge. Edgar promised the proposal would take less than 10 minutes of Mr. Mooney's time. The consummate businessman, Mr. Mooney was willing to listen to what Edgar had to say, and they scheduled a time to meet.

When they met, Edgar's script went something like this: "Mr. Mooney, I want to first thank you for taking the time out of your busy day to meet with me. I recognize your time is valuable, so I'm only going to ask for five minutes to explain a proposal I really think you will appreciate. I realize you don't know me, but my name is Edgar Rafferty and I am an aspiring real estate investor. I don't have much experience, but I'm an incredibly hard worker and I'm willing to take on any challenge. I've seen how successful you've been as a real estate investor, and I really respect how you've been able to accrue so many properties. I would love to someday learn how to be as effective as you. I would be honored if you would let me help you find opportunities to invest in. I'll do all the dirty work to research and find investment deals for you. I don't even need to be paid a bird-dog fee for it. I'll bring the opportunities to you for free. All I would hope to get from it in return would be to learn from you what you are looking for in a property and how to find real estate deals that you would want to buy. I mostly just want to be a sponge and to soak in whatever I could from you. I'm a fast learner and highly motivated. I promise I'll do everything I can to make it worth your time. Would you be willing to give me that chance?"

As you can imagine, Edgar's proposal worked. He wasn't paid anything for his work, but what he learned was invaluable. He found the perfect currency to exchange for the mentorship—his own time. As a result, he and Mr. Mooney formed a mutually beneficial relationship that helped Mr. Mooney find more investments and gave Edgar the mentorship he needed to begin creating his own real estate portfolio.

# ENCOURAGE THEM TO JOIN A MASTERMIND GROUP

Having a mentor isn't the only way to receive encouragement to work toward your goals. One of the best pieces of advice you can give your adult child is to join a mastermind group. Don't worry, we're not talking about an evil mastermind with a plot to take over the world. A mastermind group, often just called a mastermind, is a group of like-minded peers who meet regularly to give each other advice and support. Napoleon Hill is credited with creating what we now call a mastermind. He first mentioned the term "master mind" in his 1928 book *The Law of Success*, but it was popularized in 1937 when he published his landmark classic *Think and Grow Rich*, in which he used the term "master mind alliance." He describes a mastermind as, "A friendly alliance with one or more persons who will encourage one to follow through with both plan and purpose." Since then, masterminds have been espoused and championed by nearly every major self-help coach and guru on the planet. The reason? They work. Many of the world's most successful people swear by them.

Masterminds are a key part of Loral's coaching program, and they are practically required for her high-end coaching clients in the Big Table. In fact, she is part of several herself. The great thing about modern technology is that the members of a mastermind don't even have to be in the same country, much less the same town. Today, nearly everybody does videoconferencing, so there's no excuse not to meet face-to-face with a mastermind group of your choosing. Masterminds have several benefits. First, they allow you to associate with other highly motivated and successful people who can share their knowledge and talents. Mastermind with people whom you respect and who will pull you up rather than bring you down. If you indeed are the average of the five people you spend the most time with, then its best to choose mastermind partners you admire and want to be like. Next, the magic of working with people is that the synergy of your combined ideas can create a multiplicative effect on the ideas each of you could have created on your own. When two or more minds blend their innate thinking power, they create a third exponentially more powerful mind, the mastermind. This effect is accentuated if the members of the mastermind group have different skill sets or think differently than you do. This is why, although it can be helpful to have common interests, it can also be useful to have people with different talents and experiences than you. Sometimes their disparate talents will be just what you needed to solve a problem or even collaborate in your business. Finally, perhaps the biggest advantage of a mastermind is accountability. Members are encouraged to hold each other accountable to goals and tasks that each has committed to. The same "peer pressure" that is often put to negative use can be used as a motivator to help you achieve your goals. Your mastermind is like a wingman who provides mutual support but also makes sure you stay in formation.

So why does your child need a mastermind group? No matter where your child is in life or what they are doing there are people who are in a similar place and can provide the support your child needs and also need the support your child can provide. By joining a mastermind, your child can experience all the advantages we discussed above. Your child can find a mastermind group by joining a coaching community like the Make Your Kids Millionaires community, Loral or Kyle's communities, or even organically by finding people they respect and asking those people if they would be willing to meet regularly as a mastermind group. Although informal masterminds can work, coaching communities like ours usually have strict mastermind guidelines and have spent years perfecting the best ways to make masterminds productive and lasting. Thus, it's a good idea to have your first mastermind experience under the tutelage of someone who knows what they are doing. When you can no longer be there every day for your child, won't it be good to know they have a supportive group of peers who are helping them, encouraging them, and holding them accountable to perform the actions they need to achieve their goals?

For additional resources and information, go to MakeYourKids Millionaires.com, Loral's community, or Kyle's program.

# HELP THEM GET THEIR FIRST CREDIT CARDS

Credit and credit cards are such an important financial topic that we have already spent several sections in this book discussing them. Now that your child is 18, they can finally get their own credit cards, and they absolutely should. This begins their credit history.

The way we encourage your child to get credit cards at this age is to apply for two at the same time so the application for one doesn't temporarily hurt their chances for getting a second. The guideline we recommend is to make sure when your child applies that they apply with income. Throughout this book we've given your child numerous ways to make income, so they should already be making some money that they can put on the application.

When it comes to your child using their new credit card, a technique we recommend is to have one card for gas and travel and the other card for food and personal needs. This makes it easier to track and categorize their expenses and makes sure they use both cards so they will both play a role in improving their credit score. Next, they will track these credit cards in the financial tracking software we recommended in the last chapter. No matter what, they need to always pay both cards off every month.

**LORAL SAYS:** My recent experience in helping many university students is that if the student has approximately $1,500 a month in income, they can qualify for several thousand in credit.

An advanced strategy for appropriate use of your child's credit card is that, after they have had 6 to 12 months of spending, they should call their credit card company and ask for two things. The first is an increase in their credit limit. We recommend using the phrase "I have a business investment I need to make, and I need the increased limit for that purchase." The second is to tell the credit card company that they want zero percent interest on the card. The representative will probably laugh, but it will set the bracket for a negotiation that should result in an interest rate reduction. It's important to have both conversations at the same time.

## HELP THEM BUY THEIR FIRST REAL ESTATE INVESTMENT

We discussed earlier the importance of real estate in an investment portfolio. What better way to get your son or daughter (no longer children) started on their asset-building journey than to help them purchase their first real estate property? Real estate comes in many flavors, but many of the real estate investments available for adults will be difficult for an 18- or 19-year-old to buy. However, this just means your kid will have to be creative. It is quite possible for young adults to purchase a personal residence. If you followed the guidance we recommended in earlier chapters, your son or daughter now has a credit history and hopefully a solid credit score. But what about the down payment? Remember, it is possible to buy a property with very little down payment. If your child is in the military like Kyle was, they can use a VA loan, which has zero down payment. If not, they may still be eligible for an FHA loan, sporting a down payment as low as 3.5 percent. Where do they get that 3.5 percent? How about they get it from that wealth account they created from their first business that has slowly been growing? We wouldn't usually recommend it, but they could even extract up to $10,000 from the Roth IRA you helped them set up years ago. With a minimal down payment, credit history, and a form of reliable income there is no reason they can't purchase a house or condo to live in.

In a perfect world, your child's growing business is providing income, and this can be their source of repayment. The problem is that many young adults are in college during these ages and don't have a reliable income. This is where you, the parent, can help by stepping in as a cosigner or partner. We warned you your job wasn't over. As a cosigner, the parent can sign the mortgage along with their child to help secure the loan. The cosigner role provides an additional repayment source to the primary borrower and lowers the risk to the mortgage provider. Although the primary borrower will receive the loan and be responsible for the payments, the cosigner is jointly liable for the debt. The benefit is that the primary borrower may be able to receive more favorable lending terms (interest rate, down payment, etc.) than they would otherwise qualify for, and it may be the only way they will qualify for a loan.

An additional benefit is that buying a home will have a positive impact on your child's credit score. This doesn't mean you have to help them pay the loan. At some point your child needs to fly out of the nest. As a parent, we highly recommend you make it clear to your child that you don't plan on stepping in so they will need to be responsible enough to make the payments themselves. How will they do this? They need to find a way to generate the income necessary to pay the mortgage. This income could be generated either through a job or, as we prefer, a business of their own. It can also be generated from the property itself. What if your child were to buy a three-bedroom house near their college and rent out two of the rooms? In this scenario, the rent charged to the roommates could probably cover the cost of the mortgage. Your progeny could then benefit from the principle paid down on the home as well as any appreciation that might occur with the home. The same tactic can be accomplished by purchasing a duplex, triplex, or quadplex. All of these are considered residential and can be purchased with standard residential financing.

Another way your child can create income to pay the mortgage has become more and more popular in recent years. We are referring to the short-term rental craze. Rather than having long-term roommates,

**LORAL SAYS: When my son, Logan, turned 18, I actually gave him an LLC for his birthday. Since I had opened the LLC 18 years prior, it already had credibility and credit that he could put to use right away. I also let him become an active partner in some of my other businesses.**

your child could rent out the extra rooms in their house to short-term tenants via Airbnb, Vrbo, Homestay, or an assortment of other options. Although this technique is more labor-intensive, location-specific, and less consistent, it can provide more income per night if used successfully. Regardless of what technique your young adult uses to pay their mortgage, getting started by purchasing their first property will prove to be a valuable experience in learning about real estate. It may just be the launching pad they need to create their own real estate empire.

## TIME FOR THEIR SOLO FLIGHT

You've spent years preparing for the opportunity to let your child fly on their own. That time is now. Whether you are ready or not, it's time to let your child spread their wings and soar. We've both dropped kids off at college and been left with that nagging question, "Did I teach them enough?" The good news is, if you read and acted on the recommendations in this book, you almost certainly did. Be confident in the fact that you've set them up for success. Unlike some children, your child won't go crashing to the ground now that they are jumping out of your financial nest.

So what does a solo flight for your child look like? The first step is to separate them from your finances. This doesn't have to be an abrupt end if you don't want it to be, but you do need to communicate with them about what your plan will be. Will you be paying for their college? Will you still pay for their cell phone? Will you pay for their car insurance? Do they have access to any of your funds, accounts, or credit cards? If so, for how long? Eventually, the goal is to let them fly completely solo, but the transition can

**KYLE SAYS: The more you study and learn about money, the more financial tools you will have in your arsenal. As a hobbyist carpenter myself, I have pounded into my kids' brains the saying "the right tool for the right job."**

be different for different people depending on your family's circumstances. Explain to your child exactly how this transition will happen. A technique Loral and Logan use is having a regular check-in call where they discuss just the financial topics like their income, banking, credit cards, and bills.

Another aspect of your child's solo flight involves the handling of bank accounts and investments. Since you set up your child's bank accounts many years ago, they should be well prepared to manage these on their own. Likewise, they should be adept at handling their own debit and credit cards. As for investments, we mentioned in the last section the possibility of helping your child buy their first real estate investment. Another way to help your child fly solo is to give them full control of their investment accounts. This would include any custodial IRAs and education funds you may have set up for them when they were young, as we advised in the Chapter 4 sections "Open a Roth IRA for Your Child" and "Set Up a Tax-Advantaged Education Account." These usually either have to be or can be released to your child's full control at age 18. Since you taught them how to manage and conduct due diligence for these investments, they are probably more prepared to take over these investments than most adults much older.

Depending on what rules you established, this might also be the time when your child has access to any trust funds you may have set aside for them, as described in the Chapter 4 section "Create a Trust." Additionally, in most countries and states your child can own an entity once they turn 18. If they don't already have a business, it's a good idea to encourage them to get incorporated and create one. You might even be able to transfer to them one of the business or investment entities you created, as we described in the Chapter 4 section "Start a Business and Get Incorporated."

The idea is to help your child start living with a corporate life structure immediately at age 18. It may be scary, but according to law in most states, your child is an adult now. It's time to start treating them like one. If you've been training them along the way, there is no reason they can't be responsible enough to handle the many responsibilities that come with being an adult, on their own, and flying solo.

## THE FLIGHT CONTINUES

Like many things in life, learning about money isn't like hiking to the peak of a mountain where the only thing left to do is to walk back down. Instead, it's like a flight where you can fly over the summit and keep soaring higher. Your child's Flight To Financial Freedom is a life-long endeavor. You can never reach a point where you know everything there is to know about financial matters. Tax and financial laws are ever-changing, so even if you did an incredible job teaching your child, there is always more to discover. There is always a new summit to soar over and a new cloud to chase. Does that mean we shouldn't even try? Of course not. The higher you get the better the view, and the better will be your perspective of the big picture. We continue trying to learn new things about money every day. Make sure your kids appreciate this fact.

Another analogy you might want to convey to your kids is that of the carpenter. If you've taught your child all the concepts in this book, then you've given them some tools to help build their financial house. They at least have a hammer, a handsaw, a tape measure, and a screwdriver. Already they are better off than most of the world, which is equipped with only a hammer. With only a hammer you would have a hard time building a house. As they say, if you only have a hammer, everything looks like a nail. Armed with the hammer,

**LORAL SAYS: When I talk about the idea that you should "Live out loud" I am talking about the idea of being in constant conversation with your child about money. Not only this, but you must also surround yourself with and engage in conversations with people who are already financially literate and share similar financial goals. Then you have to "make it matter, say YES!, and take action!"**

handsaw, tape measure, and screwdriver, your child could successfully build a house. But how long would it take? Wouldn't it be faster if they were to add a circular saw, table saw, and a power drill? Surely some tools are more efficient than others. How much faster would it be if they had an entire garage of tools at their disposal? Building a financial house is no different.

Depending on the financial situation, the right tool might be buying real estate under market value and flipping it. It might be buying and renting it out to take advantage of appreciation and high market rents. It might instead be historically low stock valuations that warrant higher stock allocations. It could even be starting your own business in a niche you have found to be underserved. When the financial situation changes, it helps to have a wide array of money tools at your disposal so you can pick the right tool for the right job.

The only way to assemble this garage full of financial tools is through continual learning. This is the true treasure of wealth, and the reason why we do what we do. We want to help you grow your tool collection. It's also the reason why most rich people, even if they went broke, could quickly become rich again. They aren't building their financial house with only a hammer. They have all the tools they need to create wealth over and over and over. However, like all tools, they can only be continuously used if they are maintained. Financial tools are no different. Each tool has a maintenance schedule. Some are weekly. Some are monthly. Some are annual. They need to be kept sharp so they can stay effective.

If you are worried that your own garage is a little short on tools to teach your child about money, don't despair. You don't have to be a millionaire to make your child a millionaire. Besides, it's never too late to start down the road to financial literacy. The best thing you can do is start the process with them so you can learn together and you can help guide them along the way. You probably have more knowledge than you think, and you can get them started off right by teaching them what you do know at a much younger age than you learned it. Beyond that, there are a multitude of resources available these days to develop your financial tool collection. For continued information on developing your financial tools and keeping your financial literacy sharp, visit our website MakeYourKidsMillionaires.com.

We've covered a myriad of topics in this book. We've taken you and your child on a step-by-step path that started with them as a young child, learning the very basics of money. We encouraged you to establish accounts, entities, and policies to set them up for success. As they grew older your child learned about credit, banks, good and bad debt, Wealth Cycles and Lifestyle Cycles, delayed gratification, goals, leadership, teamwork, assets and liabilities, passive income, forecasting, and due diligence. You let them simulate many of the financial activities and behaviors they will use as adults, including starting their own entrepreneurial enterprises and investing. Eventually, under your watchful eye, you supervised them and led them to slowly begin to take the flight controls and start managing these accounts and business ventures and forecasting their income and expenses. Finally, you let them fly solo and take over their accounts and investments and run their own businesses.

Your child's financial journey doesn't end there. It continues with them throughout their lives. It continues with them teaching their own children what they've learned. It continues with spreading the word to their friends and other family members. It continues with an unceasing commitment to learning about money, talking about money, and creating financial freedom for their loved ones throughout their lifetime.

Congratulations for making it to the end of this book. Hopefully you've used your YES! Energy and committed to "Live out loud" financially with your child.

If you have taken action and followed along throughout, you've been able to lead your child step-by-step down their path to financial freedom. They are well on their way to acquiring the knowledge and skills necessary to become a millionaire. Even though they probably haven't reached that level yet, you have helped Make Your Kids Millionaires. We'd love to hear more about your journey so we as a community can help others be even more effective at creating financial freedom for their children. Please join us on Facebook or on our website MakeYourKidsMillionaires.com to share your stories and ideas. Thanks for letting us be your instructors on this epic financial flight. Although this book is over, the flight continues.

# RESOURCES

## Home Tasks Negotiation List

Name:                      Age:

Date:

| Check by final tasks | proposed home tasks | child rating (1-3) | parent rating (1-3) | pay rate per minute | flat rate | max time allowed | frequency | additional notes |
|---|---|---|---|---|---|---|---|---|
| | | | | | | | | |
| | | | | | | | | |
| | | | | | | | | |
| | | | | | | | | |
| | | | | | | | | |
| | | | | | | | | |
| | | | | | | | | |
| | | | | | | | | |
| | | | | | | | | |
| | | | | | | | | |
| | | | | | | | | |
| | | | | | | | | |
| | | | | | | | | |
| | | | | | | | | |
| | | | | | | | | |
| | | | | | | | | |
| | | | | | | | | |
| | | | | | | | | |
| | | | | | | | | |
| | | | | | | | | |
| | | | | | | | | |
| | | | | | | | | |
| | | | | | | | | |
| | | | | | | | | |
| | | | | | | | | |
| | | | | | | | | |
| | | | | | | | | |
| | | | | | | | | |
| | | | | | | | | |
| | | | | | | | | |

# Home Tasks Invoice

Company name:                                    Date:
Company address:                                 For the month of:

Bill to
Customer name:                                   Due date:
Customer address:

| Date | Home tasks completed | minutes | rate per minute | or | flat rate | Total | notes |
|------|----------------------|---------|-----------------|----|-----------|-------|-------|
|      |                      |         |                 |    |           |       |       |
|      |                      |         |                 |    |           |       |       |
|      |                      |         |                 |    |           |       |       |
|      |                      |         |                 |    |           |       |       |
|      |                      |         |                 |    |           |       |       |
|      |                      |         |                 |    |           |       |       |
|      |                      |         |                 |    |           |       |       |
|      |                      |         |                 |    |           |       |       |
|      |                      |         |                 |    |           |       |       |
|      |                      |         |                 |    |           |       |       |
|      |                      |         |                 |    |           |       |       |
|      |                      |         |                 |    |           |       |       |
|      |                      |         |                 |    |           |       |       |

**Total Due:** _____  Thank you for your business!

Name:                                **Balance Sheet**

Date:

| Assets | Year: |
|---|---|
| Wealth Account | |
| Car Account | |
| Charity Account | |
| | |
| | |
| | |
| | |

**Total Assets**

| Liabilities | |
|---|---|
| | |
| | |
| | |

**Total Liabilities**

**Net Worth**

**Total Net Worth**

# Income Statement

**Name:**
**Monthly Income Statement for:**                    **Date:**

| Revenue | | Forecast | Actual |
|---|---|---|---|
| | | | |
| | | | |
| | | | |
| **Total Revenue** | | 0 | 0 |

| Cost of Goods Sold | | | |
|---|---|---|---|
| | | | |
| | | | |
| | | | |
| | | | |
| | | | |
| | | | |
| **Cost of Goods Sold** | | 0 | 0 |
| **Gross Profit (Loss)** | | 0 | 0 |

| Expenses | | | |
|---|---|---|---|
| | | | |
| | | | |
| | | | |
| | | | |
| | | | |
| | | | |
| | | | |
| | | | |
| **Total Expenses** | | 0 | 0 |
| **Net Operating Income** | | 0 | 0 |

| Other Income | | | |
|---|---|---|---|
| | | | |
| | | | |
| **Total Other Income** | | 0 | 0 |
| **Net Income (Loss)** | | 0 | 0 |

# RECOMMENDED READING

*The Millionaire Maker* – Loral Langemeier

*The Millionaire Maker's Guide to Creating a Cash Machine for Life* –
   Loral Langemeier

*The Millionaire Maker's Guide to Wealth Cycle Investing* –
   Loral Langemeier

*YES! Energy* – Loral Langemeier

*Put More Cash In Your Pocket* – Loral Langemeier

*Think and Grow Rich for Women: Using Your Power to Create Success
   and Significance* – Sharon Lechter

*Exit Rich* – Sharon Lechter and Michelle Seiler Tucker

*Rich Dad Poor Dad* – Robert Kiyosaki and Sharon Lechter

*The 7 Habits of Highly Effective People* – Stephen R. Covey

*The 4-Hour Workweek* – Timothy Ferriss

*The Secret* – Rhonda Byrne

*The Richest Man in Babylon* – George Clason

*Multiple Streams of Income* – Robert G. Allen

*How to Win Friends and Influence People* – Dale Carnegie

*You Were Born Rich* – Bob Proctor

*Becoming Your Own Banker* – R. Nelson Nash

*The Misadventures of Jennifer Pennifer* – Leslie B. Kuerbitz

*Think and Grow Rich* – Napoleon Hill

*The Millionaire Next Door: The Surprising Secrets of America's
   Wealthy* – Thomas J. Stanley and William D. Danko

*Innovation and Entrepreneurship* – Peter F. Drucker

# INDEX

Page numbers followed by *f* refer to figures.

# ABOUT THE AUTHORS

## Loral Langemeier

Loral's passion to help families enjoy wealth and prosperity is what has motivated her to write five *New York Times* bestselling books (*The Millionaire Maker, The Millionaire Maker's Guide to Creating a Cash Machine for Life, The Millionaire Maker's Guide to Wealth Cycle Investing, Put More Cash in Your Pocket,* and *YES! Energy: The Equation to Do Less, Make More*). Loral, as an author, sits with an elite few. Very few American nonfiction authors have reached number one status on the Nielsen Book Scan in Australia, let alone also in the United States.

Today, under Loral's direction, Integrated Wealth Systems is a multinational organization. Loral has grown as a business developer to become a key thought leader in the entrepreneurial space.

In 1999, Loral became a millionaire in real estate in nine months when she learned she was pregnant with her first child. Since then, she has helped thousands of other people find their path to financial security. As a single mother of two children when she first became a millionaire, she is redefining the possibility for women to "have it all" and raise their children in an entrepreneurial and financially literate environment.

Loral is often booked out for months in advance on guest spots on CNN, CNBC, The Street TV, Fox News Channel, Fox Business Channel: *America's Nightly Scoreboard, Dr. Phil,* and *The View.* She is a regular guest host on *The Circle* in Australia and has been featured in articles in *USA Today*, the *Wall Street Journal*, the *New York Times*, and *Forbes* magazine and was the breakout star in the film *The Secret*.

Legacy is something very important to Loral. She is a frequent donor to charitable groups including the Boys & Girls Clubs of America, the Lake Tahoe BEAR League, Empowered Woman Foundation, Lifeschool, and Family Resource Centers. She has developed special programs for women and children, and in 2012 raised $40,000 for the Make-A-Wish Foundation. She runs Serve Out Loud, a program aimed at providing discounted education in financial literacy to United States veterans. Loral also works pro bono with college athletes looking to play professional sports by educating them on financial literacy and entrepreneurialism.

## Kyle Boeckman

Kyle is an expert on financial freedom. Financial freedom is about much more than just financial security. It's about thriving, not just surviving. Despite starting with nothing and never having a large income, Kyle was able to reach financial freedom by age 43 and leave the workforce forever. He retired as a lieutenant colonel after spending 25 years in the United States Air Force leading and instructing young people as an officer, a fighter pilot and, for 15 years, an instructor pilot.

During his time in the Air Force, Kyle was able to attain multiple degrees, travel the globe, manage $100 million dollar projects on three different continents, fly $12 million dollar fighter jets, and instruct over a thousand young students from eight countries to do the same—all by the age of 40. Kyle is grateful he was given the opportunity to teach and lead young people in the protection of freedom, and now he's excited to pivot toward teaching parents how to lead their children to a different type of freedom—financial freedom.

Kyle's journey to self-made millionaire status by age 37 and complete financial freedom by age 43 is living proof that reaching financial freedom doesn't take an incredibly high income or any version of being born with a silver spoon. He isn't an expert on financial freedom because of some fancy title or piece of paper on a wall. He's an expert because he's actually lived and achieved it. Reaching financial freedom was such a liberating experience for Kyle that he knew he had to spread the word and share his secrets for reaching financial freedom with others. He now uses his background in leadership, flying, teaching, investing, and psychology to teach people all over the world his secrets for reaching prosperity at an early age.

Kyle's program, Flight To Financial Freedom, involves leading people down their own flight path to the wealth they desire and deserve. He uses his experience as a fighter pilot and flight instructor to teach systems similar to the ones the United States Air Force has been employing for over 60 years. Some of these systems are used in this book. If you complete the education, conversations, exercises, and actions in this book, Kyle is confident your child will be well on their way to being financially literate and accelerating in their own Flight To Financial Freedom and millionaire status. Step into the cockpit and get ready for takeoff!